The
Essential
Guide to
Computing

ISBN 0-13-019469-7

9 780130 194695

90000

Essential Guide Series

THE ESSENTIAL GUIDE TO DATA WAREHOUSING

Agosta

THE ESSENTIAL GUIDE TO TELECOMMUNICATIONS, SECOND EDITION

Dodd

THE ESSENTIAL GUIDE TO NETWORKING

Keogh

THE ESSENTIAL GUIDE TO DIGITAL SET-TOP BOXES AND INTERACTIVE TV

O'Driscoll

THE ESSENTIAL GUIDE TO HOME NETWORKING TECHNOLOGIES

O'Driscoll

THE ESSENTIAL GUIDE TO COMPUTING: THE STORY OF INFORMATION TECHNOLOGY

Walters

THE ESSENTIAL GUIDE TO RF AND WIRELESS

Weisman

The Essential Guide to Computing

E. GARRISON WALTERS

Prentice Hall PTR
Upper Saddle River, NJ 07458
www.phptr.com

Acquisitions editor: *Miles Williams*
Editorial assistant: *Michael Fredette*
Cover designer: *Bruce Kenselaar*
Cover design director: *Jerry Votta*
Manufacturing manager: *Alexis Heydt*
Marketing manager: *Kate Hargett*
Project coordinator: *Anne Trowbridge*
Compositor/Production services: *Pine Tree Composition, Inc.*

Prentice Hall books are widely used by corporations and government agencies for training, marketing, and resale.

The publisher offers discounts on this book when ordered in bulk quantities. For more information contact:

Corporate Sales Department
Phone: 800-382-3419
Fax: 201-236-7141
E-mail: corpsales@prenhall.com

Or write:

Prentice Hall PTR
Corp. Sales Dept.
One Lake Street
Upper Saddle River, New Jersey 07458

ISBN: 0-13-019469-7

Prentice-Hall International (UK) Limited, *London*
Prentice-Hall of Australia Pty. Limited, *Sydney*
Prentice-Hall Canada Inc., *Toronto*
Prentice-Hall Hispanoamericana, S.A., *Mexico*
Prentice-Hall of India Private Limited, *New Delhi*
Prentice-Hall of Japan, Inc., *Tokyo*
Pearson Education Asia Pte Ltd.
Editora Prentice-Hall do Brasil, Ltda., *Rio de Janeiro*

Contents

Acknowledgments   *xix*

Introduction   *xxi*

Part 1   Computer Hardware   1

1   The Core of Computing:
How the Key Elements of Hardware Work Together   *3*

AN OVERVIEW OF HOW A COMPUTER WORKS   *4*

What Happens When a Computer Starts Up   *4*

The Computer Begins to Work   *10*

Binary and Digital   *12*

THE INTERNAL OPERATIONS OF THE CPU   *14*

Fetch   *15*

Decode (Analyze)   *16*

Execute   *16*

Store   *17*

The Clock   *19*

Interrupts   *19*

Designing a Faster CPU   *20*

ARCHITECTURE: SUITING THE CPU TO THE TASK   *26*

RISC   *27*

SIMD   *28*

VLIW   *29*

Linking CPUs   *30*

MICROPROCESSORS FOR SPECIAL PURPOSES   *31*

ASICs   *31*

DSPs   *32*

Media Processors   *33*

FPGAs   *33*

NEW APPROACHES TO COMPUTING   *34*

Supercooling   *34*

Optical Computing   *35*

Even More Exotic Stuff   *36*

CONCLUSION   *36*

TEST YOUR UNDERSTANDING   *37*

2   Memory, Storage, and Input/Output   *39*

AN OVERVIEW OF HOW STORAGE WORKS   *40*

A File is Loaded into Memory   *40*

The CPU Gets Information from Disk   *41*

A File is Saved to Disk   *43*

THE MEMORY SYSTEM   *43*

The Memory Problem   *43*

The System (Memory) Bus   *49*

Memory Chips   *51*

Some Other Types of Chip Storage   *54*

DISK STORAGE   *54*

Magnetic Storage   *54*

Optical Storage   *58*

THE I/O BUS   *60*

PCI   *61*

External I/O   *62*

CHIPSETS   *64*

CONCLUSION   *67*

TEST YOUR UNDERSTANDING   *69*

3   Computer Monitors and Graphics Systems   *71*

MAKING AN IMAGE   *71*

Pixels and Dots   *72*

Resolution   *73*

Resolution, Content, and Perception   *74*

Color   *75*

Contrast and Brightness   *77*

Image Stability and Smoothness of Motion   *77*

MONITOR TECHNOLOGIES   78

THE STRUCTURE OF GRAPHICS SYSTEMS   80

Bitmapped Images   *81*

Vector Images   *83*

Bitmaps vs. Vectors   *83*

GENERATIONS OF GRAPHICS SYSTEMS   86

First Generation Graphics   *87*

Second Generation Graphics Systems   *87*

THE KEY ELEMENTS OF THIRD GENERATION (3D) SYSTEMS   89

Changes in Graphics Software   *93*

PRINTERS   94

Printer Resolution   *94*

Major Types of Printers   *96*

Printer Intelligence   *99*

CONCLUSION   102

TEST YOUR UNDERSTANDING   102

4   Silicon Economics   105

SILICON FOUNDATIONS: MAKING CHIPS   106

Smaller is Cheaper   *107*

Smaller is Faster   *107*

Smaller Uses Less Power   *108*

New Approaches to Chipmaking   *108*

MICROPROCESSOR FAMILIES   109

  Intel Corporation   *109*

  Intel Clones   *113*

  RISC CPUs   *115*

  Summary: Can Anyone Compete with Intel?   *119*

TYPES OF COMPUTERS   120

  Mainframes   *120*

  Supercomputers   *121*

  Servers and Workstations   *122*

  Desktops   *123*

  The Set-top Box   *123*

  Portable Systems   *124*

**THE EVOLVING MICROPROCESSOR ARCHITECTURE: WHAT
DO YOU DO WITH A BILLION TRANSISTORS ON ONE CHIP?   127**

  ASIC-Oriented   *127*

  General-Purpose CPU   *128*

  Media Processors   *128*

  System on Chip   *128*

CONCLUSION   *130*

TEST YOUR UNDERSTANDING   *130*

PART 1   PUTTING IT ALL TOGETHER   *132*

  Servers   *132*

  A Graphics System   *133*

  An Analytical System   *133*

  A Desktop System   *133*

  A Portable System   *134*

Part 2   Software   135

5   Fundamentals of the Operating System   137

WHY HAVE AN OPERATING SYSTEM?   138

THE CORE FUNCTIONS OF AN OPERATING SYSTEM   138

System Supervision   139

Services to Hardware   144

Services to Software   146

Communications Services   148

Security   149

Single-User Systems in a Networked Environment   150

Directories   151

THE STRUCTURE OF THE OPERATING SYSTEM   151

The Kernel   151

User Section   153

THE CHALLENGE OF MULTIPROCESSING   153

Multiprocessing and the OS   154

Multiprocessing in Hardware   156

CONCLUSION   158

TEST YOUR UNDERSTANDING   159

6   Evolution of the Operating System   161

MAINFRAME SYSTEMS   162

MINICOMPUTER/SERVER SYSTEMS *163*

Proprietary: VMS *163*

Proprietary: OS/400 *166*

Open: UNIX and Variants *166*

CONCLUSION *172*

TEST YOUR UNDERSTANDING *173*

7 Microcomputer Operating Systems *175*

MICROSOFT'S MS-DOS *176*

An Overview of MS-DOS *176*

Memory and Task Management *177*

THE MAC OS *180*

Key Characteristics of the Mac OS *181*

Initial Development of the Mac OS *181*

Compatibility Issues *182*

The Mac Shifts to the PowerPC *183*

The Current Mac OS *183*

WINDOWS *184*

Key Characteristics of the Window OS Series *184*

Windows 1.0 to 2.0 *186*

Windows 3.0 *187*

Windows 95 and Windows 98 *188*

Windows NT/2000 *190*

OS/2 *194*

A NETWORK-ONLY OS: NETWARE *196*

VERY SMALL SYSTEM OSS   *198*

The Palm OS   *199*

Epoc   *199*

CONCLUSION   *200*

TEST YOUR UNDERSTANDING   *201*

8   Programming, Object Oriented Technology,
     and Software Development   *203*

BASIC PROGRAMMING TERMINOLOGY   *204*

Subroutines   *205*

Interrupted vs. Compiled Languages   *205*

THE SOFTWARE CRISIS   *208*

STRUCTURED PROGRAMMING   *209*

Project Modeling   *212*

Modular Programming   *213*

PROGRAMMING LANGUAGES BY LEVEL   *213*

Machine Language Programming   *214*

Assembly Language   *214*

High-level Languages   *215*

4GLs (whatever they are)   *218*

Artificial Intelligence: 5GL?   *220*

OBJECT-ORIENTED TECHNOLOGY   *221*

How OOT Works   *222*

Applying OOT   *226*

The Compound Document Concept   *227*

The Major Object-Oriented Languages   *229*

**SOFTWARE DEVELOPMENT STRATEGIES
AND PROGRAMMING TOOLS   *232***

CASE Tools   *233*

Rapid Application Development   *234*

CONCLUSION   *235*

TEST YOUR UNDERSTANDING   *236*

9   Databases, Applications, and Software Reliability   *237*

DATABASES   *238*

The Elements of a Database   *238*

Planning a Database   *239*

The Relational Model of Database Organization   *240*

Nonrelational Databases   *244*

The Power of Legacy Database Systems   *246*

Database Markets   *248*

APPLICATION SOFTWARE   *252*

Spreadsheets   *253*

Word Processing   *255*

Voice Recognition: Coming on Strong   *257*

THE SOFTWARE INDUSTRY   *258*

Microsoft   *258*

The Rest   *258*

CONCLUSION   *259*

TEST YOUR UNDERSTANDING   *260*

PART 2   PUTTING IT ALL TOGETHER   261

Choosing an OS for E-Commerce   261

Choosing a Database for E-Commerce   262

Choosing a Programming Language and Tools
for E-Commerce   262

Part 3   Networks and the Internet   265

10   Digital vs. Analog: Communications Basics   267

WAVES OF INFORMATION   268

Amplitude Modulation (AM)   271

Frequency Modulation (FM)   271

Phase Modulation (PM)   271

Bandwidth   272

Amplitude and Attention   274

Frequencies and Diffusion   274

Replacing Analog Signaling with Digital   275

DATA COMPRESSION   282

Noncontent-based Compression   286

ERROR DETECTION AND CORRECTION   289

Forward Error Detection/Correction   290

CONCLUSION   291

TEST YOUR UNDERSTANDING   292

11   Network Fundamentals   *293*

AN OVERVIEW OF NETWORK FUNDAMENTALS   *294*

A Quick Analogy   *294*

Sending a File   *296*

THE IMPORTANCE OF PACKETS   *301*

Addresses   *303*

Sequencing and Flow Control   *303*

Error Detection and Correction   *304*

Packet Size   *305*

Latency   *305*

PROTOCOL STACKS   *306*

Layer 4: The Transport Layer   *306*

Layer 3: The Network Layer   *308*

Layer 2: The Data Link Layer   *309*

Layer 1: The Physical layer   *311*

GETTING FROM A TO B: CIRCUITS, VIRTUAL CIRCUITS, AND CIRCUITLESS APPROACHES   *311*

Type One: Leased Line   *313*

Type Two: Switched Circuit   *314*

Type Three: Internet Type   *315*

Type Four: Cell or Framed Switched   *317*

MEDIA   *320*

Wireless   *320*

Wired   *322*

TOPOLOGIES, MULTIPLEXING, AND SYNCHRONIZATION   328

Topologies   *328*

Channels: Timing and Multiplexing   *333*

NETWORK CONNECTING POINTS   338

Passive Devices: Hubs and Repeaters   *339*

Active Devices: Switches, Routers and Bridges   *339*

The Issue of Multicasting   *349*

CONCLUSION   349

TEST YOUR UNDERSTANDING   350

12   Types of Networks   *351*

LOCAL AREA NETWORKS   352

Ethernet   *352*

Token Ring   *356*

LAN TO LAN CONNECTIONS: CAMPUS NETWORKS   357

FDDI   *358*

ATM   *358*

Gigabit Ethernet   *361*

Which is Best for Backbone and Campus Links?   *362*

LOCAL TO WIDE AREA CONNECTIONS: ACCESS NETWORKS   364

Carriers (Physical Links)   *364*

Network Services   *374*

WANs   381

SONET   *381*

Wave Division Multiplexing   *383*

WIRELESS WIDE AREA AND ACCESS NETWORKS **383**

Wireless Local Loop   *383*

LMDS and MMDS   *384*

Satellite Links   *385*

CONCLUSION   **386**

TEST YOUR UNDERSTANDING   **387**

13   Client/Server Concepts   *389*

NETWORK GENERATIONS   *390*

Terminal-Host   *390*

Client-File Server   *391*

Client/Server   *394*

DISTRIBUTED DATA VS. DISTRIBUTED PROCESSING   **405**

Distributed Data Structures   *407*

CLIENT/SERVER DATA SYSTEMS   **402**

Data Warehouses   *402*

Computer Telephony Integration   *402*

DISTRIBUTED APPLICATIONS/GROUPWARE   *410*

E-mail and Calendaring   *410*

Groupware: Lotus Notes and Others   *411*

Web Integration   *411*

Agent Software   *412*

CONCLUSION   *412*

TEST YOUR UNDERSTANDING   *413*

14   The Internet and Network Security   *415*

   ORIGINS OF THE INTERNET   *415*

      From DARPA to ARPA   *416*

      Early Uses   *416*

      Organization   *419*

      Virtual Private Networks, Firewalls, and the Concept
      of an Intranet   *434*

   NETWORK SECURITY   *435*

      Encryption Concepts   *436*

   DIGITAL SIGNATURES   *438*

      Digital Envelopes   *439*

      Digital Certificates/Digital IDs   *439*

      Digital Birthmarks   *440*

   CRACKING CODES   *441*

      Methodology   *441*

   SUMMARY OF DIGITAL SECURITY   *443*

   CONCLUSION   *444*

   TEST YOUR UNDERSTANDING   *445*

   PART 3   PUTTING IT ALL TOGETHER   *446*

Conclusion: The Next Stages of Computing   *451*

Glossary   *465*

Recommended Readings   *481*

Index

Acknowledgments

Many people assisted in the preparation of this work, and the space available here doesn't really allow me to do justice to their help. Here's my best shot.

The following people read and commented on parts of the manuscript. Carol Blum of Ohio University, Kate Carey of the Ohio Learning Network, and Patrick Hearne offered extremely helpful suggestions on organization and readability. Doug Gale of OARnet painstakingly reviewed and thoughtfully critiqued the networking section. Don Stredney of the Ohio Supercomputer Center, and John West of the Liquid Crystal Institute at Kent State, provided great insight into graphics technologies.

A core group of exceptional friends and colleagues read the entire manuscript several times, offering a range of invaluable advice and thoughtful ideas. They are: Ed O'Neill, Senior Research Scientist at OCLC; Al Stutz, Director of High Performance Computing at the Ohio Supercomputer Center; and Oscar Garcia, NCR Distinguished Professor of Computer Science at Wright State University. Special thanks to Oscar, who put the pieces in place.

Colin Walters provided help in research and preparation of most aspects of the text. Leon Young assisted with the bibliography and other tasks. Noelle Van Pulis took charge of the index, making the impossible occur on schedule.

John C. Dvorak's comments and encouragement have been extraordinarily important. There can't be a better team of editors than Prentice Hall's Miles Williams and Ralph Moore. Miles provided energy and vision; Ralph's consistent guidance on audience, purpose and tone made all the difference.

It's taken many years to complete this work, and a few friends and colleagues, without directly reading the manuscript, have nonetheless had a central role in making it possible. Chancellors Elaine Hairston and Roderick Chu have been patient and flexible with a colleague whose attention was sometimes distracted from academic issues; without their outstanding leadership, Ohio would be on a much less successful path. Members of the Board of Regents have been consistently supportive of all my endeavors. Regents Gerald Gordon, Elizabeth Lanier, and Tahlman Krumm, Jr. have provided exceptional encouragement and support. And, without the help of my colleague Carol Kenner, I would have been too disorganized to get *anything* done.

Finally, from the guy perpetually at the keyboard, thanks again to my amazingly patient family: my wife Noelle and children Colin, Jessica, and Mairin.

This book is dedicated to my wife, Noelle Van Pulis, and to my uncle, Raymond Walters, Jr., a scholar and mentor.

Introduction

THE ORIGINS OF COMPUTING

The story of computing's development is as fascinating as anything in history. In just more than 50 years, we have gone from some sketchy ideas and concepts to a world in which the number of computing devices is reckoned in the hundreds of millions and growing fast.

- **Early computing devices**

  The concept of a mechanical calculator dates to the Sixteenth Century, and was realized in fits and starts in various ways over the succeeding centuries. By the end of the 1800s, companies were producing devices that were sophisticated and reliable. But, even as businesses and scientists came to rely on these machines, it was obvious that the use of gears and levers would always limit their functionality. Most important, it wasn't practically possible to create mechanical devices that could be programmed. You could add a long list of numbers to get a result, then divide that result, etc. But you couldn't tell a mechanical device to add some numbers, compare the result to some other number, then either divide or multiply depending on the outcome of the comparison. You had to have people make the intermediate decisions, which meant that the operations were invariably slow and error-prone.

  The idea of an electronic computer surfaced not long after the appearance of electronics. It seemed clear to creative people (this is in retrospect, of course) that the vacuum tube, or more accurately collections of vacuum tubes, could do what mechanical devices couldn't—temporarily store the results of calculations and instructions about new ones. The actual realization of an electronic computer occurred in an American university, though which one is the subject of intense debate.

- **The University of Pennsylvania vs. Iowa State**

The University of Pennsylvania vs. Iowa State—not a football game, but a controversy over where the first electronic computer was developed. While most sources credit the first electronic computer, ENIAC (1946), to two University of Pennsylvania researchers, John Mauchly and J. Presper Eckert, there is strong evidence that the first machine was actually built in 1942 by a professor at Iowa State, John V. Atanasoff.

Whatever the verdict, we know that the American university has been a critical part of the initial and continuing development of computing. The first computer was built in an American university, and the first computer company was a direct university spinoff. Universities soon created an entirely new discipline to support the fast growing industry, and their classrooms and labs supplied the educated people as well as much of the actual knowledge that has driven an extraordinary pace of change. The university role, however, has always been in partnership with business and government.

- **The partnership of IBM and the Department of Defense**

IBM was already a mature and well-established company when the first electronic computer was created. Under the leadership of the indomitable Thomas J. Watson, Sr., IBM had taken a position of leadership in office machinery, including devices that performed calculations. The company was caught flat-footed by the advent of the electronic computer, but Watson quickly divined its importance and made an all out effort to secure leadership. There were several ingredients to IBM's rapid success, but none is more important than its understanding of the kind of businesses that would use computers. Even though the technology was new and fragile, IBM appreciated that potential customers, the kind that could afford computers, were not interested in new technology or experimentation. In fact, they were generally risk-averse. A typical IBM customer was a utility company that needed some way to deal with the huge task of calculating, printing, and reconciling its customers' bills. To companies like these, the computer presented an enormous opportunity. As the nation's population grew, and as society experienced a new level of prosperity, the challenge of hiring and housing a vast army of clerks was increasingly difficult—perhaps at some point impossible. On the other hand, the computer was a danger. If just one billing cycle was screwed up, the company would face a disaster of enormous proportions. The company would survive—people would still need electricity—but the executives surely wouldn't. IBM understood this environment perfectly, and provided systems that were amazingly secure and stable given the precariousness of the technology. This ability allowed IBM to dominate its many competitors.

Another dimension of IBM's relationship with its large and conservative customers was that there was no need for dramatic improvements in the technology. If IBM could regularly provide more for less, which was easy to do with a technology that was in its earliest stages, its customers were satisfied. Competitors could and did offer more, but their chronic inability to provide IBM's rock solid reliability and service kept them at the margins. Progress in computing might have continued at a glacial pace were it not for the Department of Defense, which was far more interested in seeing rapid advances incorporated into weaponry and related systems. The Pentagon liked IBM as a partner for the same reason as did the large corporations, and IBM obliged in advancing technology by building, in partnership with US universities, a very strong research capability. As a result, whenever competition forced IBM to pick up the pace on the commercial side, it was ready with something from the lab. This cozy relationship continued until it was broken by the accelerating pace of technological development. To understand why this happened, we need to review the development of computer "generations."

FIVE GENERATIONS OF COMPUTING

Counting computer generations is necessarily controversial—machines don't have the same pedigrees as people. But, the five generations that are described here comprise close to a consensus. We'll characterize them briefly, then discuss the fundamental changes in economics that have resulted.

- **The mainframe**

  The structure of the mainframe hasn't changed a lot since the earliest computers. Its primary characteristic is that all intelligence (computing power), as well as all storage of data and programs, is at the center; kept in the cabinet or cabinets that are the main frame(s). Users get access to the mainframe's intelligence and resources through terminals—dumb devices that are little more than a keyboard and a display.

- **The minicomputer**

  This is probably the most controversial of the generations since it is just a variation on the mainframe—the same basic centralized organization just on a smaller scale and with lower production costs. The reason that the mini is described as a generation is that its lower prices sharply increased access to computing beyond the large corporations that could afford mainframes.

- **The microcomputer**

  The microcomputer, generally synonymous with the personal computer, really is a generation since it offers a dramatic contrast to its predecessors. Where in the past individual users all shared the resources of a single machine, now a single user had direct and personal access to significant computing power as well as to stored programs and data. Eventually, this contrast was blurred as single-user machines were connected with each other over local area networks (LANs), which were then often connected back to mainframes and minis. But, even when all computer users were linked to the big systems, the relationship was fundamentally different. Now, the user had a great deal of independence, and could share with others only as desired, not as required.

- **The Internet and the Web**

  The advent of the Internet provided another dramatic shift. Suddenly, there was an all-enveloping network that meant that all users could connect to all computers. Where the evolution of the previous generation had moved toward aggregation of resources, but only within a defined group—the corporation, organization, or service such as CompuServe—now the Internet, and its graphical offspring the World Wide Web, meant that there was a universal link. With relatively trivial effort, now everyone everywhere could exchange information.

- **Pervasive computing**

  The fundamental shift in pervasive computing is away from the desktop. As advances in technology make possible devices that are both smaller and smarter, we no longer have to sit in a chair and look at a monitor to use a computer. The components of pervasive computing are a very diverse and rapidly evolving group—cell phones, personal digital assistants (like the PalmPilot), television set-top boxes, the control systems of automobiles, and more. Like the microcomputer, these devices were originally independent, but there is tremendous momentum behind the effort to get them to talk to each other, and to the world of machines on the Web, seamlessly and effortlessly.

- **The changing economics of computing**

  The economics of computing have changed with the technology. In the mainframe and minicomputer generations, because hardware was extremely expensive, programmers had to focus on the most efficient use of system resources. This meant that software development was quite conservative. Certainly, there was innovation, but it appeared in a steady, almost predictable stream.

The appearance of the microcomputer changed the dynamics in a fundamental way. The availability of cheap hardware meant that the number of computers expanded from the hundreds of thousands to hundreds of millions. This necessarily wrought an explosion in software. The first wave offered an enormous variety of choices in the basics—the operating systems that manage the computer's work and the core "productivity applications" such as word processing, databases, and spreadsheets. After a time this part of software stabilized, largely under the hegemony of Microsoft, but the shift to the Internet and the Web has produced a second wave of software that looks beyond a single desktop to all of the computers in the world. Fueled by the fact that hardware just gets cheaper and cheaper, allowing the connection of more computers holding more information, this development is changing not just the economics of computing, but the economics of society.

OBJECTIVES OF THE ESSENTIAL
GUIDE TO COMPUTING (EGC)

As I described this book project to friends and colleagues, a typical reaction was something like, "It can't be done. Things change too fast to be captured in a book. It will be out of date before it's printed." The part about things changing fast is certainly true. In the three to four months since the last edits were completed on the manuscript and until the first printed copies appear, some of the technologies mentioned will be on their way to obsolescence, and other new and exciting ones will appear. But, if the world of computing was really changing too fast to understand, the knowledge base of the people who provide the engines of innovation would be too small to sustain the rate of change. In fact, the number of people who really understand the full sweep of issues in computing and telecommunications *is* very small. If you read this book you will have a breadth of knowledge that is very rare.

And, whatever the critics say, it *is* possible to catch the train of technology and climb aboard. If you view this book as a reference to all that is new and current, you will be disappointed. For that, you need the Web, newspapers, and magazines. The real question is how do you get the foundation of knowledge that allows you to understand what the media are saying about technology—not just comprehend it, but put it in the perspective needed for employment, education, or investing? The situation for the average person with technology today would be analogous to that of an untrained person suddenly placed in a football game as a coach (the first and last sports analogy in the book, I promise). This coach doesn't know the rules, much less have any sense of how to develop a strategy, and things are changing so fast that he can't infer them from watching the game. To maintain the analogy then, the purpose of this book is to put you in the stands, and give you a rule book and a TV for instant replay (if I could choose, I would like the comparison to be with John Madden's analysis). This experience should give you the knowledge and perspective you need to be a coach, a referee, or even a player.

COMPANION WEB SITE

There are a variety of paths you can pursue when you complete the EGC. If you only want to continue to be far more informed than all but a handful of people, you simply need to use the Web, the newspapers, and magazines to keep current. To make this easier, we've provided a Web site, www.phptr.com/walters, that both provides direct information and offers links to some of the best sources for breaking knowledge (the Web site also includes answers to the questions provided at the end of each chapter). Alternatively, if you want to go deeper, this book is a foundation for more focused study. To learn in depth, you really (still) need books, and the Suggestions for Further Reading includes an array of choices. The EGC Web site updates these on a regular basis. Needless to say, there are a variety of other directions you could choose. Whatever your decision, I hope this volume launches you in a productive and pleasant direction.

Part 1

Computer Hardware

(Chapters 1 through 4)

The four chapters in this first section will introduce you to computing's foundation—hardware. It's common for people who use computers to be intimidated by hardware. They assume that only engineers can hope to understand the exotic devices that lurk inside a computer's case. In fact, computing devices employ some fairly basic principles, and any interested person can easily understand them.

Once you're familiar with how the various parts of a computer work, you'll appreciate an additional point—there are a variety of ways to accomplish most of the tasks for which computers are used. Abetted by poorly informed sales staff, many people think that computers differ only in that some parts have a higher speed rating and others have more capacity. Not to say that speed and capacity aren't important—they most definitely are—but that's not the end of the story. For example, the simple term 'speed' is deceptive. A computer that might be very fast at one kind of task could be slow at another. Further, although it's always good to have more space on a hard disk or more memory, there are other qualifying factors. For example, what kind of memory is it? Where in the system is it located? There are different kinds of memory and where the various pieces are placed in the system matters a lot. There are even different kinds of CPUs—the chips that do the actual processing. The speed of the chip, that famous "800 MHz!" or whatever it says on the ad, can even be deceptive. Some CPUs with slower speed ratings are much faster than their competitors at many tasks.

This last point brings us to architecture—a term that refers to both the way in which a computer's key parts are organized and also to the organization of the elements within the CPU. Both will be discussed in this section, and in the process you should appreciate that the kind of hardware you buy is increasingly dependent on the software you use. If games and graphics are your thing, then put your money in one place. If you are buying for work, you'll understand that it makes sense to structure the innards of your file server differently from that of your e-commerce Web server. On the in-chip side of architecture, we'll see that the choices available to designers, and of course therefore to buyers, are increasing rapidly. We're now entering the age of the "system on a chip," a concept that will be the driving force behind pervasive computing. But, these single chip computers will have an array of divergent designs. As more and more devices acquire computational power, it's likely that the number of distinct chip architectures will increase significantly.

To help you understand these issues, the first three chapters of this section are:

- Chapter 1: The Core of Computing: How the Key Elements of Hardware Work Together
- Chapter 2: Memory, Storage and Input/Output
- Chapter 3: Computer Monitors and Graphics Systems

Before leaving the general topic of hardware, however, we'll move to discuss the overall issue of change. To introduce this, think of the question of flexibility. As designs in the marketplace proliferate, it's common for buyers to be advised to look for flexibility. In computers especially, much is made of the ease with which a particular model can be upgraded. While no one is going to say that you should ignore this issue in buying a computer, in fact the chances that you will significantly upgrade any computer you buy today are very small. The truth is that, if you find that you need new capabilities in a system three years after you bought it, the pace of change is such that it's almost certain that buying a new one is cheaper than upgrading the old. Why is this? The answers are in the final chapter of this section:

- Chapter 4: Silicon economics

After reading this, you'll appreciate that we could soon see the ultimate alternative to flexibility—the special-purpose throw away computer. So plunge in to the hardware pool. You'll find that it's easy to stay afloat, and once you've learned those basic principles, you'll be way ahead of your information-illiterate colleagues.

1 The Core of Computing: How the Key Elements of Hardware Work Together

Even experienced computer users have at best a sketchy idea of how a computer really works. They know how to launch and use applications. They can connect to the Internet, surf the Web, play games, or whatever. Some of the most advanced (and fearless) users are even able to install internal components, such as memory modules or network "boards." But few people actually stop to think about how a computer carries out the functions that it is asked to perform. If they did, they would be surprised at how easy it is to understand. Like Mr. Spock on Star Trek, everything in a computer is *logical.* You don't have to be an engineer or a scientist to learn how things work. And mastering these core principles of computing is worth your while. Once you do, you will become a far more knowledgeable participant in today's "information society."

This chapter deals, for the most part, with the heart of computing—the CPU (Central Processing Unit). If you tell the computer to do something—display a character on the screen, draw a line, or add two numbers—the CPU either completes the work itself or manages the parts that do. Once you understand the role of the CPU, you can quickly and easily branch out to learn how other parts of the computing system work. By the end of this chapter, you will be familiar with

- The basic components and operations of a computer
- The functions of the CPU
- How it is possible for CPUs to become faster and more effective every year
- How the CPU is being adapted to fit a diverse array of tasks

3

AN OVERVIEW OF HOW A COMPUTER WORKS

The best way to describe a mechanism as complex as a computer is to begin with a quick overview, sort of an orientation. This allows you to get a sense of the general flow of operations, making it easier to put the individual pieces in context as they appear. The difficulty with this approach, of course, is that you will encounter in this quick introduction some terms and concepts that may not be completely clear right away. Since the overview can't explain everything in depth—that would defeat the purpose—this section will include a number of the "Tech Talks" that are used throughout the book to explain key terms. If that's not enough, remember that more detailed explanations will follow quickly.

What Happens When a Computer Starts Up

The following section describes, in highly simplified form (and slightly rearranged for purposes of illustration), what happens when a typical microcomputer *boots up* (starts). The various parts of the computer are introduced as they appear.

Tech Talk

Booting: Computers are described as *booting up* after the observation of early designers that the system should "pull itself up by its boot-straps."

Power On

Once power is turned on, electricity flows through all of the chips and their circuits. Most components just sit and wait for instructions, but one chip, called a *ROM BIOS* (Read Only Memory, Basic Input/Output System, usually abbreviated just *BIOS*), is designed to begin giving commands as soon as it receives power. The BIOS contains an entire set of instructions, in effect a computer program written into the chip, that manages the boot-up process.

Tech Talk

BIOS: The Basic Input/Output System (BIOS) refers to a chip in some types of microcomputers, especially those that use Microsoft operating systems. The BIOS, which can be thought of as an extension of the operating system, holds information about attached devices such as disk drives, external buses, etc. The BIOS also helps systems boot up. See Chapter 7 for more detail.

The CPU Begins its Work

The first stage of the boot-up process verifies that all components are working properly. When that's complete, the BIOS hands over control to another chip, the CPU (central processing unit). Unlike the ROM, which simply holds instructions, the CPU is a microprocessor. As a processor (the micro just means that it is on one chip), the CPU has two distinct capabilities.

Tech Talk

ROM [vs. RAM]:   Read Only Memory (ROM) is a kind of chip that has information permanently burned into it. Since ROM is nonvolatile, this is a handy way to provide the computer with information that has to be readily accessible but doesn't need to change. Early BIOSes used ROM, though Flash memory, which is also nonvolatile but is faster and can be rewritten, is now preferred.

Tech Talk

CPU: The Central Processing Unit (CPU) is the part of the computer that carries out the actual computation—arithmetic and logical operations. In the earliest computers, the CPU used many chips, but today's computers nearly all use microprocessors in which all functions are on one chip.

1. The CPU can carry out a variety of mathematical and logical operations. Its basic mathematical abilities include the traditional addition, subtraction, multiplication, and division. Building on these, it can also do any other kind of mathematics. The critical logical abilities of a computer focus on comparison—for example, it can determine if two numbers are equal. This seems a simple task, but it is one that is crucial to computer programs. Finally, while the CPU does all of its mathematical and logical operations on numbers, those numbers can be used to represent things that aren't numerical. For example, the letters of the alphabet, or objects such as lines in drawings, can each be given numerical codes that identify them and set them apart from others. As a result, the computer can work with text, graphic images, and so forth.

2. The second core ability of the CPU is to manage, in a very intelligent way, the flow of information (instructions and data) into and out of its circuits. We'll see why this is important when we turn to the next stage of the boot-up process.

Addresses Come into Play

The last instruction that the ROM sends to the CPU is to go to a specific location to find the next instruction. In telling the CPU where to look, the ROM provides it with what is called an *address*. Computer addresses, like those on letters, are simply directions to where something can be found. Like everything else inside the computer, addresses are numbers. We'll see later that the size of the number matters. Since CPUs use these addresses to create what amounts to a very sophisticated filing system, the bigger the number, the larger the *address space*—the maximum size of the file system.

> **Tech Talk**
>
> **Address: Computers use addresses to keep track of information in much the same way as the post office uses them to find residences and businesses. The bigger the number in an address, the more locations it can refer to. Most current computers use a 32-bit *address space* for memory, which means that there can be over four billion separate locations to hold information. See Chapter 5 for more about addresses.**

The address of the instruction the CPU is to carry out enters its chip on a set of wires that is called a *bus*. The bus that is used in this case is known as the *data bus*. This is a path that is able to carry information both into and out of the CPU's chip (see Figure 1.1).

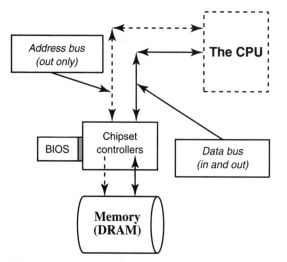

Figure 1.1 Connections through the chipset.
The address and data buses (together known as the *system,* or *memory,* bus) connect the CPU to the chipset (of which the BIOS is sometimes considered a part) and from there to memory (DRAM).

To continue with our example, the address given to the CPU by the BIOS is for something the CPU doesn't have on board. As a result, the CPU promptly puts the address on another bus, in this case the appropriately named *address bus*. When the CPU does this, it is called a *fetch*. The address bus in effect carries a request for help—the CPU is asking other parts of the computer to provide it with needed information. Unlike the data bus, this connection goes only from the CPU to the outside— nothing comes in on the address bus.

Tech Talk

Bus: A bus is a pathway that carries information between two or more parts of a computer. There are internal buses, such as the system (memory) and I/O buses, and external buses, such as USB or FireWire.

The Role of Memory

The address bus connects first to a part of the computer called *memory*. The term memory refers to a class of silicon chips that are able to hold instructions or data. The CPU can either *read* information from memory or *write* to it. The most common type of memory chip is called DRAM (Dynamic Random Access Memory). Current DRAM chips can hold 64 million bits of data (see below for an explanation of *bit*) which, at ~5,500 bits per page, translates to some 12,000 pages of simple text per chip. In most computer systems, DRAM chips are arrayed in groups of eight, with the result that they can hold quite a bit of information. Unfortunately, DRAM chips are *volatile,* which means that they need electrical power to retain their contents. Since the computer has just been turned on in our boot-up example, this means that the instruction the CPU seeks isn't to be found in DRAM.

Tech Talk

DRAM: Dynamic Random Access Memory (DRAM) is a type of chip- based storage that has the advantage of being reasonably fast and inex- pensive, but the disadvantage of being *volatile*—losing its contents when electrical power is cut off.

The Chipset

In order to get to memory, the address bus has had to travel through a small group of chips known as the *chipset*. These chips (the number varies according to the type and brand of computer) perform what is known as *glue logic,* which is to say that they bind together, both physically and functionally, the various pieces at the core of the computer. Their importance is illustrated by the fact that their individual names usually include the word *controller,* as in *memory controller.*

Tech Talk

Chipset: The chipset refers to a group of chips that provides an intelligent interface for the core components of a computer—CPU, memory, graphics, I/O system. Described as *core logic* or *glue logic.*

Back to our boot up example. When the instruction can't be found in memory, the chipset redirects it to another bus, known as the I/O (Input/Output) bus, that connects the chipset to other places where information is stored.

The I/O Bus and the Hard Drive

In a typical computer of today, the chipset will send the address over the I/O bus to what is called the *hard disk* (see Figure 1.2). This device, which consists of a series of magnetic platters, operates in a physical sense very differently from memory, but has the same functional role of allowing the CPU to read and write information. Why does the computer have two places—memory and disk—that have the same function? The answer is that the two complement each other. Memory operates very fast, but has a high cost per unit of data stored and is volatile. The hard disk, on the other hand, is much slower, but has a low cost per unit of data maintained and is not volatile. As a rough measure, for the same cost, the hard disk provides fifty times as much storage as memory. To get the best of both worlds, most desktop and similar computers combine chip and disk storage and operate them in a hierarchical fashion,

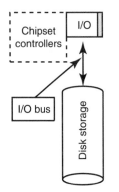

Figure 1.2 Disk I/O.
Disks connect to the CPU via the I/O bus, which is in turn connected to the chipset. See also Figure 1.1.

the voice, music, or noise waves that enter a microphone. Analog systems are well suited to carrying information, but not to modifying it.

Tech Talk

Digital: A digital system is one that translates all of the information it works with to numbers—*binary* numbers in the case of computers. Compare to *analog*.

Binary and digital systems gave birth to the term *bit,* which is a contraction of *binary* and *digit.* A bit is a single digit that can be either one or zero—in other words, it can hold just two values. But, by putting bits together in a row, you can get to bigger numbers. How big is easy to calculate—you just use the number of digits as a power of two. This is illustrated in Table 1.1 below.

When computers were first commercialized, engineers needed a standard binary value to use for the exchange of information both inside and outside of the machine. They chose eight bits since this binary number can represent 256 values and therefore can describe all of the things needed for normal commerce—every letter of the alphabet, all normal punctuation, all of the decimal numbers, and a bunch of special symbols. Thus, the term *byte,* shorthand for any eight-bit number, became the standard unit of measure in computing. IBM really made the byte a standard. Its early business computers were designed to manipulate one byte at a time in their internal circuits.

The capability of a computer in bits is a way of describing the width of its circuits. If you look at Table 1.1, you can see that moving an entire byte at once, in parallel, requires more wires than moving just one bit. So, if a computer is described as 8-bit, this means that there are eight wires that move information from place to place

Table 1.1   Binary Values

Binary Values		
Bits used/values in powers of 2	**Values expressed in binary form**	**Total values**
1	0, 1	$2 (2^1)$
2	00, 01, 10, 11	$4 (2^2)$
3	000, 001, 010, 011, 100, 101, 111, 110	$8 (2^3)$
4	0000, 0001, 0010, 0011, 0100, 0101, 0111, etc.	$16 (2^4)$
8	00000001, 00000010, 00000011, etc.	$256 (2^8)$
16	0000000000000001, 0000000000000011, etc.	$65,536 (2^{16})$
32	00000000000000000000000000000001, etc.	$4,294,967,296 (2^{32})$

Table 1.2 Bits and Bytes

Bits and Bytes			
	Thousand	**Million**	**Billion**	**Trillion**
Bits	Kbit	Mbit	Gigabit	Terabit
Bytes	KB	MB	GB	TB

in the CPU, that the circuits that do mathematics and logic are eight transistors wide, and that registers can hold eight bits at once. The various buses can also be described in terms of width. In today's desktop computers, the standard circuit size is now four bytes, or 32-bits, and all internal CPU structures are that wide, as are the various buses (some are even wider).

The common way of referring to large numbers of bits and bytes is to use a standard prefixing: *kilo* (or just K) for thousand, *mega* (M) for million, and *giga* (G) for billion, and *tera* (T) for trillion. If the prefix is in front of *bits,* it will normally be written out (e.g., 1 Mbit refers to a million bits), although a lowercase *b* is also used (Mb=Mbit). If it is in front of bytes, it will normally just get a capital *B* (1 MB is a million bytes).

With this overview behind you, you're ready to get into the core of the computer, the CPU. Until Intel's "Intel Inside" advertising campaign started in the mid-1990s, many computer users didn't even know they had a CPU, let alone how it did its work. But since CPU design is going through some major changes, ones that will present users with a lot of choices in the near future, it makes sense to get acquainted with this most essential part of computing.

THE INTERNAL OPERATIONS OF THE CPU . . . .

As noted earlier, the CPU is also called a *microprocessor* because all of its components—at least all those needed to carry out calculations—are on a single silicon chip (see Chapter 4 for a discussion of how chips are made). We'll begin our overview of the microprocessor with a simple description of its functions. The classical CPU includes a four-sequence operation (see Figure 1.4).

1. Fetch
2. Decode
3. Execute
4. Store

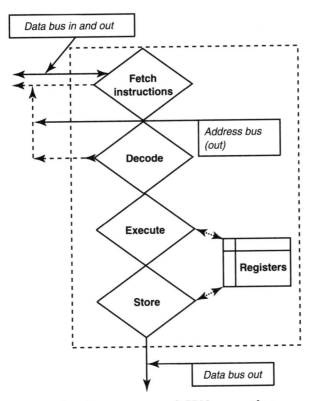

Figure 1.4 Four stages of CPU operation.
The four steps completed by a CPU include *fetching* information (instructions and data); *decoding* instructions to determine what to do with them; *executing* instructions (for example adding numbers); and *storing* the result of the instruction either on-chip in a register to await another instruction or back in memory or storage if immediate access isn't needed.

Fetch

First, instructions and data are fetched from outside the chip (usually this means from DRAM). An example of an instruction is one that contains a simple mathematical operation such as "add." In some cases, the data used by an instruction are included with it; in other instances, the instruction references the locations where the data are held. These locations are called addresses. So, an "add" instruction might carry the numbers to be added with it, or it might state that the value in *address x* is to be added to the value in *address y*. An instruction actually contains two parts: an *opcode*—the action to be performed—and the *operand*—the data it works on. So, "add" is an opcode, and *address x* and *address y* are operands.

Decode (Analyze)

Once the CPU has received the instruction, it is turned over to an area of the chip that decodes (analyzes) it in order to determine which of the chip's circuits should be used for processing. This analysis stage can also include other functions. For example, some chips will look into the stream of incoming instructions to reorder them so they can be completed in the most efficient way possible. Also, in the event that the instruction does not include the actual data that will be used, but just their addresses, this is the point at which the CPU will retrieve the data.

Execute

If the CPU is the brains of the computer, then the ALU (arithmetic/logical unit) is the part where the actual thinking (*execution* of the instruction) takes place. The ALU includes groups of transistors, known as *logic gates,* that are organized to carry out basic mathematical and logical operations. An appropriately arranged collection of logic gates can then execute a complete mathematical instruction (such as "add" or "divide" two numbers) or a logical instruction (such as "compare" two values). The instructions that a specific ALU can execute are known as its *instruction set.* CPUs from different vendors (e.g., Intel, Sun) have different instruction sets. Problems of systems compatibility begin at this level. Software written to the Intel instruction set won't work (at all) on other types of processors such as Sun's SPARC family or the IBM/Motorola Power PC series. Like different languages, instruction sets vary in both their vocabulary and their grammar (for example, they use different ways of organizing instructions).

Tech Talk

Logic gate: A logic gate is a series of transistors connected in a way that allows it to carry out a mathematical or logical operation such as addition. Logic gates are grouped into electrical circuits that execute the CPU's instructions such as to "add" two numbers or "compare" two values.

REGISTER HERE

Registers provide a good example of the connection between hardware and software. Intel's original 16-bit CPU, the 8086/8088, had only eight general purpose registers that programmers could use to hold data and instructions. As more room became available on the chip, it would have been logical to increase this number, since in most cases more registers means better performance. But Intel couldn't do this because it would have made newer chips incompatible with older "legacy" software. The number of general purpose registers finally increased—to 48—when Intel completely rearranged the architecture of its chips with the sixth generation (Pentium Pro) in 1995. Significantly, these CPUs included a mechanism for translating old register instructions to new ones.

Store

Instructions have to tell the CPU not only what operation to perform, but where to put the result. There are a number of options. If the instruction is *iterative,* for example adding two numbers then adding another to the result, the instruction will tell the CPU to place the product of the first addition in a special short-term on-chip storage area, known as a *register,* until it is needed. Because the registers are interwoven with the ALU's circuits, they allow very fast retrieval. Alternatively, if the result is not expected to be used again right away, it will be sent off-chip to memory (fast retrieval) or to disk storage (a lot slower—see Figure 1.5 for an overview of these parts).

Tech Talk

Register: A register is an on-CPU storage space where instructions and data can be transferred and held temporarily for fast retrieval.

Recent changes in computer architecture have simplified the way in which the CPU manages instructions. In the old style, it was common for a programmer to tell the computer to "add the value at memory location xx to the value in memory location yy and place it in memory location zz." The problem with this approach, often called *fetch/execute,* is that operations that need to access memory are slow. The CPU has to wait for many clock cycles while the information is looked up and retrieved. Current system strategy limits memory accesses to *load* and *store* operations. In this approach, the programmer will first give the computer instructions to load the appropriate data from memory to a register or registers. Then, an *add* instruction would be something like this: "add the value in register a to the value in register b and place the result in register c." Subsequently, another instruction could tell the CPU to "store the value in register c in memory location zz."

The value of the *load/store* approach is that every operation doesn't have to begin with a *load* since some or all of the data to be manipulated are already in registers. In considering this strategy, you will appreciate that it is important to have a lot

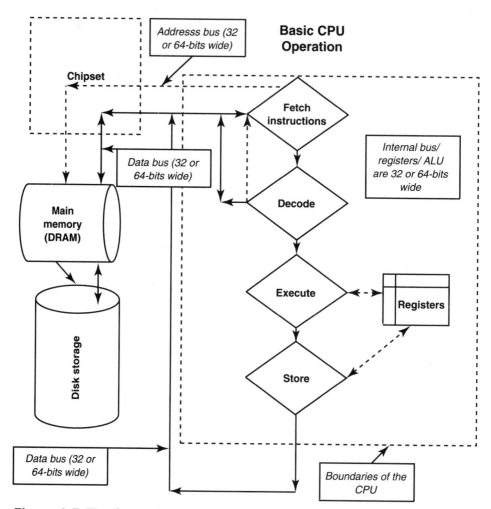

Figure 1.5 The flow of instructions in a CPU.
Note that this illustration shows bus widths.

of registers. With a large *register file*, you can use one load operation to bring an entire data series onto the CPU and do all your additions or whatever without having to access memory again. It's easy to see that adding registers is an important way of making a CPU more productive.

Tech Talk

Instruction set: The instruction set refers to both the instructions that a CPU can execute and the way in which they are organized. CPUs from different vendors have different instruction sets unless one is a *clone* of the other.

The Clock

Correctly executing instructions in a CPU depends on perfect synchronization. If instructions somehow got out of logical sequence, more of the results would be erroneous than accurate, and even worse, it would be impossible to tell which was right and which was wrong. Since even one error is intolerable, something in the system has to make sure that actions within the CPU are coherent. This management function is performed by the clock. As described earlier, the clock's circuitry is based on a quartz crystal system like that used in watches. At precisely timed intervals, the clock sends out pulses of electricity that cause bits to move from place to place within or between logic gates or between logic gates and registers. Simple instructions, such as add, can often be executed in just one clock cycle, while complex ones, such as divide, will require a number of smaller steps, each using one cycle. Chip speed is measured in cycles per second, which was once referred to by the acronym *cps,* but which is now known by the word Hertz (abbreviated Hz and named for the famous German scientist Gustav Hertz). So, a 700 million cycle per second CPU is described as functioning at 700 MHz.

Interrupts

If the CPU couldn't be interrupted until it had completed a task, its usefulness would be greatly reduced. In effect, the CPU would be like the primitive batch processing computers of the earliest days of computing; they could work on only one program at a time and were unable to do anything else until that program was completed.

To make interrupts possible, CPUs have lines (wires) that connect them to an external interrupt controller chip (part of the chipset), which contains a small database of what are known as *interrupt vectors.* When an interrupt signal comes onto the chip, the CPU saves what it is doing and goes to the interrupt vector (which is just a fancy name for a numerical table) to find the address of the instruction that the interrupt is telling it to execute instead. When finished, it goes back to the previous task. The CPU keeps track of where it was by writing the address of an interrupted task to a special register known as a *stack.* Interrupts have various priority levels that are interpreted differently according to the task the CPU is engaged in. For example, a busy CPU might temporarily ignore low priority interrupts, such as those coming from the keyboard, but would respond immediately to a high priority one that carried something like a disk error message. Similarly, a software program can be designed to *mask* lower priority interrupts if it isn't capable of being stopped.

Designing a Faster CPU

As computers become more powerful, defined as being able to do a greater amount of work in a given unit of time, they become more useful. How do you get more power? This section describes the most important strategies.

Faster Clock Speeds

It's obvious that a faster clock will allow more to be done in a given unit of time. The original IBM PC's clock ticked just under 5 million times a second (actually, 4.77 MHz). As this is written (1999), standard PCs are beginning to exceed 700 million clock cycles per second. This hundredfold-plus improvement has taken just over 15 years. And the beat goes on. Expect speeds of desktop machines to double—to a billion and a half cycles per second (1.5 GHz)—by 2001.

A chip's maximum clock speed, the fastest it can go without producing errors, is a function of how it is made. Specifically, higher speeds require that distances within the CPU have to be shorter. Thus, for the hundredfold improvement we have seen so far, the connecting lines between transistors in logic gates have to be shorter (thinner) and closer together, and these in turn have to be closer to other logic gates, registers, and other circuits. Faster chips necessarily have greater density; that is to say they have more transistors in a given area. Figure 1.6 illustrates one type of transistor.

> ### Tech Talk
>
> **Clock speed: CPUs (and other devices) are controlled by quartz crystal clocks. The consistent timing provided by the clocks helps to keep operations synchronized. Clock speed is usually measured in millions of cycles per second; abbreviated MHz.**

There are several reasons why shorter distances are essential to faster chips. One is that the speed of electricity in a wire is constant. Our speedier clock is not actually making bits move faster, it is just making them move more frequently. Since electrons won't go faster, a higher speed circuit must assume shorter distances for each clock cycle. Distance is an issue even within transistors. If the parts of a transistor are closer together, it can cycle faster. A bonus is that chips with shorter internal paths also require less power.

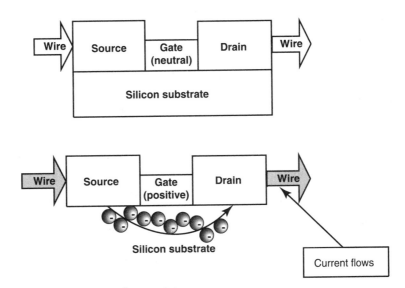

Figure 1.6 One type of transistor.
In the top drawing, the gate is neutral and there is no movement of electrical current. If a positive charge is applied to the gate, as in the lower drawing, electrons are attracted and allow current to flow from the source to the drain. If wires are attached to the source and drain, the transistor is a switch. If current flows, it is a 1; if not, it is a 0. The narrower the gate, the faster the chip can cycle, or turn a circuit on and off. The transistor is naturally a binary device. There isn't much you can do with one transistor, but put them together in groups, *logic gates,* and you have something really powerful.

TIMELESS CHIPS

Clock-driven CPUs work well, but this synchronous approach is energy inefficient. Every time the clock ticks, electricity pulses through the chip, whether any computation is going on or not. Laptops and other devices that need to save power do so in part by slowing or even shutting down the CPU when not in use. The penalty in this method, of course, is that the CPU is slow to reawaken when needed. Asynchronous (non clock-driven) chips exist, and have been shown to have much lower power consumption, but the required control circuitry uses lots of transistors that could be employed for computation. However, as shrinking parts allow more transistors on a chip, expect asynchronous designs to be used for special purposes where both low power and fast reaction are essential.

Making distances shorter in a CPU (or any other chip) means that the fundamental features of the circuits need to be smaller. Among the most important of these elements are the *traces*, microscopic equivalents of wires that make the paths between logic gates. Feature size, in the form of trace widths and transistor design rules, has gone from about 0.5 microns (a micron is one millionth of a meter or about one twenty-five thousandth of an inch) in the original PC to about 0.18 microns in the 700 million-plus cycles per second screamer of today; 0.15 design rules should be standard and 0.13 in testing by the time you read this. These successive stages of miniaturization are the result of some incredible improvements in process engineering. You would expect to be told next that these advances don't come cheap. Well they don't; the cost of chip factories, or *fabs*, goes up by huge amounts with each new generation. New ones today are in the several billion dollar range. Amazingly though, each of these fabs is radically more productive. This means that once processes are perfected, smaller, faster CPUs are also cheaper than their bigger, slower predecessors. This is the reason for "Moore's Law," which states that the number of transistors on a chip doubles every eighteen months, while the cost falls by about fifty percent. By the way, since there was no Bureau of Computer Laws where Moore could register his thought, there are a lot of variations of his law floating around.

Tech Talk

Trace: The wires that connect devices within a chip are so tiny that they are called *traces*.

Tech Talk

Moore's Law: Intel pioneer Gordon Moore stated that the number of transistors on a chip would double every eighteen months, and that their cost would fall by fifty percent during the same time.

Table 1.3 provides an example of the impact of smaller design rules on a chip's size and speed. A CPU made by IBM and Motorola, the Power PC604e, was unusual because it kept the same design through three process generations. Fortunately, this anomaly provides an excellent illustration. You'll observe that as its internal elements got smaller, the chip shrank in size while its speed increased. Most important, the smaller and faster version was also less power-hungry and a lot cheaper to manufacture than its bigger, slower, energy-gulping predecessors. The manufacturing dimension is discussed in Chapter 4, but note for the moment that it's likely that the 47mm^2 size yielded four times as many good chips from one wafer as the 148mm^2 version.

Wider Paths

In addition to a faster clock, a way of speeding up the CPU is to have it process more bits on every cycle. The first generation of microcomputers moved 8 bits at a time, the first IBM PC was 16 bits wide, the current generation of microprocessors is 32

Media Processors

A fast developing class of microprocessors is one that combines high-end DSP capabilities and some pipelines that have been optimized for graphics, together with relatively limited general-purpose integer functions. These chips, known as media processors, are aimed at the game machine and television set-top box markets. The thinking here, as with the development of RISC, is that chip real estate should be focused to the task at hand.

To give you the most realistic possible gore, your 3D game machine needs to process thirty or so complex graphical images (frames) in a second. Each of these images will have many objects, each of which will require a vast amount of computation. Originally, there were two ways to build these systems. One was to market a box whose silicon was dedicated to running games. Another was to add fast graphics processing ability to PCs. The newest alternative is to do the reverse—add some PC-type functions to a game-type chip. Of course, this kind of system won't run Word as fast as a Pentium III. However, in many cases, the slower speed won't matter since, when it comes to writing, the machine's principal users are typically still in the crayon stage. The first generation of chips to be described as *media processors* included some rather dramatic failures. As a result, the term has become somewhat unpopular. Thus, Sony and Toshiba, who created the first of a new class of super powerful media processors for the Sony Playstation, chose to call their chip the *emotion engine*.

· ·

Two for One?

Microprocessor vendors, led by IBM, are planning to use the extra transistors made available by 0.18 micron technology to put multiple CPUs on a single chip. While a single large processor might seem to make more sense, there are a number of reasons for this new approach. Interestingly, one concern is that if all circuits were combined in one CPU on a single chip, distances could become so great that a clock pulse could not get all the way across the chip in one cycle.

FPGAs

An interesting new variation on processor design is the *field programmable gate array* (FPGA). These chips use special transistors (SRAM cells, see Chapter 2) at critical junction points in their structure. The junction points can be switched, effectively altering the architecture of the chip. A relatively dumb kind of FPGA can only be programmed once, but more sophisticated kinds can be reoriented on the fly. As an example of what this technique can do, the military uses FPGA chips in target recognition computers. A chip might be programmed to look for twenty types of objects. After the system has scanned through the full set of possibilities and rejected some of them (e.g., there are no tanks present), the junction points are reset so that the entire capability of the processor is focused on analyzing the remaining options, for example, the more difficult task of finding artillery pieces. The problem with FPGAs is that the junction points use a lot of space, meaning that for the same computational capacity, they will always be quite a bit bigger than a normal CPU. Still, for some applications, FPGAs will be an increasingly popular choice. And the general concept appears to be at the heart of some of the most advanced processors now on the drawing boards (see Chapter 4).

NEW APPROACHES TO COMPUTING . . . .

There are a lot of radical ideas out there about how to make calculation much faster than it is today. We'll just mention a few.

Supercooling

Electrical circuits operate faster and more efficiently when they are cold—*very* cold, like 90° Kelvin (around –300° Fahrenheit). The biggest benefit of the CPU-in-the-deep-freeze is that it makes much higher clock speeds available. Unfortunately, there are a lot of hurdles to overcome before your desktop will feature a really cool computer. One is that the technology currently needed to supercool electronics is both expensive and bulky. If that problem is solved, there is the fact that both the CPU and the circuitry that it connects to will have to be redesigned to operate successfully in this temperature range. Still, these are not huge barriers. Supercooling is already being used in some high-end computers (supercomputer class), and a variety of companies are working to bring it to the midrange of mainframe competitors.

On a slightly different front, engineers are exploring the use of materials in the chip itself that have the property of carrying heat away. While this approach won't create dramatic changes in speed, the expected 100 percent or so improvement would be significant.

Optical Computing

As will be mentioned frequently in this book, electrical signals are vulnerable to interference from many sources. Reducing this vulnerability to zero is probably impossible; even getting close would require an enormous amount of bulky shielding. The whole concept of "micro" would disappear. Computers compensate for the probable interference by using complicated algorithms that analyze information sent from "A" to "B" in order to determine if it arrived correctly. This is true even within the CPU; it becomes a major exercise as data flows off the CPU to other parts of the computer.

An optical computer would be a great solution to this problem. Light in a vacuum is faster than electricity in a wire (~30 cm/sec. vacuum vs. ~20 cm./sec), but with current technology, this difference is of relatively little value. More important for the moment is that it is much easier to guard against interference in optics, which means that data carried by light can be transmitted with less error checking. The throughput (the real vs. the theoretical speed) of optical switches is therefore much greater than with data carried by electrons. Research has demonstrated that internal connections in a computer, say from the CPU to memory or to disk, could be accomplished much faster by light than by electricity. And it is feasible to build such a connection. So why isn't it done?

The first reason is that there isn't yet a compelling need for such speed in mainstream commercial machines. Existing computers are not yet hobbled by the problem of moving data on their very short, relatively error free, internal paths. This will likely change once the annual sixty percent or so increase in CPU speeds starts to go away—perhaps around 2015. The more important reason why optical components are not yet used inside production systems is that the increases they would bring are, at the moment, largely theoretical. The problem is that only an all-optical device will be significantly faster—translating from electronic data to optical data is a serious bottleneck. The electronics that do this are complicated and not especially fast.

So why not make the whole thing, including the CPU, optical? That's a powerfully attractive idea, and lots of scientists are working on it. Optical computers exist in the lab, but making a purely optical system, one that is able to avoid all the problems of electricity, is not yet possible on a commercial scale. Indeed, researchers appear to be quite some distance from achieving that. They need, as they say, a few "breakthroughs." Of course, breakthroughs are things that may or may not occur. Experience says that they will in this case, but when—two years, ten years, twenty years—is anybody's guess.

In the meantime, computer companies are getting lots of experience with optics. Because interference, and therefore reduced throughput, has been a real problem in computer networking, optical interconnects (fiber optics) are in wide use there and are rapidly becoming ubiquitous.

Even More Exotic Stuff

The electronic logic gate has a long way to go—to around 2010–2015—before it begins to lose momentum as the center of computation. Even so, scientists are actively exploring other, radically different techniques. One approach is to directly manipulate atoms so that the basic unit of measure becomes individual electrons (quantum computing). Expect to hear a lot about *carbon nanontubes* in the near future. Another concept is to use biochemical reactions, as in combining DNA, to execute enormously complex calculations at speeds that electronic systems could not hope to duplicate. Indeed, scientists are exploring pretty much everything that mirrors the ability of a transistor to act as a binary switch. As interesting as these ideas are, they aren't likely to have much of an impact in the near future—most definitely including the useful lifetime of this edition.

CONCLUSION . . . .

This chapter began with some basics of computation: computers work with instructions (opcodes) and data (operands). As these are fed into the CPU, the CPU goes through a standard series of operations—fetch, decode, execute, store. However, although these basics apply to all CPUs, there is considerable diversity after that. If the CPU is thought of in terms of the standard desktop system, we can observe that there have been considerable changes in architecture over a fairly short period of time.

The original complex instruction set (CISC) design has given way to one that uses, at least to some extent, a reduced instruction set (RISC) approach. Other organizational changes include the addition of multiple pipelines (superscalar) and specialized pipelines for such things as general floating point mathematics and for streaming media. Designers are also finding ways to optimize parallel execution with approaches such as having one instruction work on multiple pieces of data at once (SIMD) and including multiple instructions in one word (VLIW). At the same time that there is an increasing variety of approaches to the architecture of the standard desktop computer's CPU, there are more radical concepts for different kinds of devices. Application-specific integrated circuits (ASICs) can be added to a standard CPU "core" to make it more efficient at a limited range of tasks, while digital signal processors (DSPs) are being used to handle the increased need to work with information, such as video or audio signals, that are inherently analog rather than digital. Finally, the media processor presents a hybrid that is optimized for games and other entertainment-related computing. Given that we have seen so much change in only a quarter century or so, and given that designers have a vast increase in the number of transistors they can play with, it's reasonable to expect that we are just at the beginning of thinking about how to design CPUs. In the future, a knowledgeable person is no more likely to say that a particular computer has "a CPU" than she would be to say the she drives "a vehicle."

We'll talk at some length about directions in CPU design and manufacture in Chapter 4. In the meantime, let's remember that the CPU can't do its work alone and that its effective speed depends on what happens in other parts of the computer. In the next chapter, we'll cover where instructions and data come from (memory and storage) and how they are moved into and out of the system (I/O). Next, Chapter 3 will discuss the increasingly important question of displays—how the computer manages to take streams of data and convert them into complex graphics that are visible on a screen or a printed page.

TEST YOUR UNDERSTANDING · · · · · · · · · · · ·

1. What are the four stages of CPU operation?

2. What does an interrupt do?

3. What is the *width* of CPUs for contemporary desktop computers?

4. Why have clock speeds increased so rapidly since the microprocessor was invented?

5. Why is pipelining important?

6. What is distinctive about a superscalar processor?

7. What is the difference between fetch/execute and load/store?

8. What is the difference between RISC and CISC?

9. What is the key reason for Moore's Law?

10. What is the difference between VLIW and SIMD?

11. What is the principal advantage of optical computing? What is the principal challenge to realizing it?

12. What are examples of special purpose CPUs?

notably slower, and disk storage is *vastly* slower. Computer designers use the term *wait state* for intervals when the CPU babbles to itself and no useful work occurs because needed information has to be retrieved from the outside world. Some proportion of wait states is obviously unavoidable, but if they begin to mount up, they greatly diminish the effective speed of the CPU.

While there is bad news here, it's not quite as bad as it seems. The times shown in Table 2.1 are for *random* access—if the CPU suddenly needs to find an instruction or a piece of data that it did not expect to need. Fortunately, its quite common that accesses are *sequential*. We've already talked about the CPU "prefetching" instructions and data—if it is beginning to process a particular instruction, it will assume that the next to be needed is at the memory location just after the previous one and go ahead and get it. This sequentiality obtains quite often for both instructions and data. In cases like these, we'll see that accesses can be much faster. It's important to note at this point that different kinds of software are accessed from storage in different ways. Ordinary business software, spreadsheets and wordprocessors, for example, typically work on fairly concise data sets and often reuse instructions. Databases, particularly those that handle transactions such as sales, typically have a small number of instructions that are regularly reused, but are often highly random in their need for data. Finally, the new classes of software that go by the term *multimedia* employ a relatively small number of instructions, but rarely reuse data which are instead retrieved in large, constantly changing *streams* rather than in the small chunks used by other software. This poses a number of problems for system design.

Tech Talk

Wait state: A *wait state* occurs when the CPU has to wait for the system to fetch the next instruction or data that it needs.

The Memory Problem

We'll start our overview of the memory system by considering a key problem. The computer industry has been deeply concerned for some time now about a striking fact: CPU clock speeds are increasing at about sixty percent per year, but the effective speed of memory is going up only about 7 percent. Since CPUs get their information—both instructions and data—from memory, the speed mismatch must mean that the CPU often has to slow down and wait for information to arrive from memory. How can we avoid these wait states?

To understand the memory problem, we'll need to look at each part of the system and determine what the tradeoffs are. Obviously, the best way to avoid wait states is not to have to go to memory at all. Registers, which are close at hand and operate on the CPU's clock, can be accessed with minimal delay (see Table 2.1). Unfortunately, even the most advanced chips have only a few hundred registers. This is enough to complete some small, repetitive tasks with blazing speed, but not enough to deal with complex instructions and data.

Cache

The next logical option is an extension of the first. If you can't have enough registers right there in the thick of the computation, why not put some memory elsewhere on the chip where it can be close at hand and operate at the same clock speed? This was thought to be a crazy idea until very recently. It was hard enough to get the needed control and calculation circuits on the CPU chip, let alone put memory there as well. Fortunately, the advent of deep submicron feature sizes has radically changed both what is technically possible and what is economically feasible. In fact, CPUs have had some amount of memory "on board" since about 1990.

SRAM vs. DRAM

On-CPU memory is called cache, a term that is used in part to distinguish the fastest kind of memory from the regular kind, usually called simply *main memory*. Cache is not only faster, it is organized so as to keep the most frequently needed instructions and data in its speedy clutches. The principal reason cache is faster is that it is made from a different kind of transistor. Where main memory is DRAM (Dynamic Random Access Memory), cache is SRAM (Static Random Access Memory). SRAM has several advantages over DRAM. The first is that it can cycle much faster (the reason for this will be given later). The second is that its construction is similar enough to the circuitry of the CPU that it is relatively easy to fabricate part of the chip as logic and part as SRAM memory. It's possible, but harder, to put DRAM on the same piece of silicon as the CPU. Of course, there must be a disadvantage to SRAM or we would have lots of on-CPU cache and not have to worry so much about wait states. The problem with SRAM is that, for a given capacity, it uses about three times as many transistors as DRAM. Worse, because of the way it is built, SRAM requires something like twenty times as much space. Clearly, SRAM has to be used sparingly.

This leads to the second difference between cache and main memory. Since SRAM cache is comparatively inefficient in its use of silicon real estate, system architects used just a small amount and put it in between the CPU and DRAM. This small segment was then endowed with logic circuits that were designed to keep it full of what the CPU was most likely to want next. The *algorithms* that these cache controllers use to perform their feat of prediction can be very complex, but for the most part, the strategy is simple sequentiality: if the CPU has just asked for an instruction at memory location 555, it's very likely that it will next ask for the one at 556, and

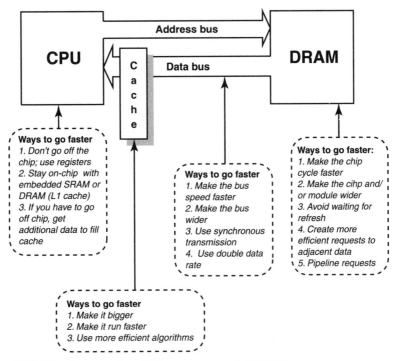

Figure 2.2 The key parts of the memory problem.

after that the one at 557, and so on. The cache's controller circuits therefore go ahead and fetch these from slow DRAM to fast SRAM. Cache started to appear in desktop computers around 1990, when mainstream CPUs passed 25 MHz (the basic technology had been used in mainframe and related systems for more than a decade). As CPU speeds soared upwards—more than a twentyfold increase in less than a decade—use of cache also increased. Cache chips got bigger in capacity (from a few kilobytes to a megabyte and more) and some was moved directly onto the CPU's chip. When this split occurred, the on-chip version became known as L1 and the separate one as L2. Today, as systems begin to move large amounts of memory directly on-CPU (both SRAM and DRAM), the terminology is confused. For example, some systems say that they have both L1 and L2 on the CPU. Logically, they would just say that all the cache is on the CPU, but logic is what drives the circuits, not the marketing.

Tech Talk

Algorithm: An algorithm is another word for "formula." It is a set of rules and/or computations that is intended to be used over and over, like a recipe.

Making Cache Faster

Can cache be made faster? Yes. Putting it on the CPU is certainly one way. On-CPU cache operates on the same clock as the rest of the CPU. This helps performance *a lot*. But remember, there isn't much spare room on this chip. So what about cache on a separate chip? Well, SRAM can be made to run very fast, as fast as current CPUs, but doing this makes it very expensive. The high-end Xeon computers of the Intel family, which are employed as workstations and servers, use a lot of separate cache (2 MB+) and operate it at the same speed as the CPU. Less expensive CPUs normally run external cache at half the speed of the CPU.

···

ISN'T *DIMM SIMM* A CHINESE MEAL?

Actually, memory chips come in multi-chip modules called SIMMs (Single In-line Memory Module) or DIMMs (Dual In-line Memory Module). A SIMM takes a bunch of chips, normally eight or nine, and groups them together into a circuit board. A SIMM has chips on one side of the board, a DIMM on both sides. This packaging greatly simplifies installation and handling. The number of chips in a module depends on a variety of rather technical factors.

Another way to make cache more effective is to use increasingly sophisticated algorithms. In other words, teach the cache controller to do a better job of guessing what it should get next. There are a variety of techniques for doing this, known by such esoteric terms as *four-way set associative* cache. Fortunately, the differences are neither great nor proprietary. As a result, most cache algorithms are very efficient. A typical *cache hit rate*—the percent of time an instruction or piece of data is found in cache rather than in memory—is usually around ninety percent for Pentium IIIs running normal business applications.

Looking back from the future, we'll be able to say that for the first decade or so, cache was an effective means of dealing with the CPU/memory mismatch, but that its value began to decline as increases in CPU speed accelerated and as people's taste in software evolved. One change that limits the effectiveness of cache is multitasking. If you jump back and forth between programs, as more and more users do, the cache algorithms can be fooled and software will have to deal with frequent wait states. As noted earlier, an even more important change is the appearance of newer kinds of software, for example, multimedia programs, that are very different from the traditional database, word processing, and spreadsheet applications that fueled the growth of the microcomputer industry. The older types of software frequently reused instructions and data, and therefore benefitted naturally from cache. But, multimedia, such as games or anything that uses a lot of video-type content, tends to reuse instructions but not data—there are long streams of constantly changing data elements that defeat the purpose of cache. To accommodate these new applications, memory has to cycle faster, and the pipeline that connects it to the CPU has to have much higher capacity. We'll talk about the pipeline—the *system bus*—next.

The System (Memory) Bus

The original IBM PC had only one bus for the entire computer. It was a paltry eight bits wide and ran at a pitiful 8 MHz (of course, at the time, this was really fast). The next generation, the AT bus, also known as the ISA (for Industry Standard Architecture bus), kept the same speed but moved up to 16 bits. As shown in Figure 2.3, memory, I/O, and video all shared this same connection to the CPU. So, if the video card needed access to its section of memory (a reserved area on the memory board) it might have to wait for the CPU or the Input/Output system if either was accessing the bus at the same time. Fortunately, since all the parts were quite slow, this contention didn't present much of a problem. However, as CPU speeds surged, and as video systems began to deal with complex graphics (see Chapter 3), the ISA bus could no longer handle all the traffic. Several things then happened. First, memory got its own direct bus connection to the CPU. Next, the ISA bus was replaced with the much faster PCI. Finally, video also got its own direct bus to the CPU. The next section will explain the evolution of the system bus (also called the *memory* or the *processor bus*); the other buses will be discussed later in this chapter.

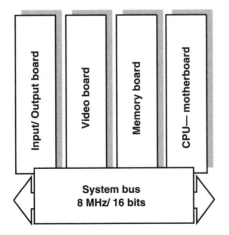

Figure 2.3 Layout of the second generation IBM PC.

Early System Buses

Early memory buses appeared at a variety of speeds and widths, but with the advent of the Pentium, stabilized for a long time at 66 MHz and 64 bits. Since 64 bits is eight bytes, you can calculate the maximum *bandwidth* of this bus as $8 \times 66 = 528$ MB. That's a lot, and indeed it was enough for quite a while. Pressure to increase the bandwidth of the bus developed as processor speeds continued to go up and as applications showed an increasing tendency to want to send vast streams of data across the bus.

Tech Talk

Bandwidth: The capacity of a communications channel is its bandwidth. In computers, this is measured in bits per second. See also Chapter 10 for a primer on digital communications.

Faster Buses

The obvious way to increase the capacity of the memory bus is to make it wider and faster. Unfortunately, that's not easy to do. The issues are complex, but two examples will illustrate. First, a wider bus is more vulnerable to *skew,* which means the problem of one or more bits in a 64-bit cohort arriving out of synch with its brethren. Surprisingly, preventing skew is mostly a mechanical problem. To work acceptably well, each of the 64 wires must have exactly the same length and electrical characteristics. Thus, the bus has to be made to very high tolerances. Taking it to, for example, 128 or 256 bits would be very expensive both for the bus itself and for the added pins needed on the CPU.

Tech Talk

Clock doubling: As CPU speeds increased in the mid-1980s, it quickly became clear that the memory bus could not keep up. This started the practice known as *clock doubling* because in the first iteration, the processor's clock was twice as fast as that of the bus. Since then, however, the difference has gotten wider. For example, a 600 MHz Pentium III runs six times faster than its 100 MHz bus.

What about faster? Well, as an electrical circuit oscillates, it gives off noise in the form of radio frequency interference (RFI) that can interfere with adjacent electrical systems such as the CPU, DRAM chips, and lots of other stuff in the computer and even nearby. RFI increases with circuit speed, and greater width exacerbates the problem. Metal shielding can defeat the effects of RFI, but if RFI is really high, the amount of metal needed creates awkward bulk and therefore design challenges. These problems also illustrate another point—both for ease of manufacturing and for minimal RFI, the bus has to be as short as possible. If you look inside your computer, you will see that the CPU and memory chips are very close together.

Current System Bus Strategies

The first stage solution to the memory bus problem has been not so much to make it faster as to make it more efficient. The standard microcomputer memory bus since about 1998 has been a *synchronous* bus. This means that the bus uses a standard clock signal so that CPU and memory don't have to waste time and capacity sending out extra bits that tell where strings of data begin and end (see Chapter 10 for a primer on data communications and Chapter 11 for more on synchronous vs. asynchronous systems). Synchronous buses are somewhat more expensive, but the greater efficiency (reduced overhead) is worth it for modern systems. Combined with increases in clock speed (first to 100 MHz and then to 133 MHz), this means that bandwidth has grown from 528 to 1.1 GB. Just as important, the synchronous bus means that in the real world, the system will more often achieve the expected bandwidth. Enough? Unfortunately, no. But before we can explain the next move in system design, we have to talk about how memory chips and associated systems work.

··

IMPROVE YOUR MEMORY AND YOUR IQ!

One way of solving the memory latency problem is to put not just cache, but all or almost all of the memory on the same chip as the CPU. When feature sizes hit .13 micron, this will almost certainly be the choice for a large number of systems. In fact, in the event that designers develop standard ways of stringing together multiple processors, a "processor in memory" chip could become the basic building block of computing. A desktop would have one or two of these chips, a workstation a dozen, a server two dozen, etc. Chapter 5 covers the complex issues involved in using multiple processors at once.

Memory Chips

Memory chips hold data the same way that a spreadsheet does, in rows and columns. When the CPU requests data from a specific address, it sends a request across the bus, where local memory module circuits translate it to the required row and column location. Other circuitry then send signals that cause the information at the addresses to be read out to the chip's output area, from which it is sent back across the bus to the CPU. The multiple steps involved in this process lead to what is called *latency*—the delay between the time an instruction or element of data is requested and the time it is ready to send back.

Tech Talk

Latency: The term *latency* is widely and somewhat loosely used in computing. Generally, it means delay—as in the delay from the time data is requested until the time it arrives.

Latency presents a tough problem. One way to deal with it is to make the memory chips cycle faster (a faster clock speed). Thus, as in the CPU, the fact that multiple cycles are needed is made less important because each cycle takes a shorter period of time. This can be done, but there are barriers. The most important of these is the problem of *refresh*. DRAM chips are volatile—the electrical charge that holds information on the chip leaks away unless it is refreshed on a frequent basis. Since this involves first reading and then rewriting the data, it slows down the overall speed because it blocks the CPU's access while this is going on. The issue of refresh and some related problems explain why DRAM cycle speeds haven't kept pace with the clock speeds of CPUs. By the way, you can now be told SRAM's key speed secret— it doesn't need to be refreshed.

But, Soft! What Error Through Yonder Silicon Breaks?

Computer chips are rigorously tested for *hard* errors—those that are the result of flaws in fabrication. *Soft* errors, on the other hand, are the result of external radiation and are far more difficult to identify—in large part because they are intermittent. Unfortunately, soft errors are becoming more of a threat as feature sizes decrease, making intruding particles relatively larger when compared to the chip's gates and wires. Designers are increasingly concerned about soft errors, and are trying to find ways to protect chips.

The most advanced memory technology, one just reaching the market in early 2000, is called *RDRAM* for *Rambus DRAM*. The Rambus approach is different in a lot of ways. First, it offsets some major problems by using a narrow system bus—16 bits vs. 64 bits for standard systems. The skinny bus is quite a bit cheaper to manufacture (it also reduces the pin count on the CPU, which can save a lot of money as

In fact, since so much information is now provided over network connections, it's a little unclear what desktop computer users will do with a 20 GB version of the DVD. However, every previous prediction that some new level of capacity wouldn't be needed has turned out to be egregiously wrong.

FEELING SLOW? TAKE TWO BUFFERS . . .

Even computers get headaches? Actually, *buffering* refers to the need for small, temporary storage areas to help deal with the fact that everything can't happen in perfect synchrony inside a computer. For example, a CPU may send a burst of data to a hard drive faster than the drive can write it; a buffer (chip-based storage, in this case) allows the faster device, the CPU, to go about its business while the slower one catches up. In some cases, the reverse occurs. For example, the CPU might be busy with a high priority task when data arrives from outside the computer at a modem or network connection. Losing the data could be catastrophic, so a buffer holds on to the data until the CPU can be interrupted. There are many kinds of buffers in computers, some of which go by different names. For example, cache memory is a type of buffer.

Holography

There's an interesting new optical technology lurking in the background—holography. The same techniques that are used to create three-dimensional images on (what appear to be) two-dimensional surfaces can be used to create three-dimensional storage on an appropriate substrate. Holographic storage uses a flat, nonrotating crystalline structure as the recording medium. Data is written by a laser beam that is split into two—a signal beam and a reference beam. When the two converge on a given location, the structure of the crystal is altered in a way that becomes a digital 1. The temporary application of a strong voltage is needed to "fix" the data. Reading uses just the reference beam (in effect, low power), but instead of reflecting light, the reference beam projects a pattern onto a photoelectric grid located on the other side of the medium.

Tech Talk

Substrate: The surface on which something is placed is called its *substrate*. Most CPUs, memory chips, etc. use silicon as the substrate, though Gallium Arsenide (GaAs) and Silicon Germanium (SiGe) are gaining somewhat. Magnetic disks use aluminum or glass as the substrate.

Holography has some tremendous potential advantages. First, it has the possibility of working with few or no mechanical parts—the laser can be refocused electrically and there is no disk to spin. Second, data can be recorded and read in parallel. Recall that all of the media talked about so far read data one bit at a time in a serial manner, then use electronic circuits to convert them to the parallel stream of 32 (or whatever) bits used by the computer. Holographic systems, by contrast, can read entire arrays almost at once. If you've ever seen the kind of punched card used by early computers, you would notice that each one had data arrayed in a tabular format—rows and columns. Holographic storage does the same; the difference is that it can read the equivalent of an entire stack of cards at one time. In holography, these stacks are called *pages* and current systems can read as many as forty. Taken together, these factors mean that holography has the potential of offering storage that is superior to traditional optical and magnetic technologies in areal density (4,000 GB per square inch), transfer speed (1 GB per second), and access times (under 1 ms). The success of holography, as with many other exciting technologies, depends on the ability of engineers to design versions that are reliable and inexpensive to manufacture.

Tech Talk

ms: A *millisecond*, abbreviated *ms*, is one-thousandth of a second. The speed of access to data on disk drives is normally measured in milliseconds.

THE I/O BUS . . . .

Computers have a number of physical paths, called *buses,* for moving data. An important one, the system bus, was discussed earlier in this chapter. Buses may not be very exciting, but as we try to find ways to make our computers faster, they're a critical part of the equation. Naval officers observe that the speed of a convoy is that of its slowest ship. Similarly, if a bus can't handle all the traffic that converges on it, the whole computer will have to slow down.

Table 3.1   Monitor Resolutions

Standard Monitor Resolutions			
Name	**Horizontal**	**Vertical**	**Total dots**
MDA	720	350	252,000
VGA	640	480	307,200
SVGA	800	600	480,000
XGA	1,024	768	786,432
QXGA	2,048	1,536	3,145,728

Note: All of these except MDA use a 4:3 aspect ratio, *which means that the ratio of the horizontal to the vertical dimension is 4:3.*

In normal use, *pixel* and *dot,* or *dot triad,* mean the same thing and are used interchangeably; the sidebar "Pixels vs. Dots" explains why this is not always the case.

Resolution

The term *resolution* is widely used but rarely explained in computing. Unfortunately, it really needs explanation because, like dot and pixel, this word is also the source of considerable ambiguity. It seems that computer makers want to confuse you by using *resolution* in two substantially different ways.

Resolution as dot matrix: In the case of a computer monitor or digital television, resolution is given as the size of the dot matrix—768 by 1,024, or whatever.

Resolution as sharpness: In the approved usage, one that extends beyond computing, resolution is taken to mean the sharpness of an image as measured by the number of dots in a given space—a linear inch is the most common measure in the decimally-challenged part of the world. And, in a return to logic, resolution in this meaning is normally given as *dpi* (dots per inch) instead of pixels per inch.

The distinction between the two meanings of resolution is important. To illustrate, let's consider two cathode ray tube (CRT) monitors, each described as having a resolution of 1,024 by 768, but one of which is listed as 17" and the other 19" on the diagonal (in fact, the actual measure is considerably less than the advertised one—the viewable area of a 17" monitor is more like 15.5"). If you measure the monitors' horizontal dimension and do a little division, you'll see that the 17" monitor has 85 dpi along a horizontal line, but its 19" sibling has only 72 dpi. So, according to one meaning of resolution, that of the dot matrix, the two monitors are the same. But according to another meaning, linear sharpness, they are quite different. You don't see this factor mentioned much, which is why some additional discussion of resolution will be useful.

Tech Talk

> **CRT:** A *cathode ray tube* is the principal type of display now used for computer monitors and televisions. The CRT uses scanning electron beams to draw an image on the surface of a tube. It is likely to be replaced in the near future for both types of applications by one or more of the flat panel technologies.

CLEARTYPE

Microsoft offers e-books under the Microsoft Reader name. These "books" use a technology called ClearType. The idea, as the name suggests, is to make a screen with the higher resolution appropriate for extended reading.

ClearType gets more dpi out of a screen without adding pixels. Sound impossible? Well, it isn't if you control sub-pixels. ClearType builds smoother text, especially text that uses diagonal lines, by borrowing neighboring red, green, or blue sub-pixels (sub-dots). If done carefully, the human eye doesn't notice that a part of the letter is in color.

ClearType works only with liquid crystal displays because they array pixels and sub-pixels in horizontal lines. CRTs don't benefit, in part because they (usually) arrange sub-pixels in triangular fashion and also because they can't control sub-pixels effectively.

ClearType could be adapted to other flat panel types, however.

Resolution, Content, and Perception

Measuring resolution is a lot easier than determining what is appropriate or required. How much resolution is actually needed depends on such things as the content (e.g., text vs. graphics) and the viewing distance. For example, the superior 85 dpi resolution of the 17" monitor described above will not seem better to most people than the 72 dpi of its 19" competitor. Why? Because the user is sitting about the same distance away and (assuming that the same amount of information is being shown) the bigger size of the text on the larger monitor makes it just as readable. It's also the case that, when using a computer monitor, most people have been accustomed to find anything above 72 dpi as acceptably sharp.

This subjectivity of resolution is illustrated by the fact that while people think 72 dpi is OK for text on monitors, it is in fact not nearly as sharp as what most people expect on the printed page for either text or graphics. The comparison to printing is difficult, since printers use yet a different way of calculating resolution (see the section on printing later in this chapter), but a quick reference to most anything printed—a book or even the product of a standard inkjet or laser printer—will show you that the text on your monitor is notably inferior. To reinforce the point about subjectivity, the reason that users don't expect 150 or even 200 dpi on a monitor is because devices with this capability don't exist. It seems probable that once a substantially higher resolution is on the market, rising expectations will change the subjective standard to a higher level. As a final point, televisions generally have much lower dpi than monitors (and measure resolution in yet another way), but this is offset by the content—viewers aren't trying to discern fine detail or read 12 point text on their televisions. Indeed, since people watching television display greater tolerance of distorted images than of sound, it seems that they are listening as much as, or more than, they are watching. Even so, the advent of digital convergence, in which many people are expected to use televisions for Web browsing, seems certain to put pressure on manufacturers to increase the resolution of these displays.

Color

We've mentioned that color displays create dots from three sub-dots (also called sub-pixels), each responsible for one of the three primary colors of red, green, and blue (printing uses the "subtractive" primaries of cyan, magenta, and yellow—see the section on printing at the end of this chapter). Since color is an increasingly important part of computing, we need to give some attention to how color images are made and what color's requirements mean for the computer.

Making black and white from a display built from RGB dot triads is easy (see Figure 3.2). If all the sub-dots in a triad are on, it will be white; if all are off, it will be black. Of course, red only is red, green only is green, blue only is blue, red plus green is yellow, red plus blue is magenta, green plus blue is cyan, and so on for a total of eight different hues. If these are the only colors available, the kinds of images you can portray will be limited to artificial things like showing some letters in red. Needless to say, if you have just one shade of green, you won't be able to depict nature, which can use dozens of greens in grass alone. Fortunately, to get a more complex image doesn't require more different color dots per pixel. Rather, one can just vary the intensity (brightness) of each dot. Thus, green only at one-third power creates a light green; a combination of a one-third power green and a one-third power blue, creates a light cyan, and so forth. The good news is that all of the different kinds of displays in wide use have little difficulty in varying the intensity of a dot. The bad news is that the computer will now have to dedicate more memory to each pixel. Let's digress a moment to see why.

Tech Talk

RGB: Color pixels in most types of monitors and televisions are built from the three primary colors of red, green, and blue. Displays using this approach are called *RGB*.

In a black and white display, a pixel is either on or off. This requires only one bit per pixel in memory, a 1 for *on* or a 0 for *off*. But with color, there are now three sub-dots (pixels), each of which requires some memory. If you give each sub-pixel only one bit, you can get as many as the eight colors described above. Mathematically, this is represented as two to the power of three (2^3). If you want 64 colors, you need two bits of memory per sub-pixel—six total—or (2^6). See the sidebar for additional examples.

Some standard levels of color, described digitally, are:	
Colors	Bits ("depth")
256	8
65,536	16
16.7 million	24

For a variety of reasons related to color theory, bits don't have to be allocated equally within the dot triad, so 8 and 16 bits will work even if the

Figure 3.2 Dot triad.
Most CRTs use spheres in a triangular shape (above), while flat panels arrange rectangular "dots" in rows (below).

> numbers aren't divisible by three. The term *depth* is used because some people think of a pixel as having 24 bits (or whatever number) behind it.

The highest level in normal use today, 16 million colors using eight bits/sub-pixel, is described as *true color* because most people consider that it can accurately reproduce nature ("most people," because these things are also subjective). To get a sense of what this 24-bit per pixel color does to memory, let's consider a screen with $768 \times 1,024$ pixels. Multiplying the total pixels ($768 \times 1,024$) by the number of bits required per pixel (in this case, 24) means that 18,874,368 bits are required for the screen. Dividing by 8 (since eight bits equal one byte) means that 2.35 million bytes, or 2.4 MB, must be held in memory to accomodate this screen. This requires about 2.5 MB of RAM. When we get to the section on the structure of graphics systems, we'll see that the first generation of computers didn't have access to anything like this amount of memory. Prices had to fall for a while before high resolution, true color display systems were possible.

Contrast and Brightness

Two elements of quality in a display that deserve mention are contrast and brightness. Contrast describes the ratio between the lightest and darkest parts of an image. While too much contrast in a color image can convey harshness, too little is sure to reduce clarity in both black and white and color. Think about trying to read dark gray text on a medium gray background and you will understand why contrast is important. As engineers try to replace the book with something electronic, achieving adequate contrast has become a major challenge. The second factor, brightness (*luminance* in technical terms) doesn't really need a description. Brightness and contrast are often linked in the sense that greater brightness can improve contrast. But you will appreciate that achieving adequate levels of brightness requires more electrical power and therefore provides a challenge to the batteries of portable systems. It may be quite some time before your electronic book can get through *War and Peace* on a single set of batteries.

Image Stability and Smoothness of Motion

When moving pictures were first created, photographers discovered that it was necessary to show at least 24 frames, separate images, in every second to make the movement of cowboys, horses, and so forth appear smooth to the typical viewer. When television appeared fifty years or so later, it employed a slightly higher rate of thirty frames per second, though this was based on electrical requirements rather than on a desire to improve the image. There's an important neurological phenomenon connected to frame rate. While decreasing the frame rate much below 24 per second causes nearly all viewers to perceive choppiness in motion, increasing it much beyond the 24–30 range doesn't produce significant benefit. This is another subjective area, but it seems that a frame rate of around 24–30 is all that is needed to fool the brain into thinking that it is seeing continuous motion. Looked at another way, since very few people would be able to notice, for example, the difference between 30 and 40 frames per second, there is no interest in changing systems to accommodate the higher speed. Obviously, frame rate isn't a concern for traditional computer applications like spreadsheets and word processing. But depicting smooth motion is an important issue for the third-generation graphics systems that support things like multimedia, especially games.

Closely related to, but different from, frame rate is refresh rate. Although 24 frames per second is sufficient to show accurate motion in objects on a screen, displaying frames at this speed makes the screen itself look unstable to most viewers. This perceived instability is called *flicker*. To counter it, movie projectors actually show each frame twice. Televisions, computer monitors, and other information displays redisplay frames at least 60 times per second. This is called the *refresh rate* and is often given in Hertz—e.g., 60 Hz. Refresh rate is related to viewing distance and content. Thus, a viewer sitting close to a display and needing high resolution (for example, for text) will be more comfortable with a higher refresh rate. As a consequence, many computer monitors operate at 80 Hz or so, but televisions stay at 60 Hz.

Tech Talk

Hertz: The term *Hertz* (abbreviated Hz) is a measure used to describe the number of cycles per second in an activity. The CPU's clock speed is given in millions (MHz) or billions (GHz) of Hertz; the number of times a monitor image is redisplayed is described in Hertz; and the frequency of electromagnetic waves (the number of wave crests passing a point in a second) is given in Hertz. For example, the frequency used by digital cellular telephones is 1.9 GHz (see Chapter 10).

We've just discussed some important similarities of computer displays and movie projectors. There are, of course, major dissimilarities. While both deal with questions of frame rate and refresh rate, the way in which computers create an image is fundamentally different. However, before we move on to consider the underlying structure of graphics systems, it's necessary to consider the characteristics of the monitor that will display the image.

MONITOR TECHNOLOGIES . . . .

The monitors in most desktop computers today are the same cathode ray tubes (CRTs) that had their first use in televisions. CRTs, which use a set of three electron guns that scan back and forth to illuminate color phosphors on the front of the screen,

then review the underlying technology. The first item, then, is to describe the two different ways of creating computer graphics—bitmaps and vectors. Since both of these approaches are in widespread use, a careful description of each is warranted.

Tech Talk

Computer graphics: The term *graphics* actually means *drawing* in both the computer and the real world. In the computer context, however, it has an additional meaning—graphics are images that are not limited to the small set of alphanumeric characters (e.g., ASCII—see next Tech Talk) of the original mainframe and personal computers.

Bitmapped Images

If you look back at Figure 3.1, you'll see the letter E shown as a series of dots in a matrix. Bitmapped images are made in exactly the same way that this drawing was done—by placing dots in a grid. If the screen supports it and there is sufficient memory to store the additional information, dots can be in color (or shades of gray) as well as in black.

Tech Talk

ASCII: *ASCII* stands for American Standard Code for Information Interchange. It uses seven bits to reference 128 letters, numbers, punctuation marks, and some symbols used for system control. A version using eight bits, *Extended ASCII*, provides the same 128 plus another 128 special characters.

Once the dots are placed and the image is made, it is possible to store a bitmap and reuse it as needed. For example, once you have drawn the E, you can keep it in memory or save it to disk. If it's needed again, you simply ask to have it retrieved. Of course, you don't have to draw every bitmapped image on your own. Operating systems have collections of letters, numbers, and symbols that are pre-drawn and ready for display. If that isn't enough, you can buy a collection of images (called *clipart*) that you can insert in any software program that will allow it. Alternatively, you can scan an existing image, such as a photograph, and create a bitmap that can also be stored and retrieved as needed.

Tech Talk

Bitmap: Bitmap has two meanings. In one, it simply refers to an image that comprises a pattern of dots. Using this definition, essentially all computer graphics—monitor or printer—are bitmaps. In the other definition, bitmap refers to how an image is made. A bitmapped image is created dot by dot for a specific size and resolution. Contrast with *vector*.

Bitmaps were first employed in microcomputers for fonts, beginning with Apple's Macintosh in 1984. As used in computing, a *font* is a collection of alphanumeric characters in a particular typeface, style, and size.

The components of a font:

- *Typeface* means a particular design approach, such as Times Roman or Helvetica.
- *Style* means such things as bold, italic, and so forth.
- *Size* is measured on the same scale of *points* that has long been used in printing. A point is 1/72 of an inch. In practical terms, 1-point type is too small to read with the unaided eye, and normal printed or computer-displayed text is in the range of ten or twelve points.

Tech Talk

Font: A font is a collection of letters (and associated characters) in the same typeface, style, and point size.

Until the Macintosh, computers had been able to display just one font. However, because the Macintosh's screen could be addressed pixel by pixel rather than in the series of blocks used by the IBM PC and other computers of the time, it was possible for the Mac to display a whole range of fonts.

One downside of the Macintosh's exciting ability was that many people, carried away with their newfound power, began to put so many fonts in documents as to induce a sort of vertigo in readers. A more lasting concern was the demand on memory made by bitmaps. In the bitmapped world, every font is a distinct collection of information. A regular 10-point Helvetica is a different set of bitmaps from a 10-point bold Helvetica and is different still from a 12-point in either style, and so forth. Given that memory was still quite limited, just 128K on the original Macintosh, using a lot of fonts really slowed things down. The memory problem was even worse for those who wanted to create complex images using the MacPaint program that came with the Mac. These images could be excruciatingly slow to work with. Also, it was a good thing that the original Mac's screen didn't support color, since there wasn't even close to enough memory available to hold more than one bit per pixel.

Of course, the Mac's bitmapped graphics, soon emulated in the PC world, would have begun to speed up before long, since the cost of memory had already begun its precipitous decline. At the same time, however, designers began to experiment with an alternative, or perhaps more accurately, a complementary, way of creating images.

Tech Talk

AGP: In an Intel system, the Advanced Graphics Port is a high speed bus that connects the graphics processor to the CPU/memory system.

Changes in Graphics Software

In Chapter 5, you will find a discussion in some depth of the important changes in software that have helped make the transition to the second and third graphics generations possible. At this point, we'll just note an essential element—there is now software in the operating system that allows programmers to make use of different graphics boards without having to know exactly how they work. The leaders among these languages are Microsoft's Direct 3D, used only with Microsoft's applications, and Open GL, which is available for the Microsoft, Apple, and Unix operating systems. An important additional dimension of these languages for 3D is that they allow computational tasks to be allocated dynamically between the CPU and the graphics processor. This is important because there is considerable interest in putting more of the geometry and ray tracing responsibilities on the graphics processor (emerging jargon refers to these two elements as *transform and lighting*). With this approach, a computer used mostly for games or other graphical applications (including digital television) could have a relatively cheap main CPU, thereby placing most of the cost in the part of the system where the action is—the graphics board. Indeed, the first generation of 3D graphics processors already had some three times as many transistors as the main CPU of the time.

Tech Talk

Transform and lighting: Transform and lighting is a new term used to describe geometry and ray tracing when they are performed by the graphics processor instead of the CPU.

Tech Talk

Open GL: Open GL is a 3D graphics language that is available for a variety of hardware and software platforms. One advantage of the language is that it allows programmers to write software that is independent of the hardware. Open GL adapts the program to the capabilities of the system.

Tech Talk

Direct 3D: A 3D graphics language that is similar to Open GL, but limited to Microsoft operating systems.

PRINTERS . . . .

Printed output seems like an old fashioned technology, but the truth is that printed material has enormous flexibility and many advantages over computer monitors. It's still a heck of a lot more convenient, for example, to take a book or two to the beach or even to bed than to take a laptop. That may change, perhaps in the near future, but in the meantime printing is doing well. Like monitors, printers have improved in resolution (the level of detail in an image) and in price. They are also much faster than in the past. The big challenge in the printer market is color. Laser technologies, which offer the best combination of speed, resolution, and price for monochrome output, have been slow in offering reasonably priced color output. As a result, inkjet printers are contenders for color, at least for low-volume applications. The appearance of digital cameras that rival regular cameras—if only for fairly small prints—means that the color printer market should continue to soar. This section will provide a brief description of the principal types of printers according to their physical operation, then will consider printing from the perspective of their intelligence. Before we get to these details, however, we need to discuss once again the vexing issue of resolution.

Printer Resolution

Printer resolution is the same as that of monitors when considered in one way, but quite different from another point of view. What does this silly sentence really mean? Most of all it means that printing introduces some new and irritating complexity with even more contradictory definitions. At this point, it would be quite reasonable for you to close the book and run shrieking from the room. On the other hand, given the importance of graphics in today's society, it's worth some effort to understand. Please stay.

Dots Again

You'll recall that the *dot triad* in a monitor is considered a single dot when measuring resolution. So, the number of dot triads in an inch is equal to the monitor's dpi. Well, that isn't true for printing. Printers don't have dot triads. Each dot is on its own, and each can be black or any of the other colors of ink or toner that the printer uses. This would naturally lead you to conclude that if a printer has 600 dpi (pretty much the minimum today), then this number is its actual resolution. Your conclusion would be correct, but only if the printed output was monochrome—for example, text in black—or if it was limited to the basic colors included in the ink or toner cartridges. If you want what printers call *grayscale* (this just means shades of gray), or if you want the equivalent in color—a range of colors usually also called grayscale—then the resolution of the printer will be quite a bit lower than 600 dpi. Don't run! We can explain!

Tech Talk

Grayscale: **Refers to an image that can show shades of black (gray), though the term is also used for color. In a true grayscale image, each dot can be a number of different shades. Most printing approaches simulate this with** *halftoning* **or** *dithering.* **A color (including black) that can be shown in 256 shades has** *256 grayscale definition* **and requires eight bits of memory (2^8).**

Graphics

The major reason that printer graphics are different from those on monitors is that printers lack the control over dot intensity that monitors have. Remember that when a monitor wants to change the shade of a color, say from dark to light green, it can vary the intensity of the electron beam and therefore the brightness of dots on the screen. The same is true if the image is black and white; the monitor can make gray by just varying the power of the electron gun. Printers (with the exception of the rare and expensive dye sublimation models) can't do this. If a printer makes a dot green, it will be green and always the same shade. A black dot is a black dot; the printer can't make a gray one.

Since you know that printers do in fact produce gray images and ones with varying shades of color, you're probably reacting to this description with some skepticism. How can it be that the printer can't make gray dots but can make a gray image? The answer is that the printer mixes white (areas without dots) and black to get what your eye sees as gray. Printers call this *halftoning,* while computer graphics often use the term *dithering.* Whatever the term, mixing in white works because the dots are so small. The same principle is employed for color; you can get a lighter color by mixing in some white areas, or a mixture of colors by combining different color dots.

Tech Talk

Halftoning: *Halftoning,* **also called** *dithering,* **is the process in printing of mixing white areas in with color to get different shades. In effect, this approach simulates grayscaling.**

Do you see the problem yet? If not, here it is. If you need multiple dots to make one dot of gray or of a blended color, then the resolution of a grayscale image can no longer be described in terms of the printer's dpi. Now, your basic unit of measure is not just one dot but a matrix of dots, called *clusters* in the graphics world. The number of dots in a cluster varies, and the whole topic is a lot more complex than this introduction (for example, in some printers dots aren't always the same size and many printers can overlay dots). The key is to remember that there is a significant drop off in effective printer resolution when working with graphics. To illustrate, the standard printer measure of graphics resolution, one which assumes the use of clusters for grayscaling, is lpi (lines per inch). By this measure, a typical 600 dpi laser printer using a typical clustering approach gets only about 80 lpi. Or, to put it another way, for a 600 dpi printer, graphics resolution is not appreciably better than monitor resolution. Again, though, remember that if you are printing in black and white or in any color combination that doesn't use grayscaling, then printer resolution is measured on the same basis as that of monitors—a resolution of 600 dpi means that there really are that many dots available to form characters. This is why printed text looks so much better than text on a monitor.

Tech Talk

lpi: Printers measure the quality of graphics output in lines per inch (lpi). This takes into account the clusters of dots needed to simulate grayscaling.

Major Types of Printers

There are three major types of printers on the market today, and they represent fairly distinct choices.

Laser Printers

Laser printers are essentially copiers with a laser and some electronics added. It's easiest to understand how they work by describing the monochrome version. Like CRTs, laser printers create a raster image (a pattern of dots produced in a scanning motion). A laser, playing the role of the CRT's electron gun, scans line by line across a drum, firing to create a dot (the equivalent of a pixel) and not firing where there will be no dot (the laser is focused by a moving mirror mechanism). Instead of hitting phosphors on a screen, bursts from the laser beam create tiny areas of electrical charge on the drum (actually, in many printers the drum is first given a negative charge so that the action of the laser removes rather than adds a charge). The drum, which is turning while the laser writes on it, then moves past a reservoir of toner. The toner has an electrostatic charge of its own. As it touches the drum, the negatively charged toner is attracted to the positively charged spots (where the laser has written) and repelled from the rest of the drum, which retains its negative charge. As the drum passes through the toner, it acquires enough toner in the right places to rub off on paper and create an image. Heat is then used to fuse (bond) the ink to the paper. The most advanced laser printers, those with the highest resolutions, need to use toner that has extremely fine particles, otherwise there would be no point in having the printer draw very small dots.

The part of the printer that includes the drum, the toner reservoir (normally in a cartridge specially designed to spread as much toner as possible on your clothes), and the paper handling areas, is essentially the same as the core of a copier; in a printer, this collection of parts is known as the *engine*. Laser printer manufacturers, such as industry leader Hewlett-Packard (HP), usually purchase the engine from another company—typically one that makes copiers (Canon has been HP's longtime partner, though HP now has a more diverse base of suppliers). The ability of laser printer manufacturers to benefit from the scale of the copier market is a principal reason for the sharp decline in prices for this device. The electronics, including the CPU, RAM, ROM, and the internal bus that connects them, are provided by the company that sells the machine. In some cases, a company buys the whole printer from another company and just puts its name on the case. Such vendors are known in the trade as OEMs (for Original Equipment Manufacturers—if the computer industry applied the same logic inside its software that it uses for naming things we'd all be in big trouble).

Laser printers are fast. A standard, if somewhat imprecise, measure of performance is pages per minute. On typical text pages, lasers put out from 5 pages per minute for standard desktops to around 40 pages per minute for advanced office systems. No other computer printing technology comes close to these speeds, especially at the high end.

••

REVERSIBLE COLORS

We have described color monitors as using the three *primary* colors of red, green, and blue. These are also known as *additive* colors because the three added together make white. Printers, on the other hand, use the subtractive colors of cyan, magenta, and yellow. These three added together make black. The principal reason for the different approach is the different backgrounds—monitors write on a black background and printers write on a white background (paper). Printers usually also have a direct source of black (e.g., a black toner) in part because this yields a truer black and in part because a printer with a separate black is much less expensive to operate; most printing is still in black, and when the black toner is exhausted, the user can replace only one cartridge (or ink supply or whatever) rather than all three color cartridges. Printers with four colors are referred to as CYMK (K stands for black—don't ask me why, I'm just an OEM).

Adding color to a laser printer is an extremely complex problem. More memory is required, of course, but while adding it can be expensive, it is easy to do. The biggest challenge has been in doing more than one color on one drum. No one has figured out a way to have the laser create charges on the drum that are somehow different in a way that allows one to pick up only magenta toner, one cyan, one yellow, and so on (printers don't use the red, green, and blue primaries employed by monitors; see the sidebar). One alternative, the one originally employed, is to have the paper pass through three separate drums, each with a reservoir of toner for one of the four colors. Unfortunately, accurately moving paper through a printer (or copier) requires careful engineering and precise manufacturing. Expecting a piece of paper to go through three separate drums while maintaining perfect image alignment (*registration* in printing jargon) is a tremendous challenge. If there is even a small amount of slippage after the page leaves the first drum, the image will look terrible. Those who remember the early days of color images in newspapers will recall the problem of two or three overlapping images.

A newer approach is to use one drum with four passes. The laser first writes the image for one color, and as the drum turns, only that color's toner reservoir is open to it. The electrostatic charge for the first image is then cleared (but the toner remains), the laser then writes the next color's image, the drum turns with only the second color's toner available, and so on. After the drum has picked up toner for all four colors, it moves across the paper. This one-drum approach adds some complexity, but this is easily offset by having only one engine; with less paper movement, it also has the potential of much better registration. Whatever the approach, though, it is easy to see that color lasers will always be significantly more expensive than monochrome lasers.

Inkjet

As the name suggests, these printers send a jet of ink from a nozzle to the page. Continuing improvements in manufacturing technology have made possible very fine nozzles and thus very small drops. The resolution of the printer is dependent on how small its dots are; current inkjets achieve resolutions of 1,440 dots per inch. Inkjets are very popular for color printing for several reasons. First, since unlike lasers these printers can print a line (or even part of a line) then stop, wait for more information and start again, they need much less memory. This in turn reduces costs considerably. In addition, they are mechanically simpler. The cost of consumables appears to be lower because ink cartridges are cheaper than toner cartridges. The real measure, however, is cost per copy factored over a few thousand pages or so. In this case, monochrome lasers and monochrome inkjets are similar, while color inkjets are usually significantly cheaper than color lasers.

LED AND LCD PRINTERS

> Some printers that are essentially similar to a laser printer use either an array of LEDs or of LCDs in place of a laser. These have been around for a while, and while somewhat successful because they have fewer moving parts, don't appear to have the potential to be a breakthrough technology. The biggest problem is that it appears not to be possible for either LEDs or LCDs to make dots as small as the laser.

Solid Ink, Thermal Wax, Dye Sublimation

Since these solid technologies are used in fairly specialized situations and appear to have little potential for the mainstream, they aren't covered in detail. The three are related in that all use heat to change a solid block of color into a form that can be applied to paper. Of the three, dye sublimation is notable in that it is the only form of color printing that allows for true halftones (variations in color intensity). Dye sublimation printers can use as many as 256 different temperatures per dot and each of these transfers a different amount of ink. The result is stunning color equivalent to regular printing. But because these printers are very expensive, very slow, and voracious in their demand for consumables, they are typically used as an alternative to small print runs rather than for typical office or personal use.

Printer Intelligence

There are a lot of ways to categorize printers, but while "dumb vs. smart" is an unusual approach, it provides a perspective that is essential if you really want to understand printing.

Dumb Printers

In one variation of printing, all the work is done by the computer and its operating system. If the application software wants to print something, it tells the operating system. The OS then calls on software specific to the printer (the printer driver) that tells it the capabilities of the printer—e.g., 300 dpi vs. 600 dpi, monochrome or color, graphics halftoning, size of page, and so on. Next, the OS constructs a bitmap of each printed page in the computer's main memory. When the page is complete, instructions about which dots are to be placed where are sent to the printer. This approach, which is often used by inkjet and laser printers working with Microsoft's Windows OS, lowers costs because nearly all memory and computational power is in the computer. One disadvantage of dumb printers is that the resources required by printing can prevent the computer from carrying out other tasks at the same time. Another problem is that if the printer is on a network, the need to send information about the location of every dot can consume quite a bit of the available bandwidth. Indeed, this problem can be serious enough that it is considered inadvisable to put a printer of this sort in a shared environment.

Smart Printers

Smart printers, which are more common than their dumb brethren, have fairly powerful microprocessors and, in the case of laser printers, substantial memory in the printer. The process here is essentially the same as in second and third generation graphics systems, in that the printer shares in the work of drawing the image. If the image is text, the OS will send commands to the printer telling it which letters, which fonts, which sizes, and so forth. The printer will then use its CPU to do the actual calculation of font algorithms and to map out the location of toner particles or sprayed ink on the page. Many printers keep commonly used font algorithms in local ROM. If a printer lacks ROM fonts, or if the desired font isn't there, the OS will send it to the printer, which will keep it in its local memory as long as it is needed. Depending on the printer and the available software, the OS can be relieved of not just font scaling, but also most other drawing and page formatting chores. For example, smart printers can draw and scale circles, squares, and so forth.

It's important to note again that laser printers require far more memory than inkjets. This is because of the physical structure of the laser and its associated drum mechanism. Unlike an inkjet, which can print a line or so of information, then pause to wait for additional commands and data from the computer, a laser printer's drum can't stop once it starts turning. This means that laser printers have to print a page at a time, and since any delay in receiving data from the printer would ruin a page, a bitmap of the entire page must be available in local memory before the drum begins to move. In the case of a laser printer, the local memory has much the same function as the frame buffer in a display adapter.

There are two principal types of smart printers: Postscript and TrueType. We'll consider each briefly.

Postscript

Postscript, developed by a company called Adobe in the early 1980s, is actually a graphics language that was designed to assist with high quality printing. Very much like the languages used to manage 3D displays, Postscript treats every element of a graphic as a vector object and allows a programmer considerable control in describing how these objects will appear on a page. Postscript printers have to be smart because the output that they receive from software programs comes in the form of a stream of instructions for drawing and placing objects; the printer's software must interpret these, including scaling them for the printer's resolution in order to create a bitmap. In addition to being a page description language, Postscript includes an extensive family of fonts built using its language. When Postscript fonts first appeared in Apple's Laserwriter in the 1980s, they were considered to be of unusually high quality. Postscript is particularly good at managing the "hinting" that allows smooth replication at a variety of resolutions and point sizes. For greater efficiency, the most commonly used fonts were placed in ROM and kept on the printer. Postscript was on its way to becoming the standard for graphics except for one problem—Adobe charged what many considered to be very high fees for the use of both its font technology and its printer language. So, under the leadership of two frequent enemies, Apple and Microsoft, an alternative was developed.

Tech Talk

Postscript: A page description language that describes how objects should be located on a printed page and how they should be scaled, Postscript uses vectors to create images and fonts and for layout commands.

TrueType

TrueType was originally intended to be a full Postscript clone, including a page description language called TrueImage, but wound up being just a font technology. Even so, it has been extremely successful both because it is good and because Apple and Microsoft chose to build the scaling technology into their respective operating systems and to make versions of common typefaces available for free. Many smart printers contain an array of TrueType fonts in ROM, and while this can speed things up, it isn't strictly necessary for efficient printing because today's microprocessors—whether on the printer or in the computer—can handle the computation without much effort. TrueType has competition, including a similar font-only product from Adobe, but the fact that it is built into the mainstream operating systems means that it has become the dominant technology for managing fonts at the low end. High-end systems, including the imagesetters used by printers, still use Postscript.

Tech Talk

TrueType: TrueType is a vector font (font scaling) technology developed by Microsoft and Apple and used in their operating systems.

CONCLUSION . . . .

We've mentioned that much of what constitutes acceptable quality in graphics is subjective. A corollary point is that the law of rising expectations applies in areas like this. For example, people once thought that monochrome monitors were great for text—after all they said, you don't need color to read a printed page. But once color systems fell in price, software designers began to take advantage of their features. Soon, no one wanted monochrome monitors—they're even hard to find now.

One change of this kind that we can reasonably expect in the not too distant future will be in monitor resolution. Once high resolution displays, e.g., 150 dpi, appear and start to fall in price, everyone will think their current 72 dpi versions are ugly and will want to throw them away. This phenomenon of rising expectations has already been demonstrated with color printing. Graphics that seemed great a few years ago now are rejected as unsuitable.

A final point about graphics is the question of when and how 3D will break out of the game arena and into the mainstream. While no one has yet shown compelling use of 3D in regular business software, it is likely to catch on quickly in the fast growing computer-based education market. The ability to create highly detailed illustrations, both real and abstract, will be valuable for instruction and appealing to a generation accustomed to high quality video since childhood (quality in the graphics, not in the content!).

TEST YOUR UNDERSTANDING . . . .

1. Why are physical screen dots and pixels not always the same?
2. What are some of the differences in describing resolution?
3. Describe the relationship between resolution and perception.
4. Why does available memory limit the number of colors that can be shown in monitors?

5. What is the relationship of flicker and refresh?

6. What are the strengths and weaknesses of the leading monitor technologies?

7. What is the difference between a bitmap and a vector image?

8. What were the principal reasons behind the shift from first to second generation graphics?

9. Why is there interest in moving all of the functions of 3D processing to the graphics adapter?

10. What are the advantages of Postscript and TrueType fonts?

4 Silicon Economics

In the Introduction, it was observed that computing is going through a period of extraordinarily rapid change. At the end of only fifty years, we are about to leave the fourth distinct generation and begin the fifth. More dramatic, there have been three generational shifts in the last two decades alone. Although there are enormous economic issues in software and networking, the fact is that the foundation for change is in hardware and that the interplay of technology and market in this area is exceptionally important and complex. As a result, this chapter will begin with the core issue of how chips are fabricated, then move on to consider the principal vendors of CPUs and the architectural choices they have made. Next, we'll cover the rapidly evolving computer family tree, noting the accelerating proliferation of computing devices that don't look like traditional computers. Finally, we'll discuss the design tradeoffs that vendors are considering as they prepare for the world of "pervasive computing." By the end of this chapter, you should be familiar with:

- How chips are made
- The major families of microprocessors
- The types of computers now in existence and how they are evolving

SILICON FOUNDATIONS: MAKING CHIPS . . . . . .

Nearly all chips—microprocessor, memory, specialized—are made from a single silicon crystal that is grown into a long salami-like shape. The current standard for these crystals is eight inches in diameter, although we should see 12-inch (300 mm) diameter sizes in a few years. When the crystal is finished, it is cut into thin slices called *wafers*. It is on these that the chips are made.

Tech Talk

Wafer: A *wafer* is a slice of extremely pure crystalline silicon on which chips are fabricated. Current wafers are about 8" in diameter, but 12" wafer production is just beginning. Once the 12" processes are perfected, the price of chips should fall even faster. Some more exotic processes use wafers made from other substances, such as Gallium Arsenide (GaAs) and Silicon Germanium (SiGe).

The process used to create the transistors and traces on the surface, *photolithography,* is basically the same as that employed in making a photographic print. The silicon is first coated with a special photosensitive chemical and exposed to light in the pattern of the circuits it will carry. The pattern is created by a *mask* that overlays the target in the same way that a negative in an enlarger sits between the light source and the photographic paper. Several processes are then used to etch the silicon into this pattern. Positively and negatively charged materials are added to the etched areas to create transistors, and tiny amounts of metal are deposited (from a vapor) to create connections. A number of layers (the state of the art is seven) are established in this way, each one using multiple masks. All chips are fabricated at once on a wafer and tested there as well. They are then cut out of the wafer, each one is placed in a package (usually plastic), and wires for connections to other parts of the computer are added.

Tech Talk

Photolithography: The process of creating patterns on a wafer is known as *photolithography*. The technology is very similar to that employed in a photographic enlarger. Current processes use visible light, but alternative approaches using x-rays or electron beams are in development.

The process of making a CPU (or any other high density chip) is complex and it is therefore not surprising that there are some continuing challenges to fabricators. The biggest problem is that if there are any impurities or other flaws in its silicon or metal, a chip will almost certainly be useless. Unfortunately, it has so far proved impossible to make a wafer that has no flaws. To give you an example of the problem, consider a CPU that is made using .18 micron technology (essentially meaning that

Table 4.1   *(continued)*

Intel CPUs					
Generation	Year	Name	Transistors	Initial speed	Special features
					* Adds Integer SIMD abilities * Lots more L1 cache
VII	1999	Pentium III	9.5 million	450 MHz	* Adds floating point SIMD abilities * Reaches 733 MHz same year
VIIa?	2000	"Willamette"	?	1 GHz	* New flagship 32-bit CPU; note only about a year behind previous redesign * Significant improvement in FPU capabilities
VIII	2000	Itanium	?	800 MHz	* True 64-bit processor * VLIW-type technology

IT'LL COST YA

The fastest chips in a family are *disproportionately* expensive. When AMD announced its Athlon (K7) line in August of 1999, this is how their chips were priced. Intel's marketing strategy is similar.

AMD K7 Prices	
Speed	**Unit price**
650 MHz	$849
600 MHz	$615
550 MHz	$449
500 MHz	$249
Source: EE Times on the Web.	

One striking thing about Intel's history is the accelerating rate of change. With the debut of the Itanium, three distinct generations will have appeared in only about five years. Clock speeds increased from just over 200 MHz to over 700 MHz in less than three years. Given this progress, you would have to think that Intel at the turn of the century was more dominant than ever. In fact, the opposite is true. Intel's market share, which stayed above 90 percent for most of the 1980s and 1990s, dipped to around 80 percent in the last years of the 1990s. The reason for this change was the appearance of the sub-$1,000 PC.

A number of Intel's competitors, led by AMD, began to offer very low priced CPUs for the new class of sub-$1,000 PCs that appeared around 1998. Since Intel did not have a competitive chip, it lost market share as the new category of machine soared in popularity. The shift was a little deceptive however; low price also means low profit, and Intel continued to dominate the high end. To understand the difference in profit, see the sidebar.

So, there's been bad news and good news for Intel. Unfortunately, there's more bad news. An increasingly serious problem for the mainstream microprocessor vendors is what appears to be increasing resistance to high-end pricing. Computer buyers, especially corporate ones, have come to realize that faster processors secure only a very small improvement in the performance of real world applications software. Beginning in 1998, when mass market CPU speeds reached 300 MHz, improvements in software performance began to diminish and vendors began to notice an increasing indifference to faster processors. People simply didn't want to pay the large price premium, for example, the 340 percent shown in the sidebar, when going from 500 to 650 MHz. Sales overall have increased, but the market growth has now shifted to the low end.

Intel currently has three different microprocessor lines, with one more soon on the way.

The Celeron

The low-end Celeron, rushed to market in 1998 to fight inexpensive rivals from AMD and Cyrix, was at first essentially a budget version of the Pentium II. Intel has since moved to give it the same SIMD instructions as the Pentium III.

The Pentium III

Distinguished initially by the addition of a special floating point pipeline, the III is now the mainstream desktop chip. It differs from the Celeron largely in the amount of high speed cache.

The Xeon

The Xeon, which is aimed at servers and workstations, appeared in the second half of 1998. It has a Pentium III core and comes with logic that allows it to be used easily in systems that have as many as eight CPUs. Xeons also have more of the highest speed cache.

The Itanium

Scheduled to appear in 2000, the Itanium will be Intel's first 64-bit chip. Like the Xeon, which it will eventually replace, the Itanium is designed for servers and work-stations.

Intel Clones

Intel CPUs were manufactured from the beginning by a number of licensees because of the need for second sourcing. Beginning with the 386, Intel decided that it would no longer license its designs. This didn't affect IBM, whose original agreement gave it the option to continue to manufacture Intel designs if it so chose (IBM exercised this right only sporadically). Rival AMD thought it also had a continuing right to fabricate everything in the Intel's x86 family and sued to enforce it. The results of the lawsuit were mixed, but AMD has grown to be Intel's principal challenger and we'll turn to it next.

Tech Talk

Clone: Historically, *clone* has meant two different things when applied to CPUs. One is a chip that is *instruction set compatible,* meaning that it can directly execute software designed for the CPU that it is cloning. The other meaning is *pin compatible,* which means that the clone can fit into the same physical socket and make the same electrical connections as the target CPU. Contemporary clones are instruction set compatible, but pin compatibility is now less common, for both legal and technical reasons.

AMD and NexGen

AMD (Advanced Micro Devices) was the most aggressive of the cloners during the 386 and 486 years. Most observers agree that AMD's success with these chips was an important factor in causing Intel to advance the development and marketing of the

Pentium. AMD's cloning took two paths; the first was a direct copy of the 386, including on-chip software known as *microcode* (see Chapter 5), which Intel challenged in court. While the mutual lawsuits wound their way through the legal system, AMD buttressed its clone with a second approach. It created a version of the 486 that was not an exact copy of the Intel original. Instead, the microcode was written by engineers who had no knowledge of the real thing. This "reverse engineering" approach had been pioneered earlier in the development of BIOS chips (also discussed in Chapter 5) and had withstood legal challenges. The reverse engineered 486 chips were very successful technically and modestly competitive in the market.

WHERE YOUR CHIP DOLLARS GO

The legal struggle between AMD and Intel, which lasted from 1987 to 1995, is estimated to have cost some $200 million for lawyers and their expenses. The results were inconclusive, in large part because changes in the technology had made many of the issues moot.

AMD became more competitive with the sixth (Pentium Pro/Pentium II) generation. The advantage for AMD was that Intel had itself engaged in a form of reverse engineering in order to graft their old CISC system into a new RISC-based one. AMD could now simply find its own ways to do the same thing. With the help of intellectual property gained through the acquisition of fellow cloner NexGen, AMD has had a string of very competitive chips. Unfortunately, the company has chronically failed to manufacture its newest chips in volume large enough to threaten Intel's leadership. Taken with the fact that, as a cloner, AMD has to charge less than Intel for a comparable chip, this has not been good for the company's profits. AMD has taken a chunk out of Intel's market share, but only in the low-profit, low end of the market. AMD's seventh generation chip, the Athlon (K7) introduced in 1999, has looked very competitive against the comparable high-end Pentium III, but to make a dent in the high end, AMD must resolve its traditional problems in getting sufficient volume to the market. Efficient, low-cost manufacturing has been one of Intel's strengths.

Cyrix

A Texas-based company, Cyrix Semiconductor was the first to make a clone of an Intel CPU without using Intel microcode. Cyrix was seduced into the market by Intel's huge profit margins and felt that it could compete by going *fabless*—IBM and others provided its foundries. Still, Cyrix always struggled to make a profit. It is now

signed to encourage the production of Alpha machines from vendors other than Compaq. So far, there have been few takers, though Korean semiconductor giant Samsung has licensed the technology and promises to advance its capabilities. The combination of Compaq's market scale, the former DEC's R&D, and the fabricating skills of Samsung could make a formidable combination.

HP: PA-RISC

Hewlett-Packard (HP) is a major player in the workstation and server markets with its PA (Precision Architecture) RISC family. The current leader, the PA-8000, is a true 64-bit CPU that has the usual state-of-the-art elements: it is superscalar, super-pipelined, and as with all workstation-oriented chips, emphasizes floating point and advanced graphics performance. The race for leadership in workstation performance is a perpetual seesaw battle, with the newest entrant usually seizing the banner and holding it for a few months until the next new version of a competitive CPU is announced. The PA-8000 has had its share of honors, especially in floating point performance, but HP's alliance with Intel to design the Itanium suggests that HP considers the PA-RISC architecture to have reached the end of its natural life.

Can Anyone Compete with Intel?

Intel has some powerful advantages in manufacturing and marketing microprocessors. First, it has the software "legacy." To quote Carl Sagan, there are "billions and billions" of dollars worth of software programs out there that are designed to operate only with Intel's x86 architecture. Even if Intel's CPUs slipped behind in performance relative to the competition, it wouldn't be enough to cause all those software developers to go to the tremendous expense of rewriting their programs to run on a different CPU family (one of the problems they would have is *which* different CPU). So, Intel would have to not merely slip, but really fall behind, to make people reconsider its CPUs for either software development or purchase.

Intel's second advantage in the market is its famed skill at manufacturing. Unlike many big companies that get sloppy when they dominate a market, Intel has given fanatical, unrelenting attention to production efficiency and quality. To illustrate this, consider Intel's "Copy Exactly" process. Instead of first using a development facility to get processes correct and subsequently a production one to adapt these to volume, Intel fine tunes for both dimensions at the same time in the same fab. Once things are perfected, all of Intel's many fabs around the world copy the process as exactly as possible. This not only speeds development time, it also means that problem solving can be replicated throughout the system almost instantly. While Intel has been challenged at the low end of the market in recent years, and lost share as a result, its problem has not been the ability to compete at a profit, but rather just how much of its existing profits it wanted to sacrifice. Intel's profits are in fact extremely high. Before the recent fight with AMD began, its margins were in the range of 40 percent—amazing for a capital intensive business. And that leads us to Intel's third advantage, cash on hand—billions and billions again. If ever Intel is beaten, it won't be because it lacks the resources to invest.

So what are Intel's weaknesses? One is technology. Its CPU's have typically just equaled the most ambitious cloners, and have rarely been performance leaders vs. the RISC world. This is deceptive, however. Just as the legacy software is an advantage for Intel, it is also a problem; the company can't easily follow radical new design strategies because it always has to worry about "backwards compatibility." So far, it has done a great job of both staying compatible and keeping its best CPUs near the top in power. It has also consistently beaten everyone in price/performance ratio.

Intel's other weakness is the breadth and direction of the microprocessor market as a whole. You would expect a company with more than 80 percent market share to be engaging in regular discussions with flinty-eyed lawyers from the Justice Department. In fact, Intel has had very little scrutiny, largely because it is a manufacturer of microprocessors, not just CPUs for desktop computers. Viewed from this broader perspective, covering devices from mainframes to cell phones, Intel's share is strong but not dominant.

Thinking of the amazing array of devices that currently employ CPUs leads us to the next topic.

TYPES OF COMPUTERS . . . .

This section will not attempt to provide a comprehensive description of different kinds of computer systems. That will only be possible in the context of a discussion of operating systems, communications, corporate issues, and so forth. The purpose at this point is simply to give you a general perspective by noting how the systems differ.

Mainframes

The term *mainframe* originally referred to the cabinet in a large computer system that housed the CPU and memory; smaller cabinets (or racks) held disk drives and such. Today the term refers to any very large scale computer system, especially to those made by IBM and its competitors (notably Hitachi and Amdahl, which makes a "plug compatible" machine in partnership with Fujitsu and NEC). To give you an idea of scale, IBM's current System 390 series of computers consists of parallel processing units that support up to ten CPUs; in case that isn't enough, as many as 32 of these ten-CPU units can be linked together (*clustered,* in the most common industry phrase). A single system can support huge amounts of main memory (for example, 2 GB for a four processor machine) and terabytes (that's trillions of bytes) of disk space. A hierarchical memory system allows a cluster of computers to share a second, expanded memory area that can reach 8 GB. In some of the largest systems, processors and disk arrays are connected with fiber optic cables (*fibre channel*). According to IBM, its newer systems, which employ single chip CPUs, use 97 percent less power than the earlier machines; this means that they can be air instead of water cooled. No more having to call a plumber when the machine goes down.

Tech Talk

Cluster: A *cluster* is a group of independent computers, typically two to eight, that are linked by high speed networks. Special software extends the operating system such that the cluster functions as one computer. Clusters are used in part to get more processing power and in part to provide extended reliability—if one machine fails, the others take over for it.

Mainframe computers also support a range of operating systems; the IBM family can even run multiple operating systems at the same time. The critical objective of these systems is handling volume—vast amounts of data, tremendous numbers of simultaneous users, and so forth. Speed of computation is a secondary objective; other kinds of computers provide much lower cost per unit of calculation. The mainframe has been portrayed as a dinosaur, and it is certainly true that the category lost market share in precipitous fashion in the late 1980s and early 1990s. But mainframes have bounced back for the simple reason that they are still the best bet for big businesses that need to manage immense quantities of data.

Supercomputers

Supercomputers are loosely defined as whatever is the fastest at a given time. This flexible definition is important, but superior becomes inferior just as fast in the supercomputer world as it does in the microcomputer arena. The famous first generation supercomputer, the Cray-1 of 1976, is long since out of service—its power would be equivalent to a desktop machine today. Traditional supercomputers had CPUs with (for the time) very high clock speeds that were very wide (128 bits vs. 32 to 64 bits), were super-superpipelined and superscalar, and had four or six CPUs.

The traditional supercomputer was also a vector computer. The best way to explain vector computation is by example. Let's say you are designing a part for a machine and need to make it just slightly smaller to make it fit, so you tell the computer to multiply each of 45 dimensions by .9872. (As an aside, note that this problem, like most scientific problems, requires floating point math, and you will want your CPU to have a fast FPU section, one that has multiplication hard-wired in rather than doing it as a series of additions.) Back to the problem—the computer does your multiplication in a series of 45 operations, one after another, then draws the result on the screen for you. So far, so good, but let's suppose you are doing calculations on weather and you now have to multiply 10,000 numbers by some factor, then take the results and multiply by another factor, and so on, perhaps a thousand times. Vector processing helps by allowing you to run the same operation (e.g., multiply) on an array of numbers all at the same time (rather than one number at a time—how big an array depends on the machine). The big difference between vector computation and the SIMD approach used in contemporary microprocessors is that the vector machines pipeline their execution units—they can do multiple parts of a calculation at once.

We talk about traditional supercomputers in the past tense because such state-of-the-art machines today no longer use specialized processors. Instead, they employ standard microprocessors in what are known as *massively parallel* architectures. IBM, for example, is building a machine with a million processors. While there was nothing wrong with the older approaches, parallelism has turned out to be a much cheaper way of getting the maximum bang for the buck. These new architectures are described in Chapter 5.

Servers and Workstations

In 1990, this section would have been called "Minis and Workstations," but the minicomputer has really ceased to exist in computing, while the server has become a central factor. And, in fact, both servers and workstations are now very similar to desktop microcomputers.

Workstations are desktop computers that are much more powerful than normal PC-type machines and that are used for computer assisted graphics, various kinds of modeling and simulation, and other computationally intensive tasks. For much of the 1980s, a big part of the workstation market existed simply for the purpose of running a computer-assisted design program called AutoCAD from Autodesk, Inc. Workstation CPUs, once usually from the MIPS, Alpha, PowerPC, or PA-RISC families, but now quite often from Intel, emphasize floating point math and will normally have a very sophisticated graphics accelerator.

Contemporary servers come in two distinct kinds: those that are built on a desktop base and those that are built on a workstation platform. One difference, of course, is that servers have more storage capacity. A more significant variation, however, is that servers are designed to cope with failure. They have redundant power supplies, and provision for a mirrored or clustered architecture that allows one machine to duplicate another so that, even if there is a major system catastrophe (for example a

PORTABLE POWER SOURCES

Probably the most disappointing technology in the computer world is the battery. To achieve the ideals of portable computing, designers have sent out an S.O.S. for very lightweight, reliable, long-lasting power supplies. They are still waiting; such batteries haven't been developed yet, and may never be. While there has been some progress in power supplies, most of the improvements in the life of portable computing devices is due to reduced consumption rather than more battery power to the ounce.

Palmtops

The first palmtops were known as personal digital assistants (PDAs). The market began, and almost ended, with Apple's Newton in the early 1990s. Grossly over-hyped by Apple's CEO and self-styled visionary, John Sculley, the Newton fell from the Apple tree and splattered. The problem was that the machine was designed to be, and promoted as, an electronic notepad. Jot down those appointments. Send a note to mom. Capture those poetic thoughts. Unfortunately, since PDAs are by definition small and portable, they don't have keyboards. This left the burden to handwriting recognition software that couldn't do the job. The comic strip *Doonesbury* lampooned it for days, and despite a number of strengths, the Newton was a flop. Specialized handheld devices of varying sizes have since done well, but quietly, in areas like inventory, sales, record information systems in hospitals, and so forth. But the big advance has come with 3Com's PalmPilot.

WEBPADS

As this is written, a new kind of handheld called the Webpad is about to make its debut. The very promising idea here is that a device with a screen shaped like an 8 ½ x 11 pad of paper and endowed with advanced handwriting recognition software, can connect seamlessly to the Web through built-in wireless networking hardware and software. Though the basic idea has been tried before, several advances make this attempt exciting. One is that a new company, Transmeta, has designed a CPU that is both very powerful and very low in power consumption; competitors won't be far behind. This class of CPU will make it possible for the user to be productive for long periods of time. A second reason is that wireless networking schemes have finally become reliable, standardized, and inexpensive (see Chapter 11). This will make it easy for users to access the Web without having to think about it.

The PalmPilot generation is smaller and less power hungry than the Newton, but at the start at least, was also less ambitious. There is improved handwriting recognition, but also an easy-to-use keyboard equivalent. Applications, including calendar, task list, notepad, and so forth, are simple and foolproof. Most important of all, 3Com was in the market well over a year before it had competition. This allowed it to build some scale, and that was enough incentive to cause developers to write software that connected Palm applications to desktop equivalents such as calendars. People could now enter appointments in the Palmtop and synchronize them with their office system. This integration then spurred a very rapid increase in sales. 3Com has licensed the Palm operating system to other vendors, including those who make clones of the PalmPilot. Competing products, which use Mircrosoft's Windows CE operating system, have had difficulty getting a strong foothold in the market.

Cell Phones

The most significant adoptions of the PalmPilot's operating system have come from leading cell phone vendors. In the late 1990s, three changes have made the cell phone ubiquitous: deregulation has led to intense competition; cell phones have moved from analog to digital technology; and advances in chip design rules have made possible the integration of a vast number of features in a very small space. The worldwide market for cell phones is now well in excess of a hundred million units annually and climbing fast. Most observers expect the palmtop and the cell phone to merge and become the standard way of providing both functions. Subsequently, the phone/PDA will be given networking abilities that will allow it to connect automatically to desktop computers, automotive computers, and other devices designated by the user.

to combine ASIC concepts with high degrees on silicon integration. This is the basis for the *system on chip* idea (SoC) which envisions special and general-purpose logic, memory, control functions, and I/O on one chip. There is a strong economic argument for this approach. The fewer chips you have in a system, the lower its cost, even accounting for the design and manufacturing expense of integration. To illustrate, with SoC, you can now do away with the circuit board and the cost of attaching pieces to it. The expensive process of chip packaging is simplified if you don't have to put pins on each chip that allow it to communicate with other chips. The downside of SoC at the moment is testing. As chips get more complex, testing becomes more of a challenge. If, instead of validating limited purpose chips for just their relativley few functions, you have to examine SoC chips for a much greater range of functions, you can find yourself with a vastly more difficult testing problem. And speaking of huge challenges leads us to the last of the integration issues—*codesign.*

Codesign is the ultimate in application-specific/integrated systems; now software is thrown into the fray. The idea is that instead of designing hardware with software in mind or vice versa, you create both at the same time. Engineers will think through the logic of a problem and develop an abstract process to deal with it. Then, an extension of the existing Electronic Design Automation (EDA) tools will plot out both the structure of the chip and the software that will run on it. The idea is that the two will work together with optimum efficiency—those functions that will operate best on the chip will be placed there, and those needing some flexibility or external control will stay outside. Think of the software as fitting the hardware just as a hand fits in a glove. Testing will also be a big challenge here, but the first problem is creating EDA software that can deal with the complexity of codesign. Since the opportunity is a major one, lots of extremely bright people are working on it. Of course, while codesigned chips will be at the maximum of efficiency, they will also be at the maximum of inflexibility. Advocates of this approach don't care, pointing out that chips will soon be so inexpensive that the devices they reside in can simply be thrown away when obsolete.

Let's conclude with a radically different idea. Many believe that when feature sizes of .13 microns become standard around 2003, it will be so cheap to put millions and millions of transistors on a chip that application-specific designs will be a waste of time. The most extreme view is taken by scientists and engineers at MIT. A subproject of their larger "Project Oxygen," which is preparing a blueprint for the world of pervasive computing, has concluded that the processors of the future will have very few predrawn circuits. Instead, they will be field programmable gate arrays (FPGAs) whose hundreds of millions of logic gates can be reconfigured on the fly to support whatever software is in use at the moment. Moreover, because these "raw processors" would be so highly customizable—paths on the chip would be optimized for the task at hand—you would have both maximum flexibility *and* maximum efficiency.

CONCLUSION ·

If the entire world of computing were to have a single slogan, it would most logically be "smaller, faster, cheaper." This phrase summarizes chipmaking and, through it, computing as a whole. Making chips smaller makes them operate faster. Also, because yields increase as size decreases, smaller chips are cheaper as well. The lynchpin of all this, of course, is the ability to continue to make chips smaller. Scientists and engineers have found ways to do this for the last quarter century, and it seems likely that they will be able to continue to work their magic for at least another decade or so with the traditional techniques of photolithography. At that point, some new approach may be needed, but in the meantime, individual chips will have many billions of transistors and will operate at speeds in the billions of cycles per second (GHz).

Microprocessor manufacturers have been the most aggressive in taking advantage of the advances in chipmaking. Although profits in this area can be huge, very high design and capital costs, together with the need to have new CPUs accommodate older software, limit the number of competitors. Intel, which benefits from both an enormous base of legacy software and an exceptionally efficient manufacturing system, dominates the market for CPUs used in desktop machines, servers, and the like. Competitors include a handful of companies that make clones of Intel's chips, and another handful that makes CPUs based on variations of RISC technology that are not in any way compatible with Intel's chips. Intel might have to contend with charges that it has a monopoly were it not for the fact that the market for microprocessors is much broader than that for desktops, servers, and related types of computers.

Computers now come in an amazing array of types. The traditional categories of mainframe, server, workstation, and desktop computers are now complemented by portable equipment such as laptops and palmtops, and the huge and rapidly growing use of microprocessors that are "embedded" in things like cell phones, televison settops, automobiles, and many, many other "smart" devices. "Silicon economics" continues to build a world in which intelligent machines coexist with humans.

TEST YOUR UNDERSTANDING · · · · · · · · · · · · ·

1. What are the three alternatives to visible light being explored for chipmaking?

2. How do the three types of Intel desktop CPUs differ?

3. What are some of Intel's advantages in the CPU marketplace?

Part 2

Software

(Chapters 5 through 9)

As you shift your attention from hardware to software, it's appropriate to think of hardware as the vehicle and software as the driver. Or, if you prefer the concept of layers of activity, hardware is the bottom layer, and software sits on top. In fact, though, we'll see that software itself comprises a number of layers. The first of these is the operating system (OS), the layer in software that is responsible for managing the hardware-software partnership. The principles of the OS are covered in:

- Chapter 5: Fundamentals of the Operating System

Over the years, systems developers have created multiple kinds and types of operating systems. Some of these variations are principally the consequence of improvements in technology, while others are largely the result of market forces. Whatever the reason or reasons, diversity in operating systems is a fact that must be dealt with by those planning to rely on computers in today's economy. Indeed, although Microsoft dominates the desktop, the choice for a system used for a complex activity like e-commerce includes quite a few viable alternatives and is not so easily made. We consider OS options in:

- Chapter 6: Evolution of the Operating System
- Chapter 7: Microcomputer Operating Systems

Continuing with the e-commerce example, the choice of OS is not the last software decision. The core of your business will be some sort of database. This is the software that will track your inventory and sales, and lots of other essential functions. One way of creating this software is to "roll your own"—hire some programmers and custom build everything you need. The process of software development, including programming languages and the hot area of "objects" is covered in:

- Chapter 8: Programming, Object-Oriented Technology, and Software Development

Of course, you don't need to write your own software from the ground up—you can buy off-the-shelf packages that are already fully functioning databases, spreadsheets, or whatever. There are a lot of choices here, and the last chapter in this section puts considerable emphasis on how databases function and the different types now on the market. The concluding part of this chapter discusses the increasingly important issue of software reliability.

- Chapter 9: Databases, Applications, and Software Reliability

5 Fundamentals of the Operating System

The first element of software that we will discuss is the part that connects the computer to the hardware—the operating system (OS). Operating systems are often defined by their role in computer I/O (input/output), which means handling communications between the CPU/memory subsystem on the one hand, and on the other, handling links to external elements such as disk drives, display systems (including printers), connections to other computers (networks), keyboards, mice, and so forth. For example, when you print a document, it is the OS that determines how to get the material from the program in which you're working through the various parts of the computer and out to the printer. But it's important to understand that the OS is not responsible only for I/O. Under the surface, there are several other actions that occur in your computer when you go to launch a program, create or save a file, or print a document. And it is with actions such as these that this chapter is concerned because it is the operating system that manages all of the basic operations of a computer system. Admittedly, this is a simplified way of explaining a complicated part of computing, but by the end of this chapter, you will understand

- Why have an operating system?
- The core functions of the operating system
- The structure of an operating system
- The challenge of multiprocessing

WHY HAVE AN OPERATING SYSTEM? . . . .

Is the OS necessary? The short answer is no. An OS is a convenience, not a necessity. There are many computer systems that don't have an OS; instead, they make the functions of the OS a part of another program. For example, many embedded processors have a single core of software that includes all functions that the computer will perform. So why have an OS if it isn't needed? The answer is to deal with complexity and to accommodate the need to revise and improve.

If you have a simple embedded system with very limited functions and just one or two connected devices, you might not want to add a big OS. When the time comes to upgrade the system, it will be relatively easy to rewrite all the software. But if the program adds more functions, or if the hardware includes more elements, the amount of software will grow almost exponentially—something that makes it more inviting to bugs. At some point, upgrading by rewriting the whole thing doesn't make sense— it's time to create individual OS and program modules that can be revised separately. Mainframe computer systems reached this stage in the late 1950s. Minis and micros followed suit; even palmtops and PDAs have a separate OS.

THE CORE FUNCTIONS
OF AN OPERATING SYSTEM . . . .

The OS is the software program that really understands the hardware and knows how to work with it. Because the OS is so knowledgeable, the programs, the hardware devices, and the user don't have to be as aware. Table 5.1 provides an overview of the five key functions of the OS. Each will be covered in turn.

Table 5.1   Operating system functions

Operating system function	Example
System supervision	manages memory, starts and controls processes
Services to hardware	drivers for various devices (drives, displays, etc.)
Services to software	support to other programs such as the user interface (UI), file systems, etc.
Communications services	redirects requests for information from the local system to an external one; connects to network device drivers (e.g. Ethernet board)
Security	controls user access to directories and files

System Supervision

One way to think of the OS is as a manager. Of all the programs in operation, the OS is the one in charge.

Managing Memory

The most important of its supervisory functions is control of memory. This will be easier to understand if you think of memory as the tables in a large restaurant. If you have one place where reservations are taken and tables are assigned, all should work smoothly. But if people are constantly coming in at different doors and asking the waiters to seat them or take reservations, things can get out of control quickly. The OS, then, is like a maître d', checking off table assignments, keeping a master list of reservations, and so on. To see why memory management is important, remember that standard computers run at least two programs at any given time: an application program and the OS (the OS is also a program; the word *application* is normally used to describe software that performs tasks directly for users). Both need to use memory, and there is danger of fatal conflict if they attempt to access the same area. The original way for an OS to cope with this was to create *partitions*. The two programs then each have an area of memory set aside for their exclusive use. Figure 5.1 shows how memory could be partitioned in the one megabyte available to the PC's original operating system, MS-DOS.

Tech Talk

Application program: A program that is at the command of a user is normally called an *application*. By contrast, the operating system and other programs are usually known as *systems software*.

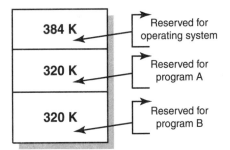

Figure 5.1 Static partitioning.
In static partitioning, two application programs and the operating system have reserved shares of memory.

Physical Memory

It helps to understand this if you think of a computer's memory as a lot of pigeon-holes on a rolltop desk. If software needs to store something temporarily, it puts it in hole number 32 (or whatever number is available); it then keeps track of that number and when it needs the information back, knows exactly where to find it. This is de-scribed as working with *physical memory*—each program gets a set of addresses that correspond to actual places on DRAM chips and that only it can use.

Tech Talk

Physical memory: The amount of memory that can be directly ad-dressed by a computer's hardware is called *physical memory*. It is lim-ited by the maximum size and number of DRAM chips that can be accommodated in the system.

Partitioning physical memory hampers system effectiveness when more than one program is running. If we assume that physical memory is limited, just dividing it into lots of partitions will mean that each program is going to get a pretty small slice (as in Figure 5.1). Moreover, such a static approach to partitioning isn't fair—at any given time it's likely that one program will be very active and struggling for as much memory as it can get, while the other is just sitting there, not doing any work but occupying valu-able memory space. Obviously, a dynamic approach to partitioning, in which memory is allocated and reallocated according to need, is preferable to static allocation. Modern OSs are able to do this, largely because they use a trick called *virtual memory.*

Virtual Memory

Dynamic allocation of memory has the potential to be much more effective than the static approach. For example, when the OS wants the word processor to yield to the database, it simply swaps the word processor out of memory to disk and moves the database from disk to memory. The challenge in this strategy occurs when, as must happen frequently (lots of times per second in an interactive system), the process is reversed. Because of changes that occur naturally in the normal execution of a pro-gram, the shape of physical memory might no longer be the same when a program is restarted—items would then be returned to different pigeonholes. This could cause big problems if the word processor, when it resumed operating, went to pigeonhole 32 for something that was now to be found in pigeonhole 49.

Tech Talk

Virtual memory: *Virtual memory* is an extension to a computer's physi-cal memory that is provided by the OS. It allows the system to more easily manage multiple programs.

IBM solved this problem for its mainframes by creating a system of memory addresses that was independent of physical memory. Called *virtual memory* (see Figure 5.2), this approach sets up a numbering scheme that is typically much larger than physical memory can accommodate—say 16 million vs. 1 million. Because there is now an almost limitless number of pigeonholes, all operating programs get unique addresses—if the word processor is assigned virtual location 32 for the storage of some piece of information, it is the only program to get it. But this number no longer represents an actual place; instead, it is a tag that identifies the information.

In order to keep track of where virtual addresses are to be found in physical memory, the system now includes a layer, the memory management system, that translates between virtual and physical memory as things are moved back and forth. Memory is now much easier to manage, and more and larger programs can be accommodated because the virtual memory is so much larger than the physical memory (virtual addresses that can't be kept in physical memory are held in disk storage). While virtual memory is a function of the OS, implementing it efficiently requires changes to hardware as well. CPUs without attached or on-chip memory management systems can't realistically handle virtual memory. Chips—CPUs or chipsets—now also include *translation look aside buffers* that keep a table of virtual-physical memory conversions close at hand. A well-designed translation look aside buffer (no acronym!) can make memory management work much faster.

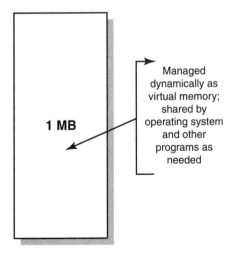

1 MB

Managed dynamically as virtual memory; shared by operating system and other programs as needed

Figure 5.2 Virtual memory.
Virtual memory management is much more flexible than the static version. The tradeoff is that it requires a more sophisticated and more capable hardware.

An important point about memory management is that virtual memory systems don't move memory around one byte or even one word at a time. Instead, memory is partitioned into blocks of around 2 to 4 kilobytes each, called *pages,* that are shifted all at once. So, when the memory management system identifies a virtual address that needs to be shifted back from disk to memory, it moves the entire page that the address is on (and if memory is full, swaps another page from memory back to disk in order to make room for it). When the memory management system discovers that a requested address is not in physical memory, it issues a *page fault,* which is the command to have it returned. Programmers, as you would guess, spend a lot of time thinking about how to organize their programs in a way that avoids page faults. One last piece of memory jargon: when a program gets confused and causes lots of page faults to occur in sequence, it is said to be *thrashing*—programmers *really* want to prevent this.

Tech Talk

Memory pages: Memory is organized into blocks called *pages* that are typically 2Kb to 4Kb in size. Rather than move an individual word from disk to memory (or vice versa), the entire page is moved.

Tech Talk

Thrashing: A poorly written program can find itself constantly moving pages back and forth between memory and disk. Called *thrashing*, this makes systems very inefficient.

The OS's supervisory role includes more than memory management. The OS also has to keep track of multiple programs. This function, called *multitasking,* is discussed next.

Multitasking

The ability of a computer to handle two or more programs at once is a key distinction of an OS. For quite some time, this was a way of separating the big guys from the little ones—mainframe, mini, and workstation systems were multitasking and microcomputer systems were not. While it would have been theoretically possible to put a multitasking OS (such as Unix, see Chapter 6) on a chip like an Intel 8088, the size of the OS, not to mention that of multiple programs, would have brought operations to a crawl. By about 1985, and with the appearance in the microcomputer world of systems based on the Intel 80386 for the PC and the Motorola 68020 for the Mac, this had changed. A workable version of Unix was ported to the Intel platform and a form of multitasking was added to the Mac OS. Windows 1.0 was multitasking too, and supposedly even on a 286, but rumor has it that various religious cults were using

The User Interface

In the early days of computing, each program was responsible for presenting itself to the user. This meant not only the appearance of the screen, but also the entire set of available commands. By the late 1970s, operating systems had taken a part of this burden on themselves. To illustrate, we'll use the familiar example of Microsoft's Windows. You know that Windows gives you a startup screen, the Desktop, which you use to find and launch programs. In addition, Windows has standardized much of the menu system. For example, most programs use the same "File" and "Edit" menu settings at the left of the top bar. Windows also provides some consistent functions, such as "cut," "copy," and "paste," that are available to all applications and normally allow movement of information from one program to another. Of course, Windows doesn't control the whole thing. The actual menu settings will vary according to the functions it provides to the user.

The first user interfaces (UIs) were character-based and command-driven. If you've seen MS-DOS, you know what this means. If not, think of a blank screen with just the prompt "C:>" or something similar somewhere on the left. Once this appeared, it was your responsibility to know what to do next. With limited exceptions, today's UIs are graphical and menu-driven. They are often called GUIs (for graphical user interface), but this acronym will be avoided for aesthetic reasons. In some OSes, such as Windows and the Mac, the UI is embedded in the OS's core software. In others, such as Unix and its popular sibling Linux, the user can choose between a variety of different UIs (see Chapters 6 and 7 for descriptions of these OSes).

Application Programming Interface (API)

The user isn't the only one who needs help in working with the OS; programs require services and assistance as well. Just as the user sees the UI as a map to the services of the OS, so the programmer has a set of *APIs* (Application Programming Interfaces) that provide a similar, but more comprehensive, map. The set of APIs published for an OS provides a library of functions that a programmer can call to do such things as open a new window or provide a menu bar. The term API is now used rather widely, often referring to any request for a function (an action) going from any program to any other.

APIs need not be static; an OS vendor can develop and publish new ones when the software is rewritten. For example, Microsoft has added TAPI (telephony API) to its newest OSes so that they can be used to support and manage a wide variety of telephone-related applications. To illustrate, programmers now have access to APIs that allow them to route a call from a company's telephone switching system (usually a PBX, or private branch exchange) directly to a PC on a local area network. From there it can be passed to an application that records it and makes it available as a substitute for an answering machine. To illustrate further, other program-to-program APIs would also make it possible for a voice recognition program to transcribe the voice message, put it in an e-mail, and send it to the user's palmtop. Without APIs, programmers wouldn't be able to take advantage of the services of the OS, and other programs and would have to create everything on their own.

SHOW US YOUR DOCUMENTS!

A hot issue in computing has been "undocumented APIs." As the name suggests, these are known to the developer of the software but not to others. Critics have accused Microsoft of using undocumented APIs in Windows as a way of giving an advantage to Microsoft's applications (Word, Excel, etc.). Microsoft has denied this, saying that there is a "Chinese Wall" between its OS and applications groups. Whatever the truth of this issue, there are more important reasons for the success of Microsoft's applications (see Chapter 9).

File Systems

Since the concept of files is a fairly basic one, it won't be covered in depth here. Essentially all computers use a hierarchical file system, with directories and files branching off from the center like roots on a tree. The way in which files are structured and organized is often an intrinsic feature of the OS; DOS has a file system of its own, so do IBM mainframes, and so forth. Some OSs, such as Windows NT, Windows 2000, and most mainframe systems, can support multiple file systems at once.

Communications Services

The OS manages not only physical connections to external devices via drivers, but also logical linkages in networked environments. This is illustrated by the simple process of saving a file. If you are on a network, and want to save a file to a drive on the server, for example, on Drive M, your application program will save it just as if it was to the local Drive C. In a networked system, the OS recognizes that M is not a local drive, and instead of sending it to a disk, forwards the file information to the section of the OS that manages communications. Once there, the file is packaged in the appropriate network protocol, given the correct address, and sent to the right output port (for example, an Ethernet card; network protocols and connections are described in detail in Part 3). Older OSs, such as MS-DOS, could be modified with driver-like software that allowed them to function on networks; an example is Novell's "requestor" modules. Modern OSs, however, have this capability built in.

Tech Talk

Port: A *port* is a place where data can enter or leave the computer through some attached device. The term *port* is used to refer to both physical connections and their software address. The OS manages the use of ports.

Security

Security isn't much of a concern in a single-user operating system, but quickly becomes a big deal when multiple users are sharing files and services. As a consequence, we'll digress for a moment to talk about multiuser systems.

Multiuser Operating Systems

A true multiuser OS is one that has only one copy of the OS that is shared by multiple users. These systems are also called *terminal-host*. As we'll see in Part 3 when we talk about networking, in terminal-host systems, only the host has any intelligence. The terminal has no CPU, little or no memory, and no storage. Terminal-host computing is the exclusive province of mainframe and minicomputer OSs (these go by confusing names such as VM and MVS from IBM, and VMS from DEC; see Chapter 6). These OSes will allow many users, perhaps thousands, to be sharing system resources at any given time. Most versions of Unix are also multiuser, and some are designed to support hundreds of simultaneous terminal users.

Multiuser operating systems are necessarily distinguished by the degree of security they provide. The level of interaction varies, but the typical system is one in which many people or client computers are using the host computer or server at the same time. Each of these users is interacting with his or her process, or they are using separate threads in the same process, or both. This level of interaction makes some kind of traffic control mandatory. Processes and threads have to be identified with their owners and, equally important, files and collections of files (directories) have to be identified in a way that makes it clear who has the right to access and change which piece of information.

Multiuser systems normally give each user a separate identification (user ID), that tracks processes and threads, as well as files. Normally, a user will see not the ID but a *username,* the system automatically handles the conversion from name to number. Users have to get these usernames and IDs from a system administrator. User IDs are normally associated with specific levels of access. For example, a member of the accounting staff would have access only to materials in the section of the computer set aside for the accounting department. Those files that she "owns" personally (usually because she created them) can be accessed and modified at will (typically called *read/write* access). By contrast, she might only have the right to look at, but not modify, files that are in a common area for the department (read-only access). Of course, she would not be able to see, much less read or modify, files in other individuals' areas.

Some other dimensions of OS-based security include internal auditing to see who used what and for how long, controls to make sure that deleted files are erased so they can't be viewed by snoopers, and other such functions. Finally, to extend the example above, none of the individuals in accounting or any of the other user departments would have any kind of access to "system" files (those that belong to the operating system itself) or to files that run system programs (such as one that shuts down the computer), etc. Access to these files is limited to system administrators (some OSs refer to them as *superusers*) and they are often protected by multiple levels of passwords.

The OS ensures that a user is who she says she is by means of passwords. A user logs in to the computer, is asked to give the password, and, if the user ID and password can be verified by the computer, is given access to whatever resources the holder of that ID is allowed to access. There are various ways of handling passwords. Unix, which is fairly secure, takes the password from the keyboard, runs it through an encryption algorithm, then compares it to the encrypted original that is in the file with the user's ID. If there is a match, the system provides access. Next, it uses information in the file to determine what files and services the user may work with. As you can see, it is no trivial matter for an OS to support multiple simultaneous users. Such systems must be designed as multiuser from the ground up if they are to be effective.

Single-User Systems in a Networked Environment

Single-user computers can be set up to facilitate connection to a multiple user host (a server) in one of two basic ways. In the first case, add-on software (normally provided by the maker of the server OS) allows the single-user system (the client) to be authenticated by the host. In the second and now standard approach, the single-user OS is designed from the beginning to function as a network client and comes out of the box with provision for password logins, file access restrictions, etc. Windows NT and Windows 95+ support this approach. Unix also has these capabilities, but doesn't fit in this category because both client and server are full-blown multiple user OSs (to

So, for the sake of efficiency, designers have concentrated on multiprocessing that is both symmetric and preemptive. The need for preemption is critical here. Letting programs run across multiple processors isn't efficient if the load can't be balanced in a dynamic fashion. Getting the best use out of the system requires that the OS be able to move tasks among CPUs according to need. The OS must also be able to preempt a running program for one of higher priority (hardware, of course, must be able to support interrupts for multiple CPUs). Despite the challenges, support for preemptive multiprocessing is now the clear standard for server OSs. As noted, we are likely to see this capability in desktop machines in the near future. As shown in Figure 5.6, OSs that support multiprocessing add a scheduling module to the kernel.

Multiprocessing also presents serious problems for application programs. Many programs, especially older ones, are written so that they will execute in a linear fashion—first this action, then that, then the next, and so on. Usually, each instruction assumes that the previous one has been completed before it executes; often it is dependent on this being the case. A program of this type will work in a multiprocessing system, but not very efficiently. For software to take advantage of multiprocessing, it has to be written in a way that allows, whenever possible, for instructions to execute in parallel. Changing a program to function in this way normally requires not just rewriting, but completely rethinking, the way the program was originally structured. As an example of the kind of problem application software developers face for these systems, consider the new issue of *thread migration*. Threads can be very efficient, but if the OS and the parent program are not written to effectively manage multiprocessing, threads can become separated from caches and data, quickly making a theoretically efficient approach inefficient in practice. It's important to remember that

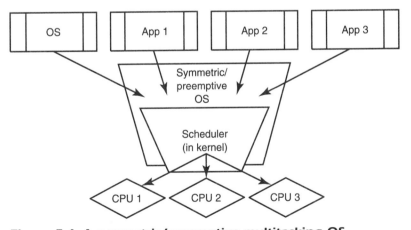

Figure 5.6 A symmetric/preemptive multitasking OS.
The scheduler sends work to the next available CPU. Interrupts can give priority as needed.

some programs are inherently linear, not just in the code but in the logic, and won't benefit, or not very much, from parallel execution of instructions. But there are important categories of software that are greatly enhanced by multiprocessing. Notable among these are databases that need to support multiple queries (especially from multiple sources). As multiprocessing hardware becomes less expensive, software designers are more likely to appreciate its benefits and introduce them in new and revised programs.

DANGERS OF SHARED MEMORY

The best way to solve the access bottleneck in shared memory systems would be to add cache to each CPU, but this can create dangerous problems. The most effective caches (*write-back* caches) can hold a write to memory until the memory system is free. If it didn't do this, the CPU would have to wait, negating much of the cache's benefit. But in a write-back cache, there is a period of time in which what should be the same data are different in cache than in memory. For example, CPU A has calculated a value and changed the number in memory location xx, but its write-back cache holds on to it for a fraction of a second. In the meantime CPU B goes to read the value at xx and gets the wrong (not the most current) information. Bang! The missiles head for Moscow. There are many other similar kinds of problems. Designers therefore have to provide for *cache coherency*, a strategy that ensures that caches are in synch.

Multiprocessing in Hardware

Moving to the hardware side of multiprocessing presents engineers with some tough choices. The most important problem is how to connect the CPUs to each other. There are two basic approaches that are usually known as *shared memory* and *shared nothing*. For reasons that will become apparent as we discuss the two architectures, shared memory tends to be limited to ~64 CPUs, while shared nothing designs can go into the thousands—a strategy also known as *massively parallel*. Shared memory is the easiest approach; it simplifies communication and saves money. It's slower, though, because the two (or more) CPUs will be contending for access to the memory system, as shown in Figure 5.7. Because simple is more attractive than fast, shared memory is the most common way to go.

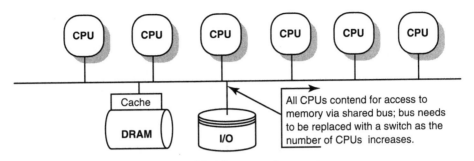

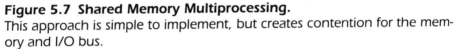

Figure 5.7 Shared Memory Multiprocessing.
This approach is simple to implement, but creates contention for the memory and I/O bus.

The biggest problem with shared memory multiprocessing is the capacity of the bus. If the bus is saturated, the CPUs will have to slow down to wait for it. Most systems use buses that are similar to (but faster than) those used elsewhere in the computer. An alternative to the traditional memory bus is the use of switched access (usually crossbar switching) instead of a bus; this approach, which we will describe in Part 3 when we talk about networks, can be faster but is generally more expensive. Overall, though, shared memory multiprocessing works well. In the Unix world, for example, 64 CPU shared memory machines are not uncommon.

What about shared nothing—connecting independent CPUs, each with its own memory system? This approach (see Figure 5.8) avoids contention for the memory bus, but substitutes for it the problem of how to connect the CPUs—remember that they still need to share instructions and data. Providing for multiple physical paths from any given CPU to any other requires a more sophisticated internal bus or switch fabric, more wiring connections, and the like. For the most part, these massively parallel architectures are built to order for spare-no-expense buyers. For example, the U.S. Department of Energy has the current state-of-the-art in massively parallel computers. Its system uses *4,096* IBM Power3 CPUs. This awesome machine can operate in the 3 teraflop (trillions of floating point operations per second) range. Of course, awesome is in the context of the times; using 4,000 processors won't seem so great when IBM finishes its planned million-processor machine.

In the mainstream market, achieving the potential of massively parallel processing will require some agreement on a standard architecture. This will make mass production and low costs possible. Current costs are high because so much of the design and manufacturing is custom—the CPUs themselves aren't very expensive. Once a standard reference model is established, software developers will invest the resources needed to allow their programs to make good use of the vast power that will become available. There is a candidate for this role now on the market. Called Non-Uniform Memory Architecture (NUMA), this approach combines the shared memory and mas-

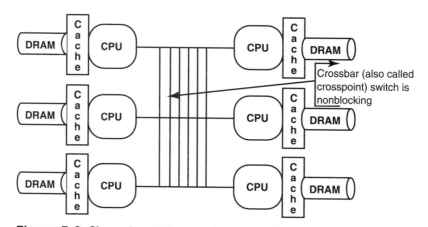

Figure 5.8 Shared nothing multiprocessing.
This strategy requires the use of switches for interprocessor communication as well as radically different software. These systems are normally known as *massively parallel.*

sively parallel approaches. Machines are built from clusters of four shared memory CPUs, which are in turn linked to each other through a complex switched network of the type used by other massively parallel systems.

The challenge for designers of multiprocessing systems—both on the software and the hardware sides—is in getting systems to *scale* effectively. Perfect scalability in this way of thinking would be that two processors would be twice as fast as one, four would be four times as fast, and so forth. In fact, we'll never see 100 percent scalability since the clock cycles needed by the scheduler to allocate tasks and the overhead in waiting for memory access or CPU-to-CPU communication will always introduce some latency. Current systems scale reasonably well, perhaps at 80 percnt or so when there are two to four processors, but get less efficient after that. However, since there is accelerating demand for more powerful computers, we can expect that engineers will find ways to improve scalability with dozens and even hundreds of CPUs.

CONCLUSION . . . .

The operating system, initially a luxury in computing, has evolved to become a necessity for all but the simplest systems. The modern OS provides a range of critical functions that include supervising the use of system resources, providing services to users and programmers, maintaining security, and managing communications in net-

Open Source

An interesting development in software is the "open source" movement. To understand what this means, you have to consider the alternative. Traditionally, programmers have jealously guarded the *source code* (see Chapter 8) that explains how their software works. The reason for doing this is that someone with access to that code could easily copy the work and market a variation as their own. In other words, protecting source code is seen as protecting profit.

The open source movement turns this logic on its head, advocating the free publication of source code. A number of programmers had done this for a long time with minor pieces of software, but the idea gained momentum when applied to operating systems. To understand why, remember that applications software, stuff like spreadsheets and databases that do the real work in computing, rely on the OS for an array of services such as managing I/O and the user interface. If applications programmers have access to the OS's source code, they will be able to do a better, more efficient job of using these services. A second reason for open source software is that it limits the power of the OS vendor. While Microsoft has regularly denied that it makes OS source code available to its applications developers, the Justice Department and the attorneys general of a bunch of states have expressed disbelief and argued that the knowledge has been shared and had given Microsoft's application groups a huge advantage over competitors. Whatever position you might take on this, the fact is that open source takes the argument away.

The open source model has been adopted by a number of major software vendors, including AOL's Netscape division. The momentum for the effort, however, comes from an open source clone of Unix, known after its developer, Linus Torvalds, as Linux.

Linux

In a world of heavyweight, corporate-sponsored OSs, Linux might seem no more than a curiosity. That would be true except for the fact that the fruit of Torvalds' labor is lean and efficient, running especially well on Intel CPUs. The Achilles heel of software like this would normally be driver support. As we have noted, drivers are essential for critical peripherals such as disk drives, displays, network adapters, and so forth. Driver software is hard to write and the constantly changing mix of peripherals makes support in the area very difficult, even for Microsoft. In its early days, Linux was able to offset, if not overcome, this obstacle because its thousands of fans around the world volunteered to provide needed software. As the OS grew in popularity, vendors began to provide drivers directly. It is quite incredible that Linux users have few complaints about missing or faulty drivers.

Aside from hobbyists, the first commercial uses of Linux were largely for Web servers running another highly regarded freeware package, Apache. It's difficult to gauge the effectiveness of one OS vs. another. "Linux bigots" claim that their OS is more stable than NT—that their servers can run longer without rebooting. NT adherents disagree, and in any case, Windows 2000 is widely considered to be a significant improvement on NT in this regard. There is little argument, though, that NT/2000 does win most server speed contests with Linux, especially under heavy loads. However, it's reasonable to expect that this lead will shrink over time. Experience, which includes both the maturity of drivers and interfaces and of the people who install them, is a key factor in system performance. Given this, it's reasonable to assume that the young Linux will progress faster than the older NT/2000.

Two things that initially slowed Linux's acceptance were the lack of both technical support and an easy-to-use graphical UI. The first challenge was effectively met by 1998, with two companies, Red Hat and Caldera, offering packaged versions of the software and the kinds of technical support options that corporate users insist on. The second issue is more of a problem. By late 1999, there were still at least three competing graphical UIs for Linux. While choice is normally a good thing, recall that if true ease of use is to be assured, applications programs will have to make calls to the UI's APIs. Given the level of effort involved, it's not likely that many vendors will want to support more than one UI. At this writing, Linux is well supported by database vendors, but Corel is the only mainstream developer of other types of applications to support it.

The UI, though, is mostly an issue for the consumer world. Server administrators are macho types who don't mind typing in line after line of arcane code (or so they say). And in the "server space," Linux is on a roll. Major database vendors such as Oracle, Sybase, and IBM have Linux versions, complete with technical support packages. Even more striking, major hardware vendors such as IBM and HP are offering Linux with new machines. The appearance, again in early 1999, of a new version of the Linux kernel that supports multiple processors, together with third-party clustering software, allows Linux to move up from the Web server in the closet to a coveted space in the glass house. Maybe. Momentum matters in the market, and Microsoft has it. Just because it's free doesn't mean that Linux will succeed.

CONCLUSION ·

The mainframe operating systems continue to be a major force in computing. They are extremely reliable and quite versatile. In the server world, the day of the proprietary OS—software designed exclusively for and sold with a specific hardware platform—seems to be fading. The most important such systems extant, VMS and

OS/400 are successful and strong, but growth is in the various forms of Unix and in its sibling Linux. Both system managers and software developers like the flexibility of having application software that can run on a variety of platforms. Of course, Unix and Linux don't define the market for server software. Novell and especially Microsoft are key players in server operating systems. We haven't covered these here, since the purpose of this chapter is the evolution of operating systems and Microsoft's and Novell's OSs evolved from microcomputer systems rather than from minicomputers. Accordingly, we'll turn next to discuss the development of microcomputer OSs.

TEST YOUR UNDERSTANDING . . . .

1. What is considered to be the first operating system, and who developed it?
2. What is the difference between a proprietary architecture and an open architecture?
3. Give three reasons why the Unix operating system is as popular as it is.
4. Why are there different "flavors" of Unix?
5. What is the purpose of Posix?
6. What does *open source* mean?
7. What are the principal barriers to widespread acceptance faced by an OS like Linux?

COMMON LAW?

Microsoft uses an object-oriented technology, called COM (common object model), for much of NT's internal workings (see Chapter 9 for a discussion of object-oriented software). An extension of COM, called DCOM (distributed COM), is used for networked applications. Rivals argue that Microsoft is using the COM/DCOM technology to extend its monopoly in desktop operating systems and applications to the rapidly growing area of distributed systems. Don't be surprised if this issue ends up in litigation.

NT's Change in Direction

Microsoft's goal for NT changed as the program developed. Its roots were in the joint project with IBM, and in the initial phase it was to use OS/2's Presentation Manager interface. This was changed to the Windows interface when IBM and Microsoft split. Fortunately, the modular design of NT made this fairly easy to do.

For quite a while, around about 1992, Microsoft trumpeted NT as its next major OS, downplaying the significance of Chicago. Redmond's hype put the industry in ferment, with many analysts predicting that NT would be the standard desktop OS within a few years. Suddenly, a few months before NT appeared, Microsoft switched the rhetoric and began to describe NT as an OS for servers and high-end workstations, and Chicago as the standard desktop OS. The reason became clear when NT appeared—it was a resource hog. The OS wanted at least 8 MB of memory (a lot then) and wouldn't run effectively with less than 12. It would work on a 486, but barely. Regular Windows applications ran notably slower on NT than on Windows 3.1. Despite its usual bravado, Microsoft seemed embarrassed by this, even though it shouldn't have been. NT was a very ambitious project. A little tuning, and the inevitable improvements in processor speed and memory cost would make it a viable competitor. By version 3.5, it was a fast-growing powerhouse. If it were not for market conflicts with Windows 95, it would be the clear choice for the standard desktop OS today. More on that issue later.

In the meantime, NT is moving past the workgroup server market into *enterprise* systems—computers (normally clusters of computers) that handle the core functions of a business such as airline reservations, billing for large mail-order companies, and so forth. When NT clusters first appeared in 1998, unlikely bedfellow IBM proclaimed that a cluster of 114 NT servers, using IBM's DB2 database, could handle in excess of 50 million transactions an hour. That's a billion in 19 hours. And that 114-server cluster costs a heck of a lot less to purchase and maintain than an IBM mainframe. The bad news is that these systems are about 99 percent reliable. Enterprise systems have to be wide awake and error-free more like 99.9 percent of the time. And it's not clear that NT will ever achieve enterprise-level reliability. A typical Unix OS has some 12 million lines of code, while NT is nearly three times as big. All that extra code increases the potential for error and exacerbates the increasingly difficult problem of testing.

Windows 2000

Windows 2000 (originally NT v5.0) had just hit the market as this text was being completed. Initial reviews are generally favorable. The OS is considered to be about as fast as, but notably more stable than, its predecessor. It is also much easier to install than NT. Additional features include better support for streaming media devices such as sound and video (both hardware and software), better integration with Web-based software, and an improved user interface. The advanced server version of Windows 2000 supports two-node clusters with a total of 64 CPUs.

OS/2 . . . .

After it split with Microsoft, IBM decided to tackle OS/2 on its own. IBM had full access to the existing source code, which was actually bad news since it was written for an obsolete CPU architecture (the 286). Still, IBM soldiered on, revealing its frequent changes of direction in press releases that simply ignored previous announcements. One of the more interesting elements was IBM's frequent boasting. When they decided that OS/2 would support Windows applications, IBM's senior executives said that OS/2 would have "better windows than Windows." Never happened.

Surprisingly, in view of all this, OS/2 v2.0, released in 1992, was a pretty good piece of software that ran only on 32-bit Intel CPUs (386–486 at that time). It was buggy, ran Windows applications slower than Windows (no big surprise), but most neutral observers agreed that it had a better interface than Windows and that, at least with applications written for OS/2, it was more stable. OS/2's first releases were somewhere between Windows and Windows NT. It was similar to what Windows 95 became—more fully 32-bit than Windows, but still some 16-bit code for compatibility.

The Palm OS

The early volume leader in the small market has been Palm Computing's Palm OS. Small and compact, this OS runs on Motorola's Dragonball processor family, which is based on that company's well-regarded 68K family of CPUs. The Palm OS is flexible, and its UI can work with another OS. The Palm OS is used in the company's own Palm PC, on a clone (the Visor) from a company called Handspring, and on some cell phones. The widespread adoption of the Palm PC has meant that many companies are or have developed applications for the Palm OS. This vault of "legacy" applications will give the Palm OS an important advantage in the escalating small system wars.

OSs for Embedded Systems

The market for embedded systems is huge. Many of these are too small and simple to require a separate OS. Of those that do, the market leader is a company called Wind River Systems, with its Vx Works and Tornado families.

Many embedded OSs are what are known as Real Time Operating Systems (RTOSs). *Real time*, one of the oddest pieces of techno-jargon, means that the OS must handle events without appreciable delay. An RTOS must, for example, respond immediately to priority events no matter what else it is doing at the time. For example, when you push down on the accelerator in your car, the fuel system has to change the flow of fuel and the air/fuel mixture right away if the car is to perform acceptably. RTOSs generally don't have virtual memory because it is too slow and because they usually don't have multiple applications that need a lot of memory. One of the most widely used RTOSs is Inferno from Lucent. Others are Neutrino from QNX and something called OS/9. At least the RTOS people know how to name things. We really don't have space to discuss RTOSs further; just wanted you to know they were there.

Epoc

The toughest competitor to Windows CE and the Palm OS is something called the Epoc OS. It is provided by a company called Symbian, which is in turn based on a consortium of telephone equipment heavyweights, including Motorola, Nokia, and

Ericsson, as well the Japanese electronics giant Matsushita (Panasonic and other brands). Most early Epoc applications are in cell phones. Since the number of cell phone users is expected to reach 600 million by 2001, and since the companies in Symbian dominate that market, the Epoc OS is likely to become a major player. Like Windows CE, Epoc is highly modular and can be adapted to work on devices of various sizes. Epoc should be widely considered for set-top boxes and the growing category of "information appliances" that are discussed in Chapter 12. To show how flexible Epoc is, it can adapt to different UIs—it is already being used to support devices that present the user with the Palm OS.

CONCLUSION ·

Microcomputer operating systems are only about 25 years old, and evolution has been rapid. Within about ten years, this category of OS had transitioned from 8-bit to 16-bit code, and was on its way to being the first type of computer to employ a graphical user interface. Indeed, by the time they were only about 15 years old, microcomputer OSs had acquired most of the characteristics of their mainframe parents, including such things as virtual memory, true multitasking, and the use of 32-bit code. Of course, much of this development was made possible by the rapid improvements in hardware. The original MS-DOS had to work with a computer whose CPU ran at under 5 MHz and which had access to only 64 Kb of memory. Today's Windows 2000 can expect to luxuriate in a machine with an 800 MHz CPU and 128 MB or more of memory. Generally speaking, progress in the OS, and necessarily, therefore, improvements in application software that depends on the OS, have significantly lagged that of hardware. For example, Intel had a true 32-bit CPU (the 80386) in 1985, but Microsoft's mainstream 32-bit OS, Windows 95, didn't appear until ten years later. These delays are partly attributable to the need to accommodate legacy software, and partly to the demands that graphical UIs and the increasing proliferation of peripheral devices have made on programmers.

The next stage of evolution in desktop OSs will be to the microkernel-kernel-shell architecture pioneered by Unix. This will make possible significantly more stable software, and will more easily accommodate the streaming media applications that are appearing with the increased integration of digital video and sound in computer programs. Windows 2000 has already evolved in this way, and the Mac OS should follow soon. Unix and Linux, which are now not all that different from regular desktop OSs, have of course implemented this approach as well. It seems likely that Microsoft will now quickly move away from the Windows 95–98 OS family in favor of a lighter weight version of Windows 2000. On the other hand, the bigger is better phenomenon has its limits. While 64-bit versions of most types of Unix/Linux are already widely available, and an equivalent for Windows 2000 should follow soon,

for insurance customers, even though most of the work of managing customers is the same in both cases. This specialization also exacerbated the challenge of interfacing different databases because most components of the program were linked to the kind of information in the database. By contrast, information hiding, which is central to OOT, creates a general design that can accommodate a wide variety of data. "Customer" would now be a class, with special iterations for utility, insurance, and so forth. Putting the data in the background accelerates programming and eases database linkages.

Structured programming also argued for careful organization of the source code, in particular for making the program as modular as possible. The use of modules has several advantages:

1. It enhances the readability of the code because blocks of related logical operations are easier to understand than a less organized approach (this is how you prevent spaghetti code).

2. The modules can manage memory separately—for example, a module could set aside a certain section of memory for its computations, then release it when the module is no longer executing.

3. Modules facilitate code reuse. If carefully written, a module (effectively a subroutine) can be used to support a number of a program's actions.

Of course, structured programming insists on extensive *commenting,* which is language inserted into the source code that explains what the program is supposed to be doing at that point.

Certainly, these recipes for good programming are not in any way revolutionary—no one is accorded a genius for thinking of them. In fact, the only reason they get so much attention is that they came at a time when software development was in crisis. As the capabilities of computers had expanded, so had the ambitions of managers to make the best possible use of their investment. Vast, complex software development projects had become the norm, especially after the appearance of IBM's System/360 computers enhanced the affordability of powerful machines. Suddenly, lots of users were observing the same phenomenon that IBM had encountered in developing the System/360's operating system—software projects don't scale well. In particular, as noted, adding more programmers increases communications problems and leads to serious bugs as the right hand not only doesn't know what the left hand is doing, but can't begin to keep track of the several hundred other hands. After the software crisis was recognized (there was actually an international conference by that name), the writing of software became a more professional activity and the term *software engineering* came into widespread use.

Project Modeling

A second major direction in the reform of programming has been focused not on the code itself but on the part of the total effort that precedes coding. This approach places an emphasis on modeling. Analysts study the program requirements and build a model (likely in a flow diagram) of the result *before* any code is written. The often used analogy is to building a house. You should no more start a program by writing code than you would begin to build a house by nailing some boards together. The classic approach to programming is the "waterfall method" (see Figure 8.3 for a simplified version).

··

FUNCTION AT THE (SILICON) JUNCTION

> More loose language from the computer front. The terms *function* and *procedure* represent an action that a computer program can perform. For example, Windows has a function for opening a new window. An application program—let's say, a word processor—issues a *function call* to Windows, asking it to do this (the syntax for this and

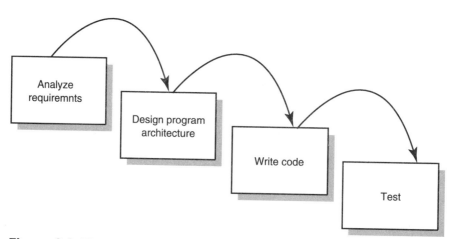

Figure 8.3 The waterfall method.
This is one of many variations on the "waterfall" approach to designing software. A very different approach is described in the later section of rapid application development.

other function and procedure calls are a part of Windows' API). Similarly, when a programmer creates a subroutine in a program, it gets a name and becomes a function that can be called from elsewhere in the program (or by another program, depending on whether the programmer publishes an API). In the minds of some specialists, there is a technical difference between a procedure and a function; for the purposes of this book, though, they are the same thing.

Modular Programming

A third major trend in programming reform has been the idea of code reuse, an extension of structured programming's call for the use of modules. Program subroutines are often painstakingly written to solve a complex problem; for example, as noted previously in this chapter, a programmer might write a subroutine that would be called every time his program needed to execute an algorithm, such as calculating an automotive lease payment or setting up optimistic estimates for Orange County investments. If written carefully, subroutines like this can be used over again, not just in the same program but in a completely different program. Obviously, the more convoluted the algorithm, the more benefit, but programmers have long appreciated the value of building *libraries* of subroutines that can be reused. Unfortunately, in normal programming, reusing code is difficult because although subroutines appear to be off to the side, in traditional programming languages it is very difficult to make them really separate. One of the principal advantages of object-oriented programming, which we'll discuss a bit later in this chapter, is that its objects are conceived and built in a way that makes them easier to reuse than subroutines.

Tech Talk

Modular programming: A hot idea in programming is to segregate code into discrete units or modules, each of which maintains responsibility for specific functions. The approach is really a more structured extension of earlier ideas; object-oriented technology is inherently modular.

PROGRAMMING LANGUAGES BY LEVEL . . . . . .

As mentioned earlier, there are basically four hierarchical categories into which today's hundreds of programming languages can be divided.

- Machine languages
- Assembly languages
- High-level languages
- Fourth-generation languages

Machine Language Programming

Machine language describes the numerical codes corresponding to the instruction set that are directly recognized by the CPU; because it corresponds to the instruction set, machine language is tied to a particular CPU. A printout of a program in machine language is a string of numbers (a very long string, even for a short program). The numbers will be written in hexadecimal for the simple reason that anyone trying to write, much less read, page after page of ones and zeros would quickly go crazy. There is very little benefit to working in machine language over assembly language. It has a section here simply because it's the first language in the hierarchy and because machine language is what other programming languages create.

Assembly Language

Assembly language also corresponds to the instruction set of a CPU. However, assembly language is represented by codes rather than by numbers. Though not nearly so widely used as it once was, a lot of programming is still done in assembly language. The problem with the language is threefold.

1. It is difficult to work with and therefore takes longer to produce usable programs.
2. Once written in assembly language, even well-documented programs are hard to read and therefore a challenge to modify.
3. Because it adheres so closely to the instruction set of a CPU, an assembly language program can only run on that CPU (porting an assembly language program to a new CPU would be essentially the same as starting all over).

So what's the benefit? The advantage is speed. Because the programmer is working directly with the CPU, with its registers and pipelines and stuff, he or she can make sure that each instruction uses the hardware as efficiently as possible (again, this is not easy to do; an unskilled programmer might make things worse).

THE BEAST IN THE GLASS HOUSE

Another reason (besides speed) that assembly language was so widely used in earlier days was simple economics. People planning to create a program normally worked at large organizations that already had a mainframe, one that was likely very heavily used. Thus, their new program had to fit into this limited resource. If Jones, who wanted a new program to analyze sales, went to visit Smith, head of his company's information systems (IS) operation, Jones could expect to grovel just to get permission to use resources to develop the program. He would be certain to be laughed out of Smith's office in the glass house (where the computers lived) if he admitted that his new program would be so inefficient as to cause the business to have to upgrade its mainframe or, heaven forfend, buy a new one. In most situations, assembly language programming was the only way to avoid this kind of crisis. Today's computing architecture, with cheap hardware that can be added in small increments, has created a fundamental change in programming.

In the old days (that is, prior to about 1985), CPU resources were so scarce that this tradeoff usually made sense. However, as the microprocessor revolution began to pump out sixty percent annual increases in CPU power, assembly language lost much of its appeal. Most assembly programmers have moved to C because that language has few of assembly's disadvantages (for example, it is portable) and because it doesn't sacrifice a great deal in speed. Assembly language is still widely used in those areas where speed is paramount. For example, a huge, klutzy operating system like Windows v3.0 would have been intolerably slow if key parts were not written in assembly language. Another area where performance is critical is in games programs; a good part of what is out there, including much of the new stuff, is still in assembly. Assembly is also widely used in embedded systems, where programs are normally fairly simple and speed of execution is often paramount. The class of software that turns assembly language programs into machine language is often called an *assembler,* and *assembly* and *assembler* are often used interchangeably.

High-level Languages

If machine is the first generation, and assembly the second, then what are known as *high-level* languages are actually third generation. These languages are fundamentally different from assembly in that they are no longer CPU-specific. Other things (like the OS) being equal, a program written in any of these languages can be ported from one CPU to another by running the source code through a compiler written for the receiving CPU. That's the theory. In practice, there are lots of pitfalls in this approach. The major reason for trouble is that the programmer, knowing the system he was writing for, may well have taken advantage of functions that exist on one CPU and not on another. For example, he may have assumed the presence of a certain kind of capability to manage streaming media. The programming language is supposed to step back from all of this, but in practice it can't; effective translation assumes the presence of true equivalents. Another problem is that, especially in commercial software, programmers will often mix in a little bit of assembly language here and there to deal with areas that had been slowing things down when written in the high-level language. Depending on a number of factors, porting a program from one CPU to another can be easy or hard. Still, the worst case with a high-level language is vastly less challenging than with assembly.

High-level languages are also notably easier to learn, to write, and to edit than assembler. The commands have meanings that are much more obvious and it is easier for the programmer to get in the flow. While the more explicit language makes editing easier, don't get carried away on this point. Unless the programmer has added explanatory comments to the lines of code, it is all but impossible for a successor to figure out what's going on from the words on the page—often it's pretty difficult for the original author.

High-level languages are a diverse bunch. The initial members of the group, Fortran (1957) and Cobol (1960), are still going strong. Basic is the least powerful of the languages but has the most overall users. C is the modern professional's language of choice (though an object-oriented version, C++, is overtaking it). The following sections discuss some of the more important high-level programming language still in use today. Note that there are a great many others that have been used through the years, but space makes it impossible to discuss them all.

Fortran

Fortran, the first of the 3GLs (third-generation languages), was developed by IBM and appeared in 1957. The name stands for *formula translator* and it is designed for scientific applications. The language has been continually improved, has been made a stable international standard, and is still very widely used in science and engineering circles. Fortran is available for essentially every OS and CPU family.

Cobol

Cobol, which stands for Common Business Oriented Language, was developed at the request of the U.S. government and first appeared in 1960. It took off quickly for two reasons: 1) the government insisted on its use, which meant that all manufacturers quickly supported it; and 2) its vocabulary and syntax worked very well for the kinds of business applications that most users of the time needed. Cobol has been implemented by many language developers, but it is also sufficiently standardized that code can often be transferred from one version to another. Cobol is also available for essentially every OS and CPU family.

If you consider the percentage of lines of code in current operation (as opposed to individual programs), you will probably find that Cobol is many times larger than all of its competitors combined. While most new code is written in other languages, it will be quite some time before Cobol sinks into a secondary position.

Basic

Basic was developed by John Kemeny and Thomas Kurz at Dartmouth University and first appeared in 1964. Its objective was to provide a simple, straightforward language that students could learn and begin to use in a short period of time. It was very successful in achieving this goal. The language has been widely adopted and widely adapted (customized). Microsoft's version, especially the graphical Visual Basic (see the section on 4GLs later in this chapter) is the most popular by far. Basic began as an interpreted language, but most implementations are now compiled. While once considered a language for amateurs and disdained by professionals because its remoteness from the hardware made it comparatively slow, the refinements to the language and the ever-increasing power of the hardware have led to its use in many professional environments. It too is available for all platforms.

Pascal

Pascal, originally designed by Nicholas Wirth as a teaching language, first appeared in the early 1970s. It remains popular for teaching, and based on the strength of Borland's Turbo Pascal, was for a while also used by serious programmers. The much greater appeal of other languages has moved it into the background, though, and it is likely to stay there.

C

The choice of serious (i.e., commercial) programmers today, C was developed by Ken Thompson and Dennis Ritchie as a part of the development of Unix, and first appeared in 1974. It has tremendous advantages: it is much easier to understand and write than assembly language, but is still close enough to the hardware that it runs nearly as fast. While it has been customized, there is an ANSI[1] standard version of C that is widely used. Available for just about every hardware/software platform, C (and increasingly, its object-oriented sibling C++) will likely maintain its leading role for years to come.

Ada

Ada, like Cobol, was developed at the request of the U.S. government, but in this case, for the military. The Pentagon was concerned that as military systems included more computers, they wouldn't be able to speak clearly to each other. For example, the cockpit computer might make a mistake when talking to the wing-mounted missiles; that could have lethal consequences for the wrong party. Using just one language would make all this easier. Ada was developed commercially (after a competition) and how good it is depends on who you talk to. Many describe it as bloated and overly complex, but many, like Boeing Aircraft, are very happy with it. Ada is employed mostly for programs that run on embedded processors.

4GLs (whatever they are)

The fourth-generation languages (4GLs) don't fit well together; they include all kinds of disparate approaches to programming. By one definition, a general characteristic is that these languages are supposed to be more "English-like" than other languages (it is a good thing for Americans, those notorious uniglots, that programming isn't centered in China, where they would be making it more "Chinese-like"). Another definition, though, is for languages that are programmed in a visual way, emphasizing "drag and drop" over the writing of code. To simplify, we'll cover 4GLs in three categories: database languages, markup languages, and visual languages. Later in this chapter, after a discussion of object technology, we'll address the related area of programming tools and the technique of rapid application development (RAD).

Database Languages

Since most computer applications are databases of one kind or another, there are programming languages that are optimized for the creation and maintenance of databases. Most of these are proprietary, while others (such as dBASE) are in the public

---

[1]American National Standards Institute

domain. The basic idea here is straightforward. The database language provides a set of commands that simplify many common operations. A programmer who is developing a database, for example, rather than "reinventing the wheel" by writing long blocks of code to perform such tasks as describing how a data structure is manipulated, how a form is developed, or myriad other operations, can use a database language that is already written for those tasks. This can save days of writing and more days of testing for even the most basic functions. Because database development is an arduous and failure-prone task, software publishers have put considerable effort into making their languages easier to use, which normally means making them more English-like. Most of these languages are flexible enough that the programmer can mix in regular programming code as needed. Since database languages are principally of interest to professional software developers, we'll not discuss them further here.

Visual Languages

Visual languages, also called *form-based* languages, take an interesting approach to software development. The designer begins with a screen that is essentially a blank form. She then begins to fill it out with menus and other common application components. As each of these elements is defined, the program automatically creates the code to support it. The program also assists the developer in writing code not directly a part of the form by offering visual modules (flowcharts, in effect) that can be used to describe program flow. The system can then write this code as well. Visual programming languages are not really new languages and they don't save the developer from writing actual lines of code by hand. Still, they take a lot of the drudgery out of programming and generally lead to significant decreases in development time. Microsoft's Visual Basic was the first of this genre and is still the leader. It has many competitors in the basic language environment. Increasingly, versions of object-oriented languages, such as Microsoft's Visual C++, are the first choice for serious developers. Visual language packages usually provide an array of tools, including editors, debuggers, compilers, and linkers. If you want to know how many people use these programs, just go to any serious bookstore and survey the shelves groaning with volumes of "how-to" stuff. A lot of folks out there are doing a lot of heavy-duty programming—or at least thinking about it.

Tech Talk

Garbage collection: *Garbage collection* **refers to the need for a programmer to make sure that code that has been loaded into memory is removed when no longer needed. If this isn't done, the "garbage" will soak up memory and possibly cause conflicts. Software tool kits for developers provide code and techniques for dealing with this problem, but some programmers manage to leave garbage behind anyway.**

Markup Languages

Markup refers to a type of language that is used to describe a document and its contents. The basic idea comes from the publishing industry and the marks that editors would make on a page to tell designers how the final version should appear. The "mother of markup languages," SGML (Standard Generalized Markup Language), was itself based on a language called GML (Generalized Markup Language) developed at IBM in the 1960s. GML's purpose was to help lawyers automate the management of documents with multiple cross-references. The more complex SGML is extremely powerful. It's most important characteristic, however, isn't in its standard set of marks (called *tags*) but in the fact that it isn't limited to a certain set of markup commands. Rather, SGML is a *meta-language*—this means that it is a language that can create other, more specialized, languages. SGML is sufficiently complex that it isn't widely used, but two of its variants are very popular.

The best known subset of SGML is HTML (HyperText Markup Language), the language that describes documents displayed on the Web. HTML has been incredibly popular, in large part because it is easy to create page layouts and because of the ease with which it supports *hyperlinks*—the ability to click on a piece of text or graphic and be taken to another place in the document, or to another document anywhere on the Web (discussed in Chapter 14). While the use of hypertext was not new (Apple's wonderful Hypercard program pioneered this), HTML and the other Web protocols took it to a new level of usefulness. The weakness of HTML is that it is inflexible. Unlike it's parent SGML, HTML isn't a meta-language—there is a certain set of commands, and that's it. This weakness is now being addressed by a younger sibling, XML (eXtensible Markup Language), that eliminates much of the complexity of SGML in favor of those things that are really needed for Web publishing and commerce, but retains the power to create new language subsets. In addition to its appeal for commercial applications (also discussed in Chapter 14), XML is rapidly spawning new dialects that are standardized for professional groups, such as mathematicians and chemists, whose work couldn't be represented easily in HTML.

Artificial Intelligence: 5GL?

In 1981, the Japanese government announced a massive project to develop a "fifth-generation" computer system. The basic idea was to create a completely new OS/applications approach that would employ artificial intelligence (AI) techniques for its core operations. No one knows how much was spent on this project, but it has long since quietly disappeared with few notable artifacts. This failure shouldn't be taken to mean that AI isn't useful. AI, which is the use of computational techniques to model the processes of the human brain, has not had the dramatic successes that at least some people hoped for when computers first appeared. The reason that progress has been so measured is not that AI concepts have been flawed, but that the available resources haven't been up to the task. In particular, CPU power and access to memory are just now approaching what is required for intelligent robotics. Equally important, the ability to easily process the senses of sight and sound is finally becoming more possible, thanks to cheap digital signal processors and electronic cameras. As a result of these advances, we should expect significant progress in AI applications. However, even with rapidly accelerating development, the year 2001 will be long behind us before we have to cope with machines like the HAL of the movie *2001*.

OBJECT-ORIENTED TECHNOLOGY . . . .

Object-oriented technology presents an unusual problem for people who attempt to describe it; it is relatively easy to explain the concepts and terminology of OOT, but it is considerably more difficult to provide real-world illustrations that fully and convincingly demonstrate its presumed advantages. The problem is not unique to authors of books about technology. Programmers, particularly those who have been trained in other techniques, have the same problem in understanding how to apply OOT to the task at hand. And that raises the question of OOT's importance. Many, both inside and outside of the computer community, have hailed it as not just the next wave, but a total change in programming that will vastly improve all aspects of software. Others, including some important veterans of software development, ridicule these claims. And, of course, there are lots of folks in between. Still, as you contemplate the following, consider that the weight of the argument is with the optimists—modern software development appears to be moving inexorably to OOT.

Tech Talk

Object: In Object-Oriented Technology (OOT), an *object* is an element that includes both program logic (a *method*) and data in a consistently structured way.

OOT is described as having two major advantages. First, because object software is so easy to reuse, total programming effort is reduced and the number of bugs declines considerably (reused objects have already been tested for reliability); and second, once programmers have learned it, object-oriented programming is significantly more productive—good software is produced faster. OK, now let's plunge into the object pool.

How OOT Works

An object is a section of software that includes (encapsulates) both one or more pro-cedures (a series of instructions to the hardware called *methods* in OOT) as well as data of various kinds. A button in a graphical user interface illustrates this concept. The button has data, which in this case is a description of what a button looks like on the screen, and it has a method, which in this case is a procedure that calls up a dialog box.

Tech Talk

Method: In Object-Oriented Technology, a *method* is program logic that is a part of an object and acts on its data.

THE GENERAL ELEMENTS OF OOT

- The use of objects rather than subroutines
  - Objects include program logic (methods) and data in a con-sistently structured way
  - Objects can communicate with each other in a standardized fashion
- Objects are organized into classes that have important similari-ties
  - An object in a class can "inherit" structure from another; this saves programming time

Let's describe each of these in a little bit more detail. Data in this case really means variables—slots in which the data are held. For example, if our button has three elements, two outer rings and a central sphere, it would have variables that would provide a description of each (e.g. ring one, radius of x, thickness of y, color of z; ring two, radius of x, thickness of y, color of z; sphere, radius of x, color of z). Actual data is then added to these variables so that a button of a certain size and color is created.

great many possibilities, and you would spend a lot of time just making sure the list was complete. Some aspects wouldn't be obvious—for example, are you better off thinking of flights or flight segments as a basic object? Remember that a segment doesn't necessarily have the same crew or, in some cases, the same aircraft. You will appreciate that a lot of thought needs to go into the creation of an object model. It isn't surprising then that veteran programmers often get frustrated with OOT (see sidebar). It's like a proficient hunt-and-peck typist trying to learn to touch type. You understand the theory that there will be greater productivity at some time in the future, but in the meantime, you know you could create the document a whole lot faster with the tried-and-true approach.

A final caution. Even if accurately implemented in the ideal environment, OOT is not the silver bullet that will kill the software crisis. OOT programs, like any other programs, need to be debugged. And just like other programmers, OOT programmers can easily find themselves in a swamp filled with alligators. Many OOT projects with capable staff have failed. But the underlying concepts of OOT are realistic. While some of OOT is conceptually new, much of it is a logical development of the thinking that went into the creation of previous software techniques, such as subroutines. OOT is consistent with the principles of structured programming. Finally, while object-oriented programs can be slower in execution than a similar program written without these techniques, the gap is now quite small. The extent to which speed of execution is seen as a problem needs to be considered differently than in the past—remember, CPU speeds are increasing at an annual rate of about sixty percent. OOT's speed of execution is now likely to be an issue only for the most complex programs.

The Compound Document Concept

One aspect of OOT that most people have seen is that of the compound document. In traditional software, a document belongs to an application and can only respond to its commands. If you have a WordPerfect document on the screen, you can only put in it those things that WordPerfect can do (mostly formatting text, though today's word processors include a lot of other stuff). The compound document concept, however, says that a single file (document) could have multiple parents (applications). So, while you might start an application in WordPerfect, if you wanted to have a spreadsheet somewhere on the page, you could create one in Excel and simply embed it in the WordPerfect document. When the cursor moves to the part of the document that has the spreadsheet, the controls in the menu bar change from WordPerfect's to Excel's. You could also add to this compound document a component from a drawing program, and other components from other types of programs. This is a description of Microsoft's Object Linking and Embedding (OLE), which is kind of a macro version of OOT; instead of little tiny objects calling each other at the atomic level, you have enormous applications communicating as objects.

Tech Talk

OLE: Microsoft's Object Linking and Embedding (OLE) allows a user to create an object (e.g., a table or a graphic) and embed it in another. For example, a table in Word could actually be a section of a spreadsheet created in Excel.

WRAPPERS

Some software approaches take a non-OOT program and "wrap" it in a way that allows it to function with objects in an object environment. Doing this requires that there be external software around the program that looks like an object to other objects. Invoking this wrapped object's methods is like working with an application programming interface (API) except that the API is now consistent in format with that of the other objects. Considered from a user perspective, this is like having a mainframe program appearing on your computer with the menus that are standard in Windows—you automatically know how to get it to open and save a file, etc. In fact, some systems do take an entire mainframe program and put it in a wrapper. While such an approach doesn't give all of the benefits of true OOT (like inheritance), it enhances the importance of OOT and its impact on the overall level of software development. Significantly, IBM is putting considerable emphasis on the use of wrappers and Java for its mainframe systems. This could significantly improve the longevity of these beasts by allowing them to function better in the Internet environment.

A more interesting iteration of compound documents is that of application frameworks. In this case, you don't even have one application, but a series of applets. These application objects work with each other as needed, but don't all have to be there at once. For example, you could buy a word processor that only formatted text—no drawing or graphing or other capabilities. If you needed to enhance it, though, you could buy the other modules and these would work with your text formatter. This idea isn't all that outrageous. Thanks to the techniques of structured programming, most programs are already highly modular. What would be different, though, if the applets were really developed with OOT techniques in mind, is that you wouldn't need to buy all the applets from the same vendor. Microsoft's spell checker would work with WordPerfect's text formatter. This idea is especially appealing to those who think that in the future, software will not be sold in shrink wraps, but downloaded over the Internet.

CONCLUSION . . . .

The following table summarizes the principal types of programming languages.

Table 8.1   *Summary of Programming Languages*

Summary of programming languages				
Language	**Generation**	**Variants**	**Strengths**	**Weaknesses**
Machine	1	One for each CPU type	This is what the machine executes. It is almost never used directly by programmers because the strings of 1s and 0s are impossible to work with.	
Assembly	2	One for each CPU type	Gives best speed of execution; used for games, sections of programs that use of a lot of CPU cycles	Hard to work with; porting to a new CPU means starting all over
High level	3	·		
Basic		Available for almost all systems	Easy to use	Inefficient
Fortran			Popular for scientific applications	Specialized
Cobol			Rich set of techniques for business applications	Specialized
C			Closest to assembly language in speed	Hard to work with
4GL	4			
Database		Available for almost all systems	Greatly simplifies development of database applications	Specialized
Markup			HTML and XML are becoming the core programming languages for Web documents and applications	Specialized
Object				
Java		Available for almost all systems	Facilitates reuse of code; works well over networks	Slow learning curve; slower execution on machine

Programming languages have evolved considerably over the years. The newer languages are easier to use and faster, and the techniques of structured programming have improved the conceptual and organizational aspects of programming. Much of the progress, of course, is due to the vast increases in the speed of the hardware. If developers thirty years ago had attempted to employ the much higher level of abstraction that is now typical with 4GLs and OOT, the sheer amount of code that would have to have been loaded into memory, not to mention its relatively slower speed of execution, would have brought their systems to a halt. Because it can support software approaches that are easier to develop and maintain, today's more powerful hardware dramatically facilitates fast software development. Offsetting this, however, is the increasing complexity of today's programs, both as separate assemblages of code and as programs that must interact with other programs over networks. There has been much hope that object-oriented technology and the associated new ways of thinking about programming would save the day. OOT has helped and will continue to be valuable, but software reliability is still a major issue. We'll discuss this at the end of the next chapter, after completing a discussion of databases and other kinds of applications software.

TEST YOUR UNDERSTANDING . . . .

1. What are the different levels of programming? Why are there different levels?
2. What is a *subroutine* and how does it work?
3. What is the difference between a *compiled* language and an *interpreted* language?
4. Give three reasons for the "software crisis."
5. How is *structured programming* different?
6. What are the advantages of program *modules?*
7. What is a *markup* language? Why are markup languages important?
8. How different is Object-Oriented Technology (OOT) from previous approaches?
9. At what stage is OOT programming faster? At what stage is it slower?
10. What are the principal advantages of Java?
11. What is *rapid application development?*

9 Databases, Applications, and Software Reliability

This chapter builds on Chapter 8's discussion of programming with an exploration of the software that computer users interact with directly, known in the industry as *applications software*. Actually, we'll treat one kind of application, the database, as a category apart from other applications. There are several reasons for this. One is that databases bridge the programming and applications world; most databases include comprehensive programming languages that are used to create applications. The typical user works with the products of database programming, not with the database software directly. Another reason for considering databases separately is that databases comprise as much a building block of information organization as they do applications for end users. For example, databases are a resource for other programs—virtually every type of software uses some type of database as part of its internal workings.

The only true applications that will be discussed here are spreadsheets and word processing. In addition to being the tools central to the work of most computer users, their development provides some interesting insights into the history and dynamics of the software industry. This provides a segue into the chapter's last topic, which is the software industry itself. After this chapter, you will better understand

- Database organization and structure
- The database market
- Software development strategies and tools
- The development of two key applications, spreadsheets and word processors
- The software industry in general

DATABASES . . . .

Databases are very much at the center of computing. Most computer applications are either designed to use databases or employ them in the course of doing their jobs. For example, an operating system maintains a database of resources, a word processor has a database of fonts, and so forth. As a way of guiding yourself through this complex subject, note that this section covers six major topics.

- The elements of a database
- Planning a database
- The relational model of database organization
- Nonrelational databases
- The power of "legacy" database systems
- Database markets

The Elements of a Database

A database is simply a way of organizing information. A bunch of books piled on the floor is a collection of information. A bunch of books placed on shelves in some logical order is a database. A computer database management system provides tools that make it possible for the computer to organize and manage the data more efficiently. Let's continue with the library example, which can be a very productive one. Perhaps you've put your books on the shelves according to their size—tall books on one set of shelves, short ones on another, and so forth. After that, volumes are added to the appropriate shelf in the order in which they are purchased. This is a technique that is widely used in European libraries and is not as weird as it sounds; it allows for very good use of shelf space. Let's say, though, that you want to find a book by a certain author. If your library is big enough, and you're over 50 like me, you won't remember where it is and will have to scan all of the books to find the one you want. This can be very tedious. The solution to this problem, having to look at everything to find a single item, is solved by the use of an index—in this case, a card catalog that lists all your books, alphabetized by author. When you find the right card in the index (catalog), you see that it has a number, let's say C124, which means that it is the 124th book on the small book stack (C). You can then go straight to the place where it should be (only to find that someone else has taken it; but that's another story). An index, then, is a list that holds current information on the location of objects—books, in this case.

Tech Talk

Transactional database (OLTP): **Transaction processing, also known as online transaction process (OLTP), refers to a database that is accessed for the purpose of making changes to its records. For example, a library circulation system, which changes the status of a book from checked in to checked out (or vice versa), is responsible for transactions.**

Another part of the library database is the catalog system. This includes author, title, subject, call number, and (maybe) circulation status. This database is used for queries—for example, does the library have books on a certain subject by a particular author? Queries to a database, especially complex ones that link a number of different fields, also make considerable demands on hardware. Typically, the computer will have to sort through one set of records to select those that match certain criteria, then sort through this subset to look for other criteria, and so on. If you can isolate queries from OLTP, you will have much better performance in both areas. One way to do this is to have the databases on a multiprocessing machine and/or on separate machines.

Modes of Database Operation

Transaction processing	In this mode, the database is able to make changes to its records. For example, the clerk at a library desk checks a book out, and in so doing, changes the database record to show that it is out and when it is due. The term OLTP (for online transaction processing) is often used, but this is redundant, since essentially all such databases are online. Fast and reliable OLTP systems, for example those used by airlines, require significant processing power and very fast I/O systems.
Query or decision support	Some databases allow you to look up information, but not to change it. For example, library patrons can find if a book is in, but cannot check it out. In a more sophisticated use, such databases are used to sort through vast data sets to provide "what if" kind of information to executives. If much analysis is to be done, this database mode will require a great deal of computational power.
Batch	Unlike the others, batch mode is not interactive. Instead, the database is given some instructions (find patrons who owe fines; calculate electric bills) and runs unattended until the work is finished. This is the least demanding function as far as the hardware is concerned.

But what if we want our query to also return information on the circulation status of the book (as is now usually done with library software)? Well, you can have the query software wait until it has found the records that the patron requested, then the catalog database can request the needed information from the circulation database. This adds some burden to the OLTP part of the system, but not nearly as much as if it had to handle queries and transactions at the same time.

A final part of your system will be one that periodically runs through the circulation database; finds books that are overdue; associates these with patrons, including their name and address; calculates a fine for each item; then creates a mailing list. This part of the system runs in batch mode. It doesn't have to respond immediately to anyone and can do its work every night after the library is closed.

The examples below illustrate the database just described. The columns of a table are called *fields,* as in the "Author" or "Fines owed" field. A row in a table is a *record;* the patron table would have a record for each patron.

The type of database described here is known as *relational* (other types—hierarchical, network, and object—are discussed later in this section). That is to say, instead of a number of separate databases, it is structured as a series of tables that can be either manipulated individually for simple operations or can be related to each other or *joined,* for more complex ones. For example, the catalog table doesn't con-

Circulation Table

Call no. of book	Date due	Patron SSN
zx34.5p	3/11/97	123-45-6789
cv52.9		

Catalog Table

Call no. of book	Title	Author	Subject	Publisher
zx34.5p	Using Upper Case	Capslock, C.	Computers	ASCII Press
cv52.9	Speaking Hexadecimal	Engineer, A Typical	Programming	EEEE Press

Patron Table

Patron last name	Patron first name	Patron SSN	Address	Fines owed
cummings	e	333-33-4190	forest lawn	
Goodwin	Archie	1886-00-1975	W. 35th St.	$1.50

tain availability information and the circulation table doesn't contain subject data. But, because both tables have call numbers associated with other information, it's possible to find out, for example, the circulation status of all books on a certain subject. Relational databases are dominant today (at least for new applications) because they offer both tremendous flexibility (separating information for different purposes) and tremendous power (because all the data are related, it's possible to ask questions about them from almost any perspective). Relational databases have their own special language for queries, Structured Query Language (SQL, sometimes pronounced *sequel*). While SQL first emerged in somewhat standardized form (from IBM), it has since evolved into a range of dialects—mostly extensions of the original rather than modifications. Organizing a relational database in a way that makes the most efficient use of tables and linking fields is called *normalizing*. While this wouldn't be hard in a simple database like the one described above, it becomes a formidable task for highly complex databases.

Tech Talk

Structured Query Language: Structured Query Language, abbreviated SQL, is a language that is employed for querying relational databases. Most implementations of SQL are specific to a particular database package.

Deciding which fields to index is also a major issue. Indexes do make a search on a field much faster; instead of having to sort through the entire set of records to find a field with a certain value, the database can use the index to find it. One downside of indexes is that they require additional storage space. Every index represents a new list of information, in effect a sub-database. Adding indexes makes the database larger and (potentially) slower. Further, indexes have to be maintained; new entries are added to the end of the index or perhaps in a separate file. If the entry isn't found in the main section, the software then has to do a second search. Once the new area or file gets big enough that second searches are common, the system slows down and the index needs to be "rebuilt" by having the new entries placed in the appropriate places in the main index. Large systems usually do this overnight (or whenever usage is lowest). If an index is really used often, it should be kept in memory rather than on disk. In the example above, frequently used fields like Call Number, Title, and Author would be indexed. A field like Fines owed would not; the rare occasions when this would be searched directly (e.g., a list of patrons with fines over a certain amount), would be done in batch mode and would not require the speed of indexing.

Tech Talk

Database tuning: Deciding how a particular database should be organized for a certain machine, for example, whether some or all indexes should be held in memory, is called *tuning* the database. For complex

systems, especially those with multiple processors, careful tuning can make a huge difference in performance.

Nonrelational Databases

The relational type of database discussed above is not the only type in wide use. Of the four other kinds, the most primitive are *flat-file* databases. These databases store information sequentially and are really just modernized versions of the original card file systems. They are not normally used today—at least for new applications. The next types in order of chronological development and degree of sophistication are hierarchical databases, network or CODASYL databases, and object databases.

Hierarchical and Network Databases

Hierarchical database systems organize information in the same tree-like structure as computer file systems. Network databases are very similar to the hierarchical kind with the exception that they make it easier to have very complex "many to many" relationships of data—for example, the kind shown in the tables of our library database in which links can be made between almost all elements. Since network databases are an extension of the hierarchical model, from here forward we'll lump the two together under the latter name, which is the more widely used. The disadvantages of these older types of database are that they are extremely complex to develop and to maintain. The latter point is particularly important and has two principal dimensions. First, changes to the underlying database structures are very difficult and require a lot of programming effort. This has always been a problem because businesses are in a constant state of flux (new divisions, new products, different procedures, and so forth) so that parts of the database are continually being rewritten. Second, asking even simple questions of these databases requires the assistance of a programmer. So even when the structure of the database hasn't changed, significant programmer effort is required to produce something as straightforward as a new report. Obviously, *ad hoc* queries are pretty much impossible.

••

QUERY STUFF

To say that amateurs can query relational databases with some success is accurate but misleading; few businesses would leave their database vulnerable to open-ended queries. While queries can't damage the database (they don't make changes to it; they just read from it) they can "bring the database to its knees" by asking the wrong kind of question. For example, innocent queries that want to find just a few records but also want to know what the value of the sum of those records is as a percentage of all records, can cause the database to have to read and copy information from every record. If the database is large, you can safely go out for a cup of coffee after starting this kind of query. Just don't let your fellow users add the cream or sugar for you. Solutions to this problem include limiting the kinds of questions that can be asked, allowing queries only at certain times of day (when transaction activity has dropped), or (best) forcing queries to be run only on copies of the database.

But these databases are still widely used. David Vaskevitch, a senior technologist at Microsoft, says that well over half of corporate databases still use the hierarchical model. One reason for this persistence is that, when skillfully written, hierarchical and network databases are much faster than relational systems. This is still an issue with mainframes, but isn't much of a factor for microprocessor-based systems, where additional speed is easily achieved with cheap hardware. Another reason is that while relational systems are much more flexible, this factor is most important for programs that do analysis. For transactional databases, by contrast, flexibility is less of a problem and the greater speed of hierarchical systems is even more of a benefit.

Object Databases

Describing the difference between object-oriented and relational databases is more complicated than explaining the difference between hierarchical and relational. One problem is that many people have trouble articulating exactly what an object-oriented database is. How is it different from its relational sibling? The relative immaturity of the technology makes it difficult to answer the question, but two examples can be given. One advantage of object-oriented databases is in dealing with unusual types of data. A normal database handles only limited types of data, which must be predefined and used in a consistent way; typical data types include text, integers, currency, and the like. A relational database can retrieve data that it doesn't understand—for example graphical data such as photos or film clips—by putting them in a special field called a BLOB (binary large object). The problem with BLOBs is that the database can only store and retrieve this kind of information; it can't manipulate it in any way because it doesn't understand it. An object-oriented database, on the other hand, includes a method, a way of manipulating the data, in each object. So an object-oriented database could not only retrieve, but also perform an analysis on, a BLOB-type object. For example, in a database that includes photographs, the object-oriented database's method could return all photos with certain combinations of colors.

Tech Talk

BLOB: A Binary Large Object (BLOB) refers to a collection of data, usually video or sound information, that a relational database is able to access, but not manipulate.

The second major benefit of object-oriented databases, according to their partisans, is the ease of integration of the database with programming languages. Most large, sophisticated projects require the writing of custom code. Because the languages are very different, it is quite difficult for programmers to make a relational database's SQL work smoothly with the programming language they are using (probably Cobol, or perhaps C). Object-oriented databases, on the other hand, interface naturally with an object-oriented language—C++, Smalltalk, or Java. This integration makes for faster, less buggy software. While object-oriented database companies are getting a fair amount of attention in the stock market, they aren't yet conquering the business world. A principal problem, as noted earlier, is that companies are unwilling to tinker with what works. Businesses that have just made the transition to relational systems are certain to stand pat, while those planning to make a move from old-fashioned hierarchical systems are obviously pretty risk-averse and are going to be reluctant to amplify their exposure by embracing what they consider to be an unproven technology. And, for those who perceive that object-oriented technology offers important potential advantage to their business model, vendors like Oracle, Sybase, and Informix are blunting the market for pure object-oriented databases by offering hybrid relational/object-oriented database products. In summary, while object-oriented databases are likely to be more widely adopted every year, the conservative nature of the database market, where terms like "mission critical" and "bet the company" are used in earnest, means that this new type of software won't have the same sweeping impact as other new technologies, such as Java.

The Power of Legacy Database Systems

It seems clear that the newer types of database—relational and object—are superior to the old time hierarchical model. So why are these "legacy" software systems still so important? The major reason is that successful database systems are very difficult to build and even harder to replace—so much so that businesses quickly find themselves adopting the "if it ain't broke, don't replace it" philosophy. If a database functions well, which means that it provides accurate information quickly, businesses are very unlikely to invest the time and money needed to swap it for something new—especially given that all big software projects carry considerable risk. It's this latter issue that explains why so many older systems are still functioning with no plans for replacement.

pursuing new opportunities, such as the management of streaming media. Also in the billion dollar range are companies like SAP and PeopleSoft, which have discovered a huge business in Enterprise Resources Planning (ERP) software. Smaller, but still potent, are specialized vendors like SAS for statistical packages and Autodesk in computer assisted design. The quick rise of companies like SAP and PeopleSoft shows that it's still possible to come out of nowhere and pull in huge revenues.

Below the biggest guys is a market of thousands of firms that supply software tailored to particular kinds of businesses. Such companies are often very stable and quite profitable. Growing fast in this sector are companies that provide software for embedded systems; as pervasive computing takes over from the desktop-centric world, this area should continue to be one of rapid growth. The bottom, the developer market, comprises mostly small companies that do custom programming. All in all, software companies are more popular with investors than are their hardware brethren because the initial investment is smaller and because returns can often be higher. But the biggest reward obviously comes with the greatest risk—generally meaning new types of software that may or may not catch on. Even the mainstream software business can be volatile. When the economy is bad and revenues are down, companies behave much like consumers who quickly dump discretionary expenditures, such as meals out. IS managers will often resist new software versions unless the need is compelling. The desire for stable income has driven software vendors of all kinds to try to get their clients to accept a subscription model, in which a contract with annual payments covers upgrades and support. While this approach has long been standard in the large systems world, it has been much less attractive for managers of microcomputer systems, particularly the smaller organizations. This latter group tends to be more price sensitive and more skeptical of the value of new features. The consumer market is similarly erratic.

CONLUSION ·

The database, very much at the center of computing, illustrates the stresses that obtain in the software industry as computing takes its place at the hub of society. New technologies, relational and object databases, have shown themselves to be effective and efficient. But, also because computing has now become so important, the old-style hierarchical and network databases are holding firm in the market. The move to e-commerce will accelerate the use of new technologies, but will also reinforce the importance of the old—in the online world, it will be even more of a disaster for businesses if their core software systems fail.

The software industry has given users an array of applications beyond databases. Two of the most critical, spreadsheets and word processors, have matured in just a few decades to the point that their presence is almost taken for granted. The development of these two applications shows the cycles that the software industry has experienced. In the beginning, forty years ago, the market was diverse and vibrant, with many vendors vying for each segment of the market. Over the next twenty years, there was a strong trend toward consolidation, and relatively few serious vendors were left in the mainframe/minicomputer world when microcomputers appeared.

The appearance of the microcomputer created another explosion of software offerings in every part of the market, but the smaller and weaker again fell away as microcomputers proliferated. After two decades, only a handful of important vendors were left. But the underlying hardware paradigm has changed again, this time in favor of a worldwide network of autonomous devices, and the software industry is likely once more to become vibrant and diffuse. Just as IBM tried to manage the transition from mainframe to micro, stumbled badly but finally emerged as an important player, so it is likely that Microsoft, despite far greater awareness at the management level than IBM two decades earlier, will stumble before stabilizing as a major, but no longer a dominant, player. To understand the dynamics of this emerging software market, we need to understand the network that undergirds it, and that topic is the focus of Part 3.

TEST YOUR UNDERSTANDING . . . .

1. What are the major characteristics of the relational type of database? What advantages do they provide?

2. Would it make sense for every field in a database to be indexed?

3. What are three modes of database operation, and how are they different?

4. Why have large businesses and organizations been reluctant to give up their legacy database systems?

5. How do the three markets for database software differ?

6. What were the reasons for Lotus 1-2-3's striking initial success?

7. What made WordPerfect so successful in its early years?

8. What were the reasons for the decline of Lotus 1-2-3 and WordPerfect?

PUTTING IT ALL TOGETHER . . . .

It's difficult to synthesize such a complex subject as software, but the challenge of supporting e-commerce provides an excellent vehicle for describing how the pieces go together. To close this section, and to prepare you for the next one on networks, the e-commerce example is extremely useful.

Choosing an OS for E-commerce

As noted in the closing section of Part 1, in e-commerce, a request for information enters a computer over a network connection, is passed over the I/O bus to the CPU, and from there goes to software that serves Web pages, and most likely after that to a database system that locates the item or items to be sold, or service to be provided, or whatever. There's more, but let's back up to think about what this means for the OS. Of course, since multiple applications are running at once, it's a good thing that all modern OSs are multitasking. Its sister capability, multiprocessing, requires careful evaluation, however. The reason multiprocessing is important is that it is central to scalability. While desktop computer users are rather unlikely to upgrade their computers, people who own e-commerce servers better hope that this issue comes up—if it doesn't, the business isn't growing. If the server is handling lots of requests for Web pages and/or database requests simultaneously, an OS that can move up to support multiple CPUs is a real asset. Different OSes have different capabilities in this area. An OS that can support multiprocessing efficiently—that supports a high degree of scalability—can be a critical asset.

A second, and complementary, approach is to have an OS that allows "clustering"—lashing multiple computers together to form a single one. This path provides even more scalability as well as greater reliability—something that is essential for a business that is selling things (or providing services or support) over the Web. Remember that you can cluster multiprocessor systems. Reliability also brings up the structure of the OS. A system that is layered, using the kernel/microkernel approach, is not only more stable but also more flexible; though as with multitasking, nearly all modern server OSes have this characteristic. As a final point, a really serious server is a mainframe. These are super reliable. If you find yourself needing one of these quickly, you've done well indeed. However, in today's environment mainframes are used mostly by older organizations with legacy applications. Few systems are scaled up to a mainframe, since clustered high-end servers can provide nearly all of the same capabilities at much lower cost.

Choosing a Database for E-commerce

The array of database offerings for e-commerce today is huge. Whatever the choice, any new database is likely to be based on the relational model, something that permits considerable flexibility and scalability. In the meantime, old-line hierarchical databases will continue to be very successful in running legacy applications in mainframe environments. The object-based approach is still waiting in the wings.

If your goal is getting up to speed quickly in e-commerce, you will want to buy as much off-the-shelf software as possible, since developing and testing software systems is a slow process. You can buy excellent database software from a variety of vendors for a variety of OS platforms. Leaders are Oracle, IBM, Informix, Sybase, Microsoft, Compaq/DEC, and some others. Scalability is a challenge here, however. The more complex, fully featured databases just mentioned usually require more development time and more skilled staff than PC-based software. To be sure, you will likely be able to get up to speed faster with a PC-level database such as Access (Microsoft), Approach (Lotus-IBM), or Paradox (Corel). The disadvantage here is that these programs won't scale to the enterprise level. PC software vendors, as well as an array of third parties, do provide tools for porting the simpler applications to the more complex ones, but not all are equal. Tradeoffs, tradeoffs.

Choosing a Programming Language and Tools for E-commerce

Realistically, you won't be able to build a sophisticated e-commerce system without doing some programming. Database systems require customization, which can usually be accomplished with either a built-in language or with one of the standard languages such as C, C++, Visual Basic, Java, and more. Since we're planning for the e-commerce system described here to be planted in the nourishing soil of venture capital and grow like crazy, and since we're going to have to tie several disparate applications together, let's assume that programming is needed.

A first decision is whether to go to object-oriented technology (OOT) or not. The advantages of OOT are that, once completed, software is likely to be more flexible and adaptable than an equivalent program not using OOT. The disadvantages are a potential one—that programmers aren't familiar with object approaches—and a real one—that the system will run slower than something built with a more efficient language like C. How to decide? Well, first note that there are excellent programming tools—visual development environments, etc.—for all these languages. The e-commerce example, though, really points to a single solution. For this environment, Java, with it's "write once, run anywhere" capability gives you a lot of choice about hardware and OS compatibility in your server "farm" and attached systems. Also, the Java expertise you develop will be useful in creating little Java programs, "applets,"

Each sample is given a numerical (binary) value. The result is that the digital system sends a stream of bits rather than an analog wave. The original wave can then be reproduced at the end. The more frequent the sampling, and the greater the range of values each can contain, the more accurately the wave can be reproduced.

Smoothly Sampling a Wave • Each vertical line represents a sample, each of which is assigned an eight-bit number (see Figure 10.11). As a result, our analog waveform has become digital—a stream of ones and zeros. The wave is sampled so frequently that when we want to change it back to a wave (which is necessary for analog devices such as television sets, telephones, and most computer monitors), we are able to do that very accurately.

Coarsely Sampled Wave • In this case (see Figure 10.12), in order to avoid having to transmit so much digital information, we didn't sample the wave as often. This saves bandwidth (also storage space and processor power), but it produces a less accurate representation when the signal is returned to analog form (see Figures 10.13 and 10.14).

To illustrate the problem of sampling, think of a slightly different context, that of a televison picture. Remember that a normal television picture is actually thirty individual frames—separate pictures—in one second. You see it as one image because of the way your body works; the human eye cannot distinguish much faster changes and to the extent it can, the brain adjusts to smooth things out. But let's say you decided to change the frame rate from thirty per second to ten per second. This could be very helpful technically, because in cutting the sampling rate by one-third, you would also be reducing the amount of information you would have to send, and therefore the bandwidth needed by the same amount. Unfortunately, the human eye *can* discern change much faster than ten times a second, and in this case, the brain will not compensate. The received picture will look terrible, especially if it has to represent a lot of motion. Those who have used mid-1990s vintage video conferencing will appreciate this.

Figure 10.11 Sampling.
In this figure, every vertical bar represents a sample. Each sample is given a value (see the scale on the left) which is translated into a binary number and sent to the receiver. This example shows a wave that is sampled very frequently and with a large array of possible height levels.

Figure 10.12 A recreated signal.
The receiver gets the digital stream and uses the values to recreate the wave. In this case, while the reconstruction is not perfect, it is fairly close. You can see that it would increase the accuracy if you sampled more frequently and had more possible values. You won't do this unless you have to, though. More sampling is more work for both sender and receiver. Also, more possible values means a bigger number (more bits). Obviously, if you have more samples or more values per sample or both, you will have more bits to send and this will require more bandwidth.

To carry the illustration to its logical conclusion, if you changed the frame rate in the opposite direction, to ninety per second, you would triple the bandwidth needed and produce an image that was better, but not proportionally better because you would be changing frames much faster than needed to fool the human eye and brain. Thus, the sampling rate needed to convert an analog video or audio signal to a digital one is not derived from some law of physics, but from an understanding of what is necessary to produce a rendition that appears accurate to the person seeing or hearing it.

Let's consider a real world analog to digital problem. What would happen if you wanted to make television digital? OK, let's do some math. The number of lines measured vertically in a standard U.S. televison display is about 486, and although this analog system doesn't have true horizontal resolution, the number of pixels across a horizontal line is about 720 (we're not making this up—486 × 720 is an actual digital television standard). So, 486 × 720 is 349,920. Normally, we would as-

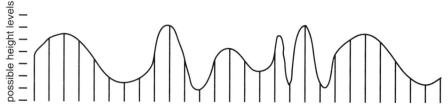

Figure 10.13 Lowered sampling.
For this example we have halved both the sampling rate and the number of possible values for each sample. There is now much less information, and it will use much less bandwidth to transmit. But . . .

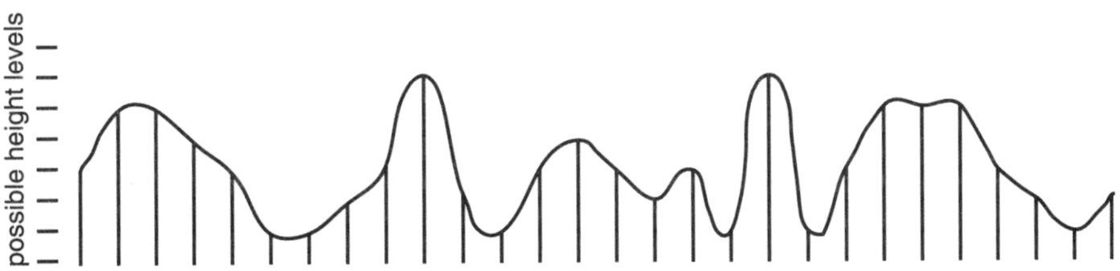

Figure 10.14 Recreated with lower sampling rate.
This wave looks quite a bit different from the original, right? You can see that
there is a penalty for taking fewer samples and/or fewer values per sample.
What kind of difference an error like this makes depends on how big the error
is relative to the overall signal rate. The subjective factor is often critical; in
video and, to a lesser extent, sound, many errors aren't normally noticed.

sume eight bits for each subpixel (red, green, and blue), but there's a clever way of
coding color that uses only ten bits per pixel. So, we multiply by ten to get the bits in
one frame (3,499,200), then times thirty for the number of frames in a second which
yields 104,976,000 bits that must be sent every second. This is on the low side, since
we haven't accounted for overhead.

So how much do we have available? We know that television uses a 6 MHz channel. Of course, all that isn't available for video—a little bit has to go to audio and some
to the guard bands that help prevent interference from adjacent channels. Let's say we
have 5.5 MHz of bandwidth. To get the data rate from this, we need to see how many
bits per Hz our signal will carry. As noted earlier, different approaches to modulation
can increase the amount of information carried in a given amount of bandwidth. This is
true for both analog and digital data. In the case of a digital source, the number of bits
that can be transmitted per Hz varies from about one at the conservative end to ten at the
aggressive end. As with analog transmission, whether you are conservative or aggressive in the way you code your wave depends on how much noise you have to deal with
and the ability of your receiver to decode complex waves. The amount of power (energy) is a factor here as well; the more power you have at the transmitter, the less you
have to worry about noise and the more aggressive your coding can be. (Put another
way, more power means that the amplitude of the signal can be higher than that of the
noise in the circuit; this is where the term *signal to noise ratio* comes from.) For broadcast television, which can get knocked around a bit as it moves through the air and which
normally has to travel quite a distance, we should therefore be conservative and use a
popular coding scheme, 8VSB, that employs both amplitude and phase modulation to
yield about 3.5 bits per Hz. This works out to 19.3 Mbps, which is now a standard for
the digital capacity of a 6 MHz television channel.

Now, we have a maximum data rate of 5.5 million times 3.5, or 19.3 million
bits per second. This is about one-fifth of the 105 million or so that we need. You see

why digital didn't look like such a great idea to people? It was this kind of calculation that caused engineers to say that it was foolish to consider digital television (or radio or telephone). That was before the computer revolution—data compression to the rescue. We'll turn next to the question of how to get all those bits into this little pipe.

DATA COMPRESSION . . . .

Both analog and digital information can be compressed—made to fit into a smaller bandwidth than it would normally occupy. But compression of digital data works much better—from the perspectives of both quality and efficiency. Essentially, there are two kinds of digital compression: content-based and noncontent-based.

Content-based Compression

Content-based means that the compression scheme understands the content it is working with and adjusts the compression to the special characteristics of the data. The best example, a standards-based approach, is that of the Motion Picture Experts Group (MPEG). The MPEG standards, the widely used MPEG-1 and the more powerful and currently ascendant MPEG-2, were developed to deal with the critical problem of finding adequate bandwidth for digital video and audio.

All approaches to compression work their magic by dealing with redundancy. Content-based schemes, as the name suggests, respond to the kinds of information in televison or other streaming video frames. There are two content-based approaches. The first is called *spatial compression,* and refers to the ability to compress the information in a single frame (or other block of information). The second, *temporal compression,* works to eliminate redundancy from one frame to another. The two operate in sequence. The brief description of these that follows is based on how MPEG-2 works, but please appreciate that the real thing is a great deal more complicated than these examples.

Tech Talk

MPEG: The Motion Picture Experts Group (MPEG) has developed a series of techniques for compressing streaming digital information so that it can be used more efficiently, employing less bandwidth in transmission or less capacity on a disk (DVD disks use MPEG coding). MPEG-1, which can deal with low to medium resolution video, has been replaced in most uses by MPEG-2, which can accommodate the original standards for high definition television. The most recent standard, MPEG-4, is being designed to get even greater efficiency through the use of vector graphics.

FEC depends on the noise potential of the medium. Direct broadcast satellites might add as much as thirty percent or so of FEC overhead, while in digital cable television 10 percent or less would be more common. Whatever is required, errors do occur in broadcasting and FEC is absolutely essential. Note that FEC is inherently lossy; it does happen that the needed data isn't available. The receiver then has the choice of displaying an inaccurate image or dropping the frame entirely. Television systems choose the latter course. You've probably been watching television when the set gives off the sound of static but the screen, instead of showing a distorted image, seems to freeze for a second or so. This ragged action means that the receiver has dropped some defective frames, leaving the last good one on for fraction of a second until the next good one arrives. When you see this digital artifact on a normal analog TV, it's because the interference with the digital image occurred somewhere upstream—probably in a digital satellite link between the network headquarters and the local station.

Tech Talk

Forward error correction: Systems like voice or video that can't resend bad information without a penalty in quality add redundant information to the bitstream. If the receiver finds an error, it can use the redundant data it has received, as opposed to a new transmission, to correct it. FEC is not flawless, but it is highly effective.

CONCLUSION   . . . .

Analog communications created a true revolution in society. The telephone, radio, television, and fax were based on tremendous ingenuity both in understanding nature and in manipulating it. The very idea of modulating waves to carry information shows creativity. Producing systems that, like television, could change the amplitude, frequency, and phase of waves to provide both detailed images in color and high quality sound, has to be viewed as a stunning technical achievement, even when considered in the larger historical context. Given these achievements, the rapid ascendancy of digital systems is all the more remarkable.

The digital approach is inherently better than its analog competition in accuracy. At first, it didn't seem that this would matter—the telephone, radio, and television had prospered as lossy media. People had learned to accept errors in transmission. But, digital systems, emerging from the world of data transmission where lossless communications were essential, offered a new dimension in quality. By using sophisticated forms of error detection and correction, the data communications people had learned how to keep their transmissions lossless, even in the face of the interference that plagues all wired and wireless links. But improved quality was just the bonus that came with digital communications. The data compression strategies that are possible only with digital systems turned the bandwidth issue upside down. Instead of requiring far more bandwidth than analog, digital compression allowed, especially in areas like telephony and television that permit lossy links, the use of far *less* bandwidth than before—you can put six digital television channels in the space required by one analog channel and still get superior quality. The remaining chapters in this section will return the focus to the fundamental elements of computer communications, but you should appreciate that these links are increasingly being used to carry images and sound, as well as traditional data.

TEST YOUR UNDERSTANDING . . . .

1. What are three ways to modulate a wave?
2. What is *bandwidth?*
3. What are the advantages of digital communications over analog?
4. What are the two components of *sampling?*
5. What difference does compression make in digital communications?
6. Describe MPEG compression.
7. What is the difference between *spatial* and *temporal* compression?
8. Give examples of *lossy* compression.
9. How does a cyclical redundancy check work, and what is its purpose?
10. When is forward error correction used?

11 Network Fundamentals

Networks are extraordinarily difficult to describe. While a reasonable person would think of computer communications as an area in which logic and order would be of paramount importance, the reverse seems to be true. The chaos is in part due to the proprietary nature of the computer and telecommunications businesses, but there are also more benign explanations. The fact is that there are a great many possible methods of transmitting information electronically, and different organizations have used pretty much all of them to deal with varying problems. For example, the most efficient software/hardware mechanism for getting data from A to B on a copper wire isn't the best means for getting there over fiber optic cable. Another reason for different approaches, of course, is the march of technology—analog signaling over copper wire made sense at one time, but it doesn't now. Finally, while technology marches and vendors learn to work together, the legacies of past approaches linger. Thus, virtually all of the data communications structures that have been invented, however obsolete, are still operating somewhere. This means there is a continuing need to make the old, the new, the open, the proprietary, the fast, and the slow work together. Networking is complex, but it's important. Computer networks are transforming the economy and are about to change daily life in fundamental ways.

This chapter will introduce the basic concepts of networking. By the end of this chapter you should understand

- What data packets are and why they are important

- What network protocols do
- The difference between connections that use circuits and those that are circuitless
- The kinds of media used for networks
- The patterns in which network connections are made
- Routers, hubs, and switches: the connecting points of networks

AN OVERVIEW OF NETWORK FUNDAMENTALS

Networks are sufficiently complicated that, as in Chapter 1, a novice will benefit from an overview before plunging into the detail. The purpose of this section, then, is to introduce and explain in general terms the key concepts of computer networking. To keep things flowing, relatively few technical terms will be employed. As before, remember that these topics are covered in more depth in this and later chapters.

A Quick Analogy

Descriptions of networks often use long, complex postal analogies. While these can easily become strained to the point of confusion, they do offer the potential for some insight. As a compromise, therefore, we'll use this brief analogy to illustrate some key points.

Let's say you're in a company that is sending parts to another company for assembly. Every so often, you complete a part. When you do, you take three envelopes. The first is a special "part container" envelope for the assembler in the other company; you put the part in it and write on the cover the name of the assembler and a number that shows which part is enclosed, "part 11 of 27," for example, and also provide a return address. The second envelope is a U.S. mail envelope, addressed to the company and department of the person doing the assembly. This would seem like enough envelopes. However, yours is a big company and you aren't allowed to leave your work to go to the mail room, so you put your two-envelope set in a third envelope, one provided for company mail, and address it to the mail room. At regular intervals, one of the company's mail boys passes by. He reads the envelope and takes it to the mail room. He doesn't know or care what's inside.

The clerk in the mail room opens the company envelope and throws it away. She reads the address inside and sees that it needs to go via the company's package delivery service, UPS, rather than to any of the company's other locations, so she puts the envelope in one provided by UPS and it is duly collected.

The use of new envelopes stops at this point, but the analogy doesn't suffer because UPS will now use containers instead of envelopes. At its local hub, a machine will look at the address and determine that the closest UPS office is #456. UPS staff will then put the envelope into a container marked "456." On its way through the UPS system, the various handlers will see only the number on the container—like the mail boys in the office, they don't know or care what's inside.

Once the envelope reaches the UPS center on the other end, the previous process begins to reverse itself. UPS delivers to the receiving company's mail room. The mail clerk there opens the UPS envelope, throws it away, and takes out the U.S. mail envelope inside. She looks at the address, then at a directory on her desk, in order to see where in the company the addressee works. Once this is done, she puts the envelope in a company mail envelope and a mail person takes it to the addressee. The addressee pitches the company envelope, opens the US mail envelope, then, taking note of the sequence number, opens the internal envelope to get the part.

This analogy is a bit tedious, and occasionally a bit strained, but it illustrates what happens in modern networks. Let's consider some of the most important elements of the process.

First, the envelope has an important role. It allows the parts of a shipment to be mixed with other parts, from other sources, and which are going to other destinations on various stages of the journey. This is much more efficient than if each of the supplier's parts had to be carried separately, and by courier, all the way from source to destination.

Second, there is a universal addressing system, the postal address, that can uniquely identify an individual at any location, anywhere. Not only is it universally capable, it is universally understood—you can be confident that the right people on the way will understand it.

Third, despite the advantages of the universal addressing system, it doesn't have to be used by all of the people who move the envelopes. Putting one envelope in another that has a specialized address means that people with little skill or training can do part of the carrying and even some of the sorting. The system operates on a "need to know" basis and some of the people—the mail boys and the UPS container handlers—don't need knowledge of the overall postal system to be efficient.

Fourth, the system does provide for intelligence; the various shipping clerks can make very sophisticated decisions about how best to get envelopes or containers to the right place.

Fifth and finally, the system provides a way—the sequence number—of ensuring that all envelopes are delivered. Even better, if the part maker put a pressure sensitive device in each part envelope, one that would make a colored stain if the envelope was hit hard enough to damage the part, the receiver would know not only if all parts were received, but also if any were damaged.

If you're environmentally conscious, you've probably seen a disadvantage of the approach given in this analogy—all those envelopes being torn up and thrown away. Well, it's just an analogy, and in the real world, the envelopes would be packets that are just a bunch of electrons.

Sending a File

Our real example will use the case of a user sending a file to another user. To the sender, the process is simple. He first opens the program that is responsible for this chore; in the case of transfers using the Internet it is called an *FTP (File Transfer Protocol) program.* The sender then selects the file and tells the program the address of the destination computer. Off it goes.

Tech Talk

FTP: The File Transfer Protocol (FTP) is one of the original applications that were specified for the Internet Protocol suite (usually known as TCP/IP). FTP, as the name suggests, is responsible for transferring files over an IP network.

While this may be a simple chore to the user, there's a lot of complicated stuff occurring under the hood. Let's trace the process step by step.

Protocols

When our user hits the "send" button, the file is passed to another layer of software called the *TCP/IP protocol stack* (or *suite*) that is responsible for getting it ready to send. While computing uses a lot of terms loosely and often borrows them from other domains in a rather sloppy fashion, the word *protocol,* in this case, is most appropriate. A *protocol* in the nontechnical world is a set of rules, normally complicated ones, that people are expected to follow so that relationships can be managed smoothly and effectively. The term is very appropriate in this case because, if ever there was a situation in which clear rules were needed to ensure effective progress, it is in computer networks. The added term *stack,* or *suite,* is used because protocols have multiple layers to deal with a variety of different situations.

Tech Talk

Protocol: A protocol is an agreed-upon set of rules for the transmission of data. In packet networks, protocols usually have a variety of layers called *stacks.*

entire wire from one end to another (more on this in the next section). The use of packets also has an advantage in that they simplify error detection and correction—only the bad or missing ones, not the entire group, have to be resent. Second, there is a universal addressing scheme, in this case TCP/IP, that allows packets to be addressed directly to any program on any computer that is part of the network (in this case, the Internet). Like a standard mail address, it is something that can be understood by computers around the world. Third, not all parts of the system have to use TCP/IP. Some specialized segments, like the local area network's Ethernet, or the wide area network's ATM, can be simple and dumb, using their own frames or cells to move the TCP/IP packets from place to place. Fourth, like the shipping clerks, the routers at key points provide the intelligence needed to manage traffic with efficiency. Fifth and finally, TCP/IP's packet sequencing and error detection/correction properties make sure that all of the packets arrive without damage.

We'll see that networks are more complicated than described in this overview. In particular, there are a lot of choices that haven't been described here. But the key elements of packet-based transmission, universal addressing, levels of activity employing a "need to know" approach, routing intelligence, and verification of accurate receipt are what make today's networked world possible. We'll now turn to the detail, beginning with a focus on packets.

THE IMPORTANCE OF PACKETS . . . .

When organizations first wanted to connect computers to other computers, they did the same thing that people did when they wanted to talk—they made a phone call. Since computers use digital signaling to send information, but telephone networks send everything in an analog format, these connections employed modems at each end to convert between the two kinds of signaling (see Chapter 10 for more on the difference). Companies that did a lot of data networking often leased a line from the phone company (or companies, after deregulation). This meant that they had a permanent connection—no dialing needed.

As computer networking grew in importance, the telephone method of making connections became more and more of a problem. One issue was that it was hard to make modems fast enough to handle the speeds (volume of information per second) that computers were capable of. A more important concern, however, was that standard telephone connections, whether dial-up or leased line, were very expensive. This was especially true if long distance was involved, as it often was. The problem was that prior to deregulation of the telephone network, and even for some time thereafter, telephone companies overcharged their customers for long distance in order to subsidize local service, as required by law (and also as a way of making fat profits). Big companies could often negotiate large discounts, of course, but even for them, data networking was expensive. For others with more limited budgets, for example, research universities and affiliated laboratories, the problem of cost became more daunting as they began to see the advantage of connecting researchers on a more or less continuous basis. Since these organizations couldn't get rates low enough to do what they wanted, they began to think of ways of making networking more efficient. The concept of packet-switching was the fruit of that work.

We've said that telephone networks are inefficient. Why is that? Let's use an analogy. If freeways were used in the same manner as telephone systems, they would work like this. If, for example, you wanted to send a truck from Glendale to Anaheim, you would call up the highway patrol and ask them to reserve a lane of the freeway all the way from end to end (including the interchanges). Once your truck arrived at its destination, you would tell the cops to take the pylons and orange barrels down. While they were up, though, only you could use the path that had been created for you. A telephone call does something similar. When you dial through the network (and of course, when you lease a line) you get a link from one end to the other that is all yours until you hang up. This is called *circuit switching* because it is similar to an electrical circuit.

It doesn't take any genius to realize that it would be a lot more efficient if the telephone network worked like the freeway, where trucks and cars from various destinations share the capacity of the road on an as-needed basis. The analogy actually is a good one, since nearly all data connections are "bursty"—meaning that there are lots of empty spaces in between transmissions of information. Actually, this is also true of voice conversations—even the most talkative people use only a fraction of the available capacity of their circuit. Telephone engineers had dealt with one aspect of the traffic problem earlier through the mechanism of *multiplexing,* which allows more than one circuit to use a single wire. It's scary to think of the alternative—we wouldn't be able to see the sky if each voice connection required a single wire. Still, the problem of expense remained.

Engineers and scientists working with the Departments of Defense's Advanced Research Projects Agency (ARPA) came up with a solution. If you put data into little packets, each with the address of the computer it was being sent to, then they could share a circuit. When packets reached connection points in the network (equivalent to freeway interchanges), special computers would read the addresses, determine what route they should take from there, and send them on their way (the computers came to be known as routers because of this function). With this approach, for example, you could lease a single cross-country circuit from the phone company and have hundreds of computers use it at once (it's millions at once today, of course).

Packet switching was originally thought to be kind of a crazy idea, the sort of thing that only university weirdos would spend their time on. But ARPA, which was intended to be a risk-taking kind of organization, financed the work and well, packet-switching is not only here to stay, it actually looks like it's going to make circuit-switching disappear in the not too distant future.

Packet-switching presents some interesting challenges. First, and most important, is the fact that there has to be some common understanding of addressing within a particular network. Second, in the event that a network extends beyond a local area where every computer knows how to find every other, there is a need to do *routing*. In its simplest form, routing means just knowing how to read the addresses of incoming packets and send them in the right direction. In its more complicated aspects, routing can include not just finding a path to the destination, but finding one that is least congested or least expensive, or some combination of these. Third, there is the question of sequencing. Since packets from a particular transmission don't necessarily take the same path to their destination, there has to be some way of getting them in the right order at the end. Fourth, there is the important question of accuracy. All electronic and optical connections are vulnerable to interference, and there has to be some means of making sure that what is received is what was sent. Fifth and finally, there are the questions of latency and jitter—do the packets arrive in an appropriate period of time, and is the time sequence consistent? These latter factors are not an issue for normal data, but become a major challenge for things like voice and video that lose coherence or aesthetic quality, or both, when delay is too long or timing is disrupted. We'll talk about each of these factors briefly, then go on to examine protocols, which are code languages that manage all of these issues for different kinds of networks.

Addresses

For reasons that are fairly obvious, the first thing in a packet is normally the destination address. While every type of network has an addressing scheme, there are conceptual differences. For the moment, we'll leave it at that, but, when we get to protocols, you'll see that there are additional issues. In particular, note that since communication isn't from one computer to another but from one *program* to another, addressing has to be more sophisticated than just a single address. Hint: Other addressing information can be in the "payload" part of the packet shown in Figure 11.1.

Sequencing and Flow Control

Unless packets are given some kind of sequence number, the receiving system has no way of knowing how to put things in the proper order. Most packets include some form of sequence number early in the packet. The concept of *flow control,* familiar to those who fly into busy airports like Chicago's O'Hare, means that the receiving computer is able to tell the sending computer to adjust the speed of its transmission. Most often, the result is that the receiver tells the sender to slow down because it

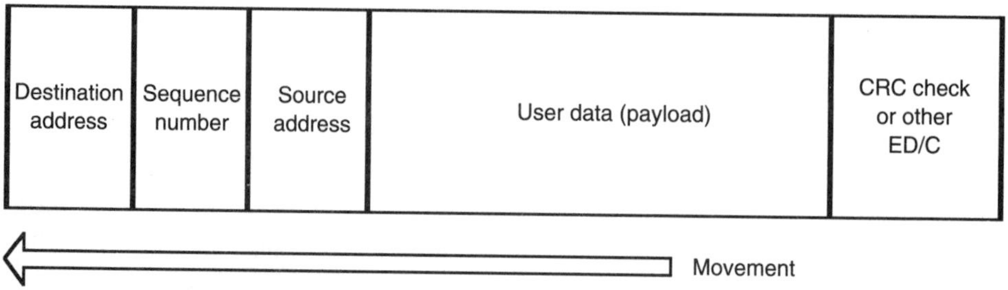

Destination address	Sequence number	Source address	User data (payload)	CRC check or other ED/C

← [==] Movement

Figure 11.1 Anatomy of a packet.

can't assimilate packets at the original speed. Obviously, a conversation like this requires that packets include the source address.

Tech Talk

> **Flow control: When two computers are connected, they can use *flow control* information to manage the data rate to a level that the receiver can handle.**

You are probably wondering what happens to packets that the receiver couldn't handle because they came too fast? It's a good thing you did, because that brings up our next topic, error correction and detection.

Error Detection and Correction

A receiver that can't cope with the flow of incoming packets typically responds by just throwing them away. This isn't a huge problem since once things slow down, the receiver will know from the sequence numbers what is missing and will ask to have them sent again. But it can also be the case that packets are damaged in this process (or because of interference in the circuit). How does the receiver know that it has a damaged packet? The answer is that the sender includes with each packet or group of packets a code that allows the receiver to verify accuracy. The simplest form of this is a *checksum*. The sender modifies the value of the payload by a predetermined algorithm, then appends a number that is the product of that computation. The receiver uses the same algorithm on each packet and compares its result to the one appended. If they don't match, the receiver asks for retransmission. The best known of these algorithms is the cyclical redundancy check (CRC). There are a number of approaches to error detection/correction (ED/C), including some that can restore corrupted data without retransmission. See Chapter 10 for more information on this. A variation on ED/C works not on single packets, but on large groups at once, often called *blocks*. This leads us to the related question of packet size.

Error detection/correction: Since most computer connections require that the same data be received as is sent, error detection and correction information is added to a packet or group of packets so that the receiver can be sure that it has accurate information. If not, it can ask that the packets or group of packets be resent.

Packet Size

The size of packets varies quite a bit. Some systems use very small packets, normally called cells, which are in the range of 53 bytes. Others, like Ethernet, use larger packets, called frames, that can accommodate thousands of bytes. In another variation, some approaches use packets of fixed size, while others allow them to vary within a specified range. The tradeoffs will be discussed when we cover specific types of networks.

Latency

You'll recall that *latency* is computer jargon for *delay*. In a circuit-switched network, where information flows without impediment from end to end, latency is minimal and consistent. Packet-switching, by contrast, puts up a number of barriers. First, packets may have to slow down if there is not enough capacity in the circuit because others are also trying to use it. Second, the process of reading packets in routers or switches introduces delay, and contention at these points can easily make that delay variable. For example, the first part of a stream may get through with the same amount of latency, but a second part might be held up because packets from another source interfered. Thus, there would be timing inconsistency when the packets arrive at the receiver. Again, this is not a concern for normal data transmissions, but does pose a big problem for voice or video.

Latency: In communications, *latency* refers to delay in transmission of packets. While data connections can normally tolerate a fair amount of latency, anything more than a very small quantity will degrade the quality of voice and video connections.

PROTOCOL STACKS · · · · · · · · · · ▪ · · · · · · ▪

A set of computer communication codes, which are known generically as *protocols,* normally are provided in a series of layers called a *stack,* or sometimes a *suite.* Different layers have different responsibilities. Most models of computer to computer communications describe something on the order of seven layers. While this can be a good choice for teaching future specialists in telecommunications, it's confusing to the less focused student. To simplify things, we'll just cover the bottom four layers and illustrate their relationships using the popular TCP/IP protocols, which operate at Layers 4 and 3, respectively.

If you like complicated things, don't despair. Using just four layers will leave plenty of room for complexity. Frankly, we'd ignore the whole stack of stuff if it weren't for two points. First, it's really hard to acquire a basic understanding of computer communications without some sense of protocol layers. Second, like the two strange bedfellows in Khartoum, there is widespread discussion, even controversy, about which layer should do what, and with which, and to whom. These discussions transcend the nerds and enter into mainstream business operations. Please be warned that in order to provide a coherent overview, this section will have to use some terms not previously explained. Rather than make the "explained below" phrase ubiquitous, it is provided just this once. Everything will get more detail later on—if it bothers you, feel free to just flip back and forth.

Please note again that even these four basic layers don't provide a clean separation of functions. In the real world, layers overlap and have exceptions. So here we go.

Layer 4: The Transport Layer

This layer takes collections of bits (files) from an application and assembles them into packets. An example would be the earlier description of taking a file for transfer by an FTP program. Almost always, this requires breaking up a sequence of bits in order to allow them to fit in the space available in the packet. A TCP/IP packet, for example, is limited to about 65,000 bytes (a page of text is 6,000 to 10,000 bytes) so a file will often comprise many packets.

Tech Talk

TCP: The Transmission Control Protocol, TCP, rides on top of IP and manages a connection for purposes of flow control, etc. Its sister Layer 4 protocol, UDP, is connectionless.

A Host of Confusion

> Official networkspeak refers to the computers at the ends of connections as *hosts*. This is a carryover from the days when most every computer on a network was a mainframe or mini to which terminals were attached—it was host to these devices. Today, all but a tiny fraction of the computers on networks are single-user machines. We tend to think of the term *host*, if we use it at all, as something akin to a server. So, we'll go with the modern context and talk about computers rather than hosts. Expect confusion on this score if you move from this book to more technical ones.

Packets created in this layer include

- *Destination* port address—the address of the *process* (program or sub-program) in the remote computer that will be the recipient of the data.
- *Source* port address—this is needed in case packets need to be retransmitted or for communication about error detection/correction.
- Error detection/correction information
  - Cyclical redundancy check (or similar)
  - Packet sequence number

Tech Talk

UDP: The User Datagram Protocol, UDP, is an alternative to TCP. Like TCP, it rides on top of IP, but does not manage a connection for purposes of flow control, etc. It is truly connectionless.

The only way to make error detection/correction function is to require some communication between receiver and sender. TCP, which works at Layer 4, does this by having the receiver send an acknowledgment, or *ack*, packet to verify that it has received a certain number of bytes correctly. When errors are discovered, packets are retransmitted.

Flow Control (Optional)

Flow control also requires an ack packet. The receiver uses this packet to tell the sender how fast it can send information; there will be a message to slow down if too many errors are discovered.

Typically, the control information described above is put in the leading part of the packet, known as the *header*. Overall, it is useful to think of a Layer 4 protocol as the supervisor for the communications mechanics that sit below them.

> **Tech Talk**
>
> **IP: The Internet Protocol, IP, is a Layer 3 routable protocol that can deal with very large networks. It carries either TCP or UDP and can ride on a range of lower level protocols.**

Layer 3: The Network Layer

This layer takes packets from the layer above (or creates them if not already done) and puts them into packets of its own. The header includes something like the following:

- Destination addresses—the address of the computer that will be the final recipient of the data.
- Source address (the sending computer)
- Other control information such as the length of the packet, the name of the protocol carried inside the packet (e.g., TCP), the route to be taken (sometimes specified in advance), etc.

In the case of the Internet Protocol (IP), which functions at Layer 3, the total length of the packet can be no more than 65,535 bytes (including information from other layers, such as TCP). While some networks will have sophisticated error/correction detection information in this layer, IP has only a rudimentary form, since it relies on TCP (or its sister protocol, UDP) to do this. IP is said to *encapsulate* TCP (or UDP), as shown in Figure 11.2.

THE OSI SUITE

The most common way to explain protocols is to begin by describing a stack developed by an international standards group, the International Standards Organization (ISO), which created the Open Systems

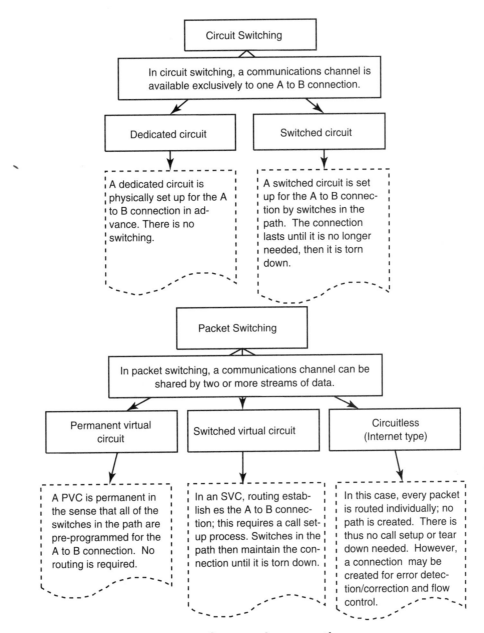

Figure 11.8 A summary of network connections.

MEDIA . . . .

Communications media fall into two categories, wireless and wired, with a fair number of iterations in each.

Wireless

The various frequency bands used for wireless transmission belong to what is known as the *electromagnetic spectrum*. This topic, together with descriptions of how waves carry information, is covered in Chapter 10.

Radio

Radio waves, roughly 1 KHz to 1 GHz in the frequency spectrum, carry radio, television, cellular telephone calls, and communications from ships, planes, drug dealers, cops, good buddies, garage door openers, and lots more. Altogether, a heck of a lot of stuff is carried by radio waves. Still, relatively little of that is data. The problem with using radio frequencies for data is that this is both a very crowded and a rather noisy part of the spectrum. The most reliable way of modulating a wave, the method least vulnerable to interference, is frequency modulation (see Chapter 10). But this is also the least efficient, since using two sets of frequencies for the binary numbers uses more bandwidth than amplitude or phase modulation.

Given all the competition for the use of radio waves, conserving bandwidth is a real issue. On the other hand, all that stuff being broadcast creates lots of interference—mostly through waves that are reflected by earth, sky, or buildings, and bounce back at the wrong frequency and/or the wrong phase. Also, as we've already noted in Chapter 10, interference with a signal's amplitude is very common. There are some radio-based local area networks, used mostly where cables just don't work, for example, where people are moving around a hospital with laptops or PDAs. There is also increasing use of radio for campus-type networks (as noted, campus in this case means a cluster of buildings—more than a LAN but less than a WAN). However, both types of use are usually for short distances and low data rates, for example, e-mail or similar messages.

The future will bring a sharp increase in digital connections in the radio band; the first change has already begun with the introduction of personal communications systems (PCS, digital cell phones) that provide both voice and pager-type functions. Next, digital television (DTV) will appear, and with it, some related information services. DTV broadcasts will have huge information carrying capacity, but it will be only one-way (television sets are receivers, not transmitters, and even if they could

fairly stable and includes many known quantities, the protocol used by interior routers, open shortest path first (OSPF) provides for router to router communication only when some important element in the network has changed. For example, if there was heavy congestion in one part of the network, a router would signal that to its neighbors, which would add this information to their tables and send packets on alternate paths.

Tech Talk

Open shortest path first (OSPF): The most popular router to router communication protocol for interior networks, OSPF, which uses a link/state algorithm, is more efficient than the older RIP (Routing Information Protocol) because routers exchange only a subset, the active links, of their tables.

EXTERIOR ROUTERS • Exterior routers, sometimes called *edge routers,* communicate between domains. One side of an exterior router is simple—this part connects to the interior network and is essentially an interior router. However, the other side, the part that looks outside the domain, has a more complicated task because, lacking any direct knowledge of the networks to which it connects, it must communicate a great deal of information on a regular basis. A particular function of exterior routers is helping to ensure that packets won't be placed in loops—sent on a route that causes them to be redirected endlessly in a circle. To avoid this, exterior routers need to tell each other something about the interior side of their network. This is a good time to mention another component of the IP packet—the *time to live* segment. This field is created by the sender with a specific value (normally 15) and is then decremented each time a packet makes a hop (enters and leaves a router). If a receiving router gets a packet with a value of 1—for example, it has made 14 hops—it assumes it is in a loop and discards it. Exterior routers originally used a protocol called the Exterior Gateway Protocol (EGP) to do this, but a replacement called Border Gateway Protocol (BGP) is now dominant.

Tech Talk

Border gateway protocol: Used in wide area networks, BGP is a router to router protocol that allows exterior routers to communicate with each other. BGP is more efficient than its predecessor, Exterior Gateway Protocol (EGP), because routers exchange only changes to their tables, not the entire table.

Tech Talk

Network loop: To illustrate a network loop, consider the case of router A sending a packet to router B, thinking that it is on the path to network node C. But router B has a damaged routing table, which tells it

that the way to get to C is through A. So it sends the packet to A, which consults its routing table again and sends it to B. . . .

Routing and Security • Routing presents some security problems. The most serious occurs when a router sends out a bad routing table, which others then pick up and send on. Bad tables can wreak havoc for a number of reasons. One concern, of course, is that packets will arrive by a slow route.

A much worse problem, though, occurs when a packet is mistakenly sent to the wrong router. In such a case, which includes a packet with too small a time to live value, the receiving router politely tells the sender that it is in error; the packet can't be delivered via that network. If there are enough incorrectly routed packets, this courtesy will result in *packet storms*—a wave coming from one router and another going back. This kind of thing can lead to a major network collapse, something that has happened on a few occasions when a central router propagated erroneous tables. Router crashes can also happen for malicious reasons. There have been cases where disgruntled, or perhaps just evil, individuals have sent a constant stream of bad packets to an ISP's router, bringing it to its knees while it attempted to respond to each one. There are fixes to these problems, but the point is that complex, routed networks, because they depend on a continuous exchange of information from autonomous sources, are somewhat fragile and moderately vulnerable.

....

BAD, PACKET! BAD!

One method that a malicious user can employ to attack a router or other network computer is to send it bad (corrupted) packets. For example, the user might write a program that changes packets to give them a defective network address and then send them to a specific router. The router would reply with a message saying the address was incorrect. Responding to a constant stream of these "bad" packets would slow the router, and therefore, of course, traffic trying to go through it. This would presumably satisfy the ego of the juvenile who started the process.

Multiprotocol Routers • Some routers have more responsibilities than just routing. Many also handle more than one set of protocols. For example, certain routers can simultaneously route and even translate between such disparate networks as the Internet's TCP/IP, IBM's SNA, and Compaq/DEC's Decnet. It's like a post office that not only has to sort envelopes, it also has to deal with different languages—some envelopes are addressed in Latin script, some in Cyrillic, and others in Chinese.

12 Types of Networks

The traditional way of categorizing networks is according to the level at which they connect computers—local, campus, or wide area. In this taxonomy, *local* is equivalent to the computers in a department or some other small organizational subdivision. A local area network goes by the widely used handle of *LAN*. The next kind of network, called a *campus* network, is simply one that connects two or more LANs in a building or cluster of buildings. LANs and campus networks are distinct in that they use hardware, software, and wiring that is provided locally—by the business, organization, or even the family that actually uses the network. When you leave the local or campus environment, however, it's no longer possible to do it on your own. The government won't let you string wire or set up microwave towers wherever you want to (fortunately). This means that you have to get bandwidth, and likely also hardware and software, from some external provider—typically a telephone company but increasingly an array of companies that don't have roots in the old telephone systems. Actually, it's more complicated than that. Since very few companies or organizations have direct connections to a wide area network, the real next level is what we'll call an *access* network. This type of network connects LANs, or campus networks, or individual computers, to the *wide area network,* or WAN. Access networks are the source of technological and business ferment as the industry tries to find cost-efficient ways of getting high bandwidth Internet connections to homes and businesses—"the last mile problem" as it is known in the telecommunications world. Today, for most people, businesses, and organizations, the WAN is in fact synonymous with the Internet. This chapter will cover the technological foundations of wide area networking; the structure of the Internet will be covered in Chapter 14.

This chapter will build on the basic concepts of networking from Chapter 11 by providing descriptions of the types of networks used at the various levels. By the end of this chapter you should understand

- What local area networks (LANs) are and how they operate (Ethernet, Token Ring)
- The kinds of links used for campus networks and the technologies used to support them (FDDI, ATM, Gigabit Ethernet)
- The different ways that individuals, businesses and organizations can connect to wide area networks (dial-up, leased lines, cable modems, DSL)
- The technologies that underlie WANs (SONET, WDM, and DWDM)

LOCAL AREA NETWORKS . . . .

Early in the microcomputer era, there were a variety of contenders in the LAN arena. However, the dust has now settled, and there are only two important ones left—Ethernet and Token Ring. Others, such as ARCnet and Appletalk, have shares of the market that are vanishingly small.

Ethernet

Ethernet, originally developed at Xerox's Palo Alto Research Center (PARC), is a bus-based local area network strategy. Ethernet is also baseband—only one connection can operate on a wire at one time. The wire is shared through an approach known as *Carrier Sense Multiple Access/Collision Detection (CSMA/CD)*. Ethernet nodes listen to the wire to which they are attached to see if anyone else is broadcasting (carrier sense). If all is quiet, and they want to use the wire, they send out a frame (Ethernet's version of a packet) and then listen again. If another node has also tried to broadcast during this time, their frames will collide and make a distinctive sound (collision detection). If this happens, both nodes will wait a random amount of time and try again. Believe it or not, this weird system works very well. In case you're skeptical, just observe that there are estimated to be on the order of a hundred million Ethernet "nodes" (connected computers or other devices) in operation around the world.

protocol (notably SONET) while using its own Layer 2 switching capability to carry Layer 3 and Layer 4 traffic (usually TCP/IP).

ATM is a cell-switched system. All traffic coming into ATM is broken up into 53-byte cells. No exceptions. Rigidity extends to the format of its very short protocol data unit; the first five bytes hold header information, the next 48 carry the data "payload." Always. The fixed cell length and structure has important advantages in switching. The switch hardware can be custom designed to handle the cells, with the result that, once the circuit is established, transferring cells from the incoming to the outgoing port can occur very, very fast—much faster than with any other approach. Most ATM links are permanent virtual circuits, PVCs, that are set up in advance by the network provider. But ATM also offers switched virtual circuits (SVCs) which are equivalent to dial-up connections. Some systems use ATM SVCs as backups in case a primary link goes down.

The small size of the cells is an advantage and a disadvantage. It can hurt in that the process of breaking up packets to fit into the cells adds overhead (remember that IP packets range up to about 1,500 bytes). It also hurts in that the payload-to-header ratio is unusually low (another way of saying this is that overhead is high). Data people argued against the 53-byte cell size as ATM was being developed, but the advantage of the small cell comes in handling voice and video. These *streaming* connections can't suffer more than a small amount of delay. Because it requires another stage of analysis to determine a packet's length, a normal switch, such as that on an Ethernet LAN, introduces latency as it processes packets of varying size. Also, if there is contention for an output port, a long data packet can hold up another transmission, forcing it to sit in a buffer and wait. This problem is much worse in routers, which are already a lot slower than switches. Variable latency in switches and routers introduces "jitter" that degrades the quality of audio and video. Audio can become choppy sounding, video can flicker, audio and video can get out of synch, and so on. The ATM approach, both because of its short cells and because of its more efficient Layer 2 focus, does a much better job of keeping traffic flowing smoothly through the switches.

Uses of ATM

In its Layer 1 clothing, ATM is specified for fiber optics and for UTP. The UTP specification, which came late and which is only popular with a few vendors (notably IBM), operates at 25 Mbps. The standard ATM is 155 Mbps (fiber only), scaling up to over 2 Gbps. It's not clear when ATM hits the wall, but it can certainly go faster than the 2 Gbps level. In terms of sheer bps, ATM is the fastest higher-level protocol around. It can also go the distance. Unlike Ethernet and Token Ring, whose broadcast technologies limit their range, ATM links can be as long as the fiber connection they run on (e.g., 80 km or so).

While ATM can work directly with the media at Layer 1, the heart of the protocol is at Layer 2. Like X.25 and Frame Relay (see sections later in this chapter), ATM either uses static connections (permanent virtual circuits) or employs a call setup phase to create virtual circuits through the network. Once the call is set up and the best path from sender to receiver has been determined, the path gets an ID number, which is registered in the databases of each switch. Cells then carry just the path ID; destination and source addresses are not needed. This simplified system helps make the switches function as fast as possible. Actually, ATM has several ID levels. A path can be host to many channels, so once a path from A to B has been set up, a number of processes at A can communicate with a number of processes at B, without having again to go through the entire call setup process. Most ATM based systems use permanent virtual circuits, but businesses often employ switched virtual circuits as a way of getting extra capacity on the fly—"bandwidth on demand."

Tech Talk

Virtual circuit: A defined path from one point in a network to another that relies on switching created by software rather than on the physical switching used by a regular circuit is called a *virtual circuit*.

Paths and channels can be established in ways that determine how much bandwidth they will receive from the switches. Thus, if a channel has been guaranteed 155 Mbps, each switch on the path will keep information about bandwidth levels and will make sure that cells on that channel can move at the guaranteed rate. When combined with the fixed cell size, these guarantees ensure that video and voice can move through the network without encountering inappropriate latency. The guarantees are referred to by the generic phrase *quality of service* (QoS). ATM is a protocol that is known for its "promised" ability to provide QoS. "Promised" is put in quotations because this function, which adds a great deal of complexity to the switches, has been difficult to implement. Quite a few of ATM's users don't actually attempt to use QoS functions because they fear they will bring the network down.

ATM in Today's Market

ATM hasn't been around all that long (planning took place throughout the 1980s, but products have been on the market only since about 1991, and really useful since only about 1994) and it was a while after that before it was fully specified. This lack of complete and final specifications was a problem, since it forced vendors to try to solve things on their own, resulting in incompatibilities. In networking, caution is advised when mixing and matching hardware from different vendors. In the early days of ATM, this approach was particularly risky. The situation continues to improve, but

with new electronics that allow additional, high quality channels for data. Better still, junk the analog stuff and make the whole thing digital. Unfortunately, these advanced solutions not only require rebuilding more of the network, they also assume replacing all the set-top boxes as well. This poses a big financial problem for the financially challenged cable companies. Costs would be lower if the cable companies could develop a standard digital set-top architecture. CableLabs, which is a research and standards organization funded by cable providers, has been hard at work on such a standard. The biggest challenge to this process comes from Hollywood. The moguls are very concerned about the advent of a new generation of cable boxes that allows direct connection to digital televisions and recorders. In such a scenario, technically the most desirable one, it will be easy for people to make perfect copies of movies. As this is written, there is hard work but little agreement on a scheme to prevent this.

HOT WIRED CONNECTIONS

There's another possible solution to the "last mile" problem—the electrical grid. Power companies have found that it's possible to carry data over the lines that bring electricity to homes and businesses. Since power lines are, to put it mildly, an electrically noisy environment, a lot of error detection and correction is needed, and this limits bandwidth. But the real issue, not resolved yet, is whether the available capacity can be cost-effective in the surging market for home bandwidth.

A cable modem network uses the tree and branch topology because that's how cable television networks are set up. At the user end, there is a cable modem that connects on one side to the PC (usually by Ethernet) and on the other to the cable. The cable then connects to other cables and ultimately to a switch of some sort. The key point here is that the part of the network that extends from the customer premises to the first switch functions like a bus-based LAN—it has shared bandwidth (compare to the star topology of xDSL and other telephone-based approaches). Depending on the situation, any given user has a lot of potential competitors for network access—120 to 500 in current systems, with the average being about 200. Where I live, in Ohio, this isn't much of a problem; my neighbors mow their lawns and watch TV. On the other hand, at my sister and brother-in-law's place in southern California, where every house has at least one fanatical cybersurfer, competition for bandwidth is fierce. The solution to this problem is for the cable companies to push fiber optic multiplexers and switches closer and closer to the customer premises, making for an ever smaller number of users sharing the same bandwidth. And, by the way, users need to protect their computers from intrusion—the shared nature of cable networks means that nosy neighbors could get access to your drives and printers.

Network Services

The communications systems described in this section—dial-up analog lines, ISDN, Switched 56, X.25, Frame Relay, and Switched Multimegabit Data Service—are different from the dedicated line/carrier systems described earlier (leased digital lines, xDSL, and television cable lines, summarized in Figure 12.4), which are just means for putting data over a wire. Some network services are dumber than others; dial-up phone lines, ISDN, and Switched 56 only provide the means for making a point-to-point connection. They are sort of intelligent Layer 1 systems. By contrast, the other network services that we will discuss, X.25, Frame Relay, and Switched Multimegabit Data Service, include some error detection/correction and flow control. These operate (more or less) at Layer 2.

Dial-up Analog Lines

The standard telephone line from a home or business is analog and limited in bandwidth to about 4 KHz. To use these lines, computers have to have modems at either end. The modems convert the digital data coming from a computer to analog, modulate (code) it, then send it over the line. The modem at the other end decodes the data and converts it back to digital. Modems, which work through the dial-up telephone system, create switched circuits (see Figure 12.8). The modems will provide flow control and error detection/correction, but don't handle any addressing and don't know or care what kind of data they are carrying.

The modulation (coding) employed by modem vendors has become ever more sophisticated, employing amplitude, phase, and frequency modulation all at once.

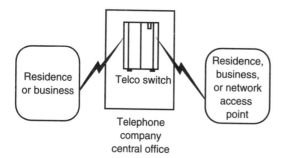

Figure 12.8 Switched phone lines.
Both analog lines and ISDN connections go through the telephone company's switching network. ISDN speeds are only available if the destination also supports ISDN.

The result is that as much as 33.6 Kbps can be stuffed into 4 KHz. Since the bandwidth actually used by the telephone electronics is about 3.3 KHz, modems are now getting 10 bits per Hz. This is very close to the theoretical maximum. In the real world, of course, noise in the line makes this aggressive modulation infeasible, and the modems often drop back to a slower speed.

ISDN

ISDN (Integrated Services Digital Network) is the digital equivalent of the analog phone line. The standard form of ISDN, called Basic Rate, includes two 64 Kbps channels plus another 16 Kbps for signaling, on a single pair of wires. This means that ISDN has a capacity of 144 Kbps (full duplex). Since normal analog lines only carry the equivalent of 64 Kbps, ISDN produces what the industry calls *pair gain.* This phrase describes a technology that allows a pair of wires to gain capacity.

ISDN normally functions as a switched service. Unlike a leased line, it isn't open all the time. Instead, just as with a regular voice phone call, you make a call to the telco switch to set up a circuit and it lasts until someone does the equivalent of hanging up. Needless to say, there is no point in making a data call via ISDN if the party called doesn't have ISDN service as well. ISDN is provisioned on only one twisted-pair and can be as far as 18,000 feet from the telephone switch. Since most homes and businesses (about 90 percent) are that close and have at least one pair available, existing wiring can be used in the vast majority of cases.

ISDN is flexible. The standard ISDN service, Basic Rate (BRI, for basic rate interface), is known technically as 2B+D, because it has two *bearer* channels of 64 Kbps and one signaling channel (the *D*) of 16 Kbps. The D channel is actually a packet-switched link that is always open to the switch. When a phone call comes in from the switch, it is signaled over the D channel; when the phone is picked up, the B channels are opened for the conversation. The same process can be used for data, with a variety of possibilities, the most important of which is that the full 128 Kbps (2 × 64) can be used at one time (in one direction). ISDN is full duplex—these capacities are available in both directions at the same time.

Installing ISDN • At the telephone company end, installing ISDN is fairly straightforward. First, the central office switch has to be ISDN-capable, which means that its software must be able to talk to the ISDN system. Second, the interfaces to the incoming line, *line cards,* have to be swapped from analog to digital. Connections can then go through the switching system just like any other 64 Kbps voice circuit. At the home or office end (*customer premises* in telco jargon), the situation is more difficult. You need black boxes. One kind of box is used to connect a computer to the line (the wall jack); the link from this box to the computer is normally Ethernet. Both the computer and the ISDN line are digital, but manipulation is required both to fit the computer's data signal into the ISDN format and to manage bandwidth. By definition, an ISDN line can handle voice, and if you happen to have a couple of ISDN-compatible digital phones sitting in your attic, that's all you need. More likely, though, you have a bunch of "free gift" analog phones that you don't want to give up. No problem, you can buy another black box that will allow you to connect these. An arcane feature of ISDN is that it can allow one physical line to carry a bunch of different phone numbers. This will allow people to have separate numbers for voice, fax, and computer. There is usually an extra charge for this feature, though. Phone numbers are in short supply.

Options and Costs • There is another kind of ISDN, Primary Rate ISDN (PRI), which has the same bandwidth as T-1, 1.544 Mbps, and also requires either one or two wire pairs, depending on the local service situation. Since both Primary Rate ISDN and T-1 can carry switched-voice conversations as well as data at varying rates, the principal difference between the two is that ISDN connects directly to the telephone company's switched network and T-1 is just a vehicle for getting bits from A to B—it has no switching capacity. PRI is more flexible, but usually more expensive.

Depending on the carrier, you will not pay a higher monthly charge for a longer ISDN line. Local calls will be billed at either a flat rate or based on time of use, again depending on the phone company. ISDN long distance calls are like telephone long distance.

ISDN is a simple enough idea. When first developed, about 1984, it also seemed feasible. Telephone companies were well along in the process of converting their long distance systems to digital circuits and the move toward all digital local switches was rapidly gaining momentum. Converting the "local loop" to digital seemed a logical next stage. That was the theory, anyway. The fact is that ISDN didn't happen on the scale intended, and it appears it never will. Interestingly, there were no technical barriers; the problems had to do with standards and market.

Problems with ISDN • Telephone companies, which have to connect with each other to provide national and international long distance service, have a good record of cooperation on technical standards. As an example, while the European equivalent of the T-carrier is different from the American (it has 32 channels and carries about 2 Mbps), the signaling standards are the same and the two can interoperate easily. ISDN, on the other hand, is a local technology and interfaces directly only with the company's own equipment (the central office switch). Thus, while international standards were developed for ISDN, as often happens they didn't specify everything in full detail—it usually takes quite a bit of time and experience to do that. So different companies implemented ISDN differently. This fragmented the equipment market and helped keep prices high. These incompatibilities are now largely solved, but they impeded progress for many years.

The market problem is more serious. When ISDN was first deployed, the Internet didn't exist except for a handful of users with esoteric interests. Data users at that time were almost exclusively large companies who met their needs with leased lines. Small businesses used dial-up analog lines. Most businesses and nearly all individuals had no data connections. ISDN's switched 128 Kbps was too little for the leased line users and too much for everyone else. Also, it was very expensive and not widely available (remember that availability is two-edged—it doesn't matter if you have ISDN if the system you want to connect to doesn't). For a decade or so, ISDN was like the weather; it was much discussed but little was done about it. With the exploding popularity of the Internet, and especially of the Web, fast modems quickly seemed slow and phone companies moved to expand ISDN offerings. Pretty much universally, they did a bad job of this.

Because of their long experience as monopolies, phone companies have a record of not understanding marketing (they do know how to advertise, but that's just a part of the deal). Indeed, providing a complex product in a way that "delights the customer" was not in their usual bag of tricks. And from the telco point of view, ISDN was not just any service. Making it happen required intra-company communications on the part of groups that didn't know each other existed. Horror stories about trying to order ISDN and getting a confused answer, followed by a promise of installation that took months to fill, followed by a nonfunctioning system, were commonplace. ISDN pricing has also been a problem. A number of telcos initially promoted the service by offering a monthly flat rate for local calls. When they discovered that many, even most, of their users were Internet junkies who left the line open 24 hours a day, they expressed shock and tried to change the pricing. Needless to say, this didn't lead to a high level of customer good will.

After a few years, the phone companies got their stuff together and made ISDN reasonably quick to order and install, and somewhat affordable. Unfortunately, at this point, ISDN's 128 Kbps was nice, but not exciting. It looks like cable modems, xDSL technologies, direct broadcast satellite, and wireless local loops, all of which offer far more capacity, will keep ISDN from being a factor in the access market.

The gnomes at the International Telecommunications Union (ITU, née CCITT) are working on a high-speed extension of ISDN called Broadband ISDN. This will be a protocol structure that sits on top of SONET and ATM, and goes to about 600 Mbps, or something like that. Don't hold your breath. History suggests that once complex schemes like this make it through the standards process, something better will have gained a strong lead in the market.

Switched 56

Switched 56 is a bit of an in-between strategy. A pure data service, it's cheaper to install than a fractional T-1 and has the advantage of being dial-up, so subscribers pay only for the bandwidth they use. On the other hand, it has less capacity and less flexibility than ISDN. Given that it can't command much market scale, it probably won't be around long.

X.25

X.25 is little known by the general public, but it is a very widely used "back end" technology. X.25 is responsible, among other things, for automatic teller networks used by banks, for credit card verification services used by hundreds of thousands of merchants, and for some low-speed, low-traffic terminal-to-host connections. There are a number of network providers. The local end, including lines and terminating equipment, is normally maintained by telephone companies. Once at the telco's central office, packets flow into a broader switching network that could belong to the telco itself, to a long-distance carrier, or to a third party like CompuServe. Charges to the customer depend on a variety of factors and may come from multiple sources (the local connection provider and the network provider). Permanent circuits are likely to be charged according to packets sent, while temporary circuits will be charged on a time-connected basis or perhaps some combination of the two. From the customer's point of view, the advantage of X.25 (or other carrier-switched services like Frame Relay) vs. a network built from leased lines and locally maintained switches is that the user doesn't have to be in the networking business. The service provider handles all the plumbing and is responsible for being sure that packets get to where they are supposed to go. In addition, since other businesses are also connected to the same network, it is possible to have an array of links beyond your own organization.

X.25 is a packet-switched network, one that uses a call setup procedure to establish virtual circuits, either permanent or temporary. Once the path through the network is established, individual packets carry a virtual circuit identification rather than full destination and source addresses. Because each packet (usually) follows the same path, packet sequencing isn't a problem. On the other hand, X.25 is especially serious about error detection/correction and flow control. Each receiving switch checks each packet for errors and returns an acknowledgment to the sender before another packet can be sent. Individual switches also handle flow control. One reason that X.25 does error detection/correction and flow control in the switches rather than at the ends of the network is that it was created for a world in which the devices at the ends—terminals—were too dumb for these tasks. Another reason for X.25's paranoid approach is its heritage as a technology for old-fashioned copper wire telephone connections, in which errors were quite common. X.25 normally runs on a line set up for 56 or 64 Kbps, though the extensive error checking means that throughput is quite a bit lower than this. While still widely used today for low-speed connections, X.25 has been by-passed for advanced data exchanges by its younger, sleeker sibling, Frame Relay.

Frame Relay

Frame Relay is a very hot technology that is offered by telephone companies (mostly) as the logical step up from X.25. It is in many ways an enhanced version of X.25. As with X.25, the telco provides the user with a dedicated line and terminating equipment that connects to an internal computer network (usually to a router) (see Figure 12.9). Where X.25 uses its own physical layer, Frame Relay sits on top of an existing carrier—Switched 56, ISDN, or T-carrier. Frame Relay frames (which can be as long as 4,096 bytes), like X.25 packets, are switched through virtual circuits following a call setup process that replaces packet addresses with virtual path identifiers. With minor exceptions, these circuits are permanent virtual circuits that the user establishes by agreement with the telco. In other words, you designate the connections that you will want to make (e.g., to remote offices and to an Internet Service Provider) and these connections are put into routing tables in the switches. Switched virtual circuits (equivalent to dial-up connections) for Frame Relay are a relatively recent innovation.

As with ATM, to which it is closely related, with Frame Relay, the user's permanent virtual circuit connections are programmed into the appropriate switches so that when a frame leaves a network site with the appropriate circuit identification in

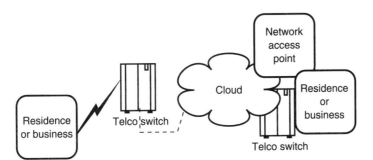

Figure 12.9 Frame Relay/X.25.
A Frame Relay, or X.25, connection also runs over a leased line. It enters the front end of the telephone company's central office, but does not connect through the regular switch. Instead, it is passed on to the Frame Relay, or X.25, packet switching "cloud" where it can connect, probably through another telephone switching center, to other residences or businesses, or to a network access point.

its header, the switches in its path recognize it and know exactly where to send it. Not only do the switches know where the frame should go, they also know how much bandwidth it can have. The user and the telco have agreed in advance on the average circuit speed, which is called the *committed information rate,* and a *burst rate,* which is the amount over the committed rate that the circuit can go for brief periods. Some Frame Relay providers also offer *bandwidth-on-demand,* which means that if the network has excess capacity, users can temporarily get a data rate higher than the burst rate by requesting it from the carrier. Of course, the pipes into and out of the network (the leased lines) dictate the maximum end-to-end speed—you can't get T-3 out of a T-1.

Another way in which Frame Relay is different from X.25 is in error correction and detection—X.25 does a lot and Frame Relay does almost none. Frame Relay detects, but does not correct; "bad" packets are simply thrown away. Frame Relay, together with other protocols that don't do error correction or flow control, is called a *fast packet* technology. When it was first marketed in the late 1980s, most of the telephone network consisted of high-quality digital circuits, including virtually error-free fiber trunks. In this environment it doesn't make sense for each switch to verify each frame; instead, the upper layer protocols employed by the user (e.g., TCP) can deal with the relatively rare problem of corrupted or missing packets by asking for retransmission. While Frame Relay switches do less work than their X.25 counterparts, they are more intelligent. The bandwidth-on-demand option is one example; multicasting is another. X.25 allows only a one-to-one transmission, but Frame Relay allows one-to-many connections.

Frame Relay specifies how a network is accessed, not necessarily how it works internally. Thus, telcos increasingly are using Frame Relay as an interface to internal networks that use other protocols, notably ATM over SONET, to move information around inside their "cloud." Once user data, chopped into cells and stuffed into slots, reaches the other side of the cloud, frames are recreated and sent to the addressee (which will then strip off the Frame Relay frames, look inside to find the TCP/IP address of the ultimate destination, then put the packets inside Ethernet frames). A lot of electronic slicing and dicing goes on in networks, and it's really amazing that it all works.

Frame Relay has a variety of uses. Many companies employ it as an alternative to leased lines for connecting remote LANs. The T-1 speed is the likely choice for this use. Frame Relay's big advantage over leased lines is that one site needs only one line to connect to multiple other sites—e.g., both to remote offices and to the Internet. The alternative, multiple leased lines with a user-provided switching center, is likely to be much more expensive. Because Frame Relay's variable length frames can introduce latency, and because its switches aren't designed to manage quality of service constraints, it is not considered suitable for video or voice. However, in the tradition of people adapting the tool they have to whatever task is in front of them, some vendors are now trying to add quality of service elements as well as voice to Frame Relay.

Frame Relay tariffs are normally a composite of the cost of the physical connections to the carrier's network and a per-frame charge. A low speed/low use link might run a few hundred dollars a month. A highly utilized T-1 connection could be several thousand. Remember, though, that in a fast-changing, competitive environment, both the variables and the rates are subject to frequent change.

Switched Multimegabit Data Service (SMMDS)

SMMDS, like X.25 and Frame Relay, is a data networking service offered by telcos to businesses. It is a much higher speed system, provisioned at rates up to 45 Mbps, though 1 Mbps or so is most common. At the physical level, SMMDS uses something known as a Metropolitan Area Network (MAN), which you can think of as a city-wide LAN run by a telephone company or Competitive Access Provider (CAP). We won't go into the technology here, just note that MANs use a time slot organization, have a dual bus rather than a dual ring topology, and are also designed to have a high level of resistance to failure. For the upper layers, SMMDS uses a cell-based switching approach that is very similar to ATM; its packets are, in fact, the same as ATM's. The real question with SMMDS is whether it is a viable alternative to ATM itself. More and more telcos and competing access providers are offering ATM services directly. Given the market scale of ATM, especially when combined with SONET, it seems that SMMDS has little long-term potential.

WANs . . . .

The best known wide area network is, of course, the Internet. Its area is now pretty much all of the populated world. In addition, however, many businesses have created wide area networks of their own. Most of these use IBM's SNA protocol suite, while others use TCP/IP with wires, routers, and switches that are physically separate from the Internet. Nearly all wide area connections currently use the SONET protocols, but there is intense interest in moving to simpler approaches. We'll discuss SONET first.

SONET

SONET, which stands for Synchronous Optical Network, takes us back to Layer 1. This is a physical transport that uses (exclusively) optical cable and synchronous time slot data management. SONET, also known in international standards as SDH (Synchronous Digital Hierarchy), is a brilliant design that has been adopted very rapidly by telephone companies and a few of their competitors (remember Qwest, described in Chapter 11).

SONET's topology is the self-healing, dual counter-rotating ring. The redundancy is especially important for SONET networks because in a WAN, lines don't live safe and secure in the walls of buildings. Rather, they are outdoors, mostly buried underground and occasionally suspended in air. As a result, the danger of damage to a cable is much higher than in other systems. The "self-healing" aspect of SONET's ring architecture means that it can survive a cut without the network going down—the other cable takes over automatically, becoming the main circuit until the original cable is restored.

SONET's synchronous nature makes it much easier to switch. When two SONET rings meet, the fact that their slots are synchronized at the same speed means that it is relatively easy to move the contents of a slot from one ring to another. SONET is also easier to multiplex and demultiplex. T-carrier frames have to be completely torn apart to extract one channel, then rebuilt before they can be sent on. SONET, by contrast, allows information from within a slot to be pulled out without interrupting the flow of data. Incredibly, synchronization flows from a central clocking system. At one point, there was a single master clock for telephone and connected SONET networks. Currently, networks use something called *Stratus 3 clocks* in central offices or network hubs. These clocks are accurate to a level of just over one part in a billion. These are fairly technical points; you may recall that SONET is considered to be a first-rate technology, one with no significant flaws other than overhead.

The speed of SONET is specified in Optical Carrier (OC) levels. The major levels defined to date are

OC-1	51.8 Mbps
OC-3	155.5 Mbps
OC-12	622.0 Mbps
OC-24	1.24 Gbps
OC-48	2.48 Gbps
OC-192	9.92 Gbps

Unlike T-carrier and DS levels, SONET/SDH's OC specifications are the same around the world. This standardization helps both in developing a competitive market for equipment and in ensuring that international links are efficient and easy to effect. Remember, though, that SONET is just a carrier. While SONET does provide some error detection and some control functions, it isn't capable on its own of setting up and maintaining end-to-end communications. For telephone connections, the world's telcos have settled on a protocol called *Signaling System 7*. For data, and for mixed

and cranks out its analysis. Even though this chore might take a while, it isn't a problem because this server is separate from the normal LAN file server—it's called an *application server*. It could be located on a LAN or, if the company has many LAN users who need its services, somewhere on a central backbone. When the application server has finished its work it sends its data to the client, which loads it into Excel. The user then runs his macro (program).

In an even more sophisticated version of this three-tier client-server model, the process begins with software at the client, formatting the initial query in a way that is easily understood by the host and optimized for execution on its database software. This is important because a database query can be executed very fast or very slow, depending on how it is structured. While the optimized query might come from Excel itself, it is more likely in a case like this that it comes from a "front end" program written specifically for the host's database. The front end will have knowledge of how the database is organized (record structure, indexes, etc.) and will be able to do the complex calculations needed to make sure that the query can be executed in the shortest possible time. It can also enforce rules, such as preventing the user from doing dumb things like needlessly looking at every record in a large database or, worse, doing this more than once. Poorly constructed queries can bring even a powerful system to a halt. Since a modern database, particularly one used in a three tier client/server environment, is likely to be relational, the query will be formatted in SQL.

The number of layers in a distributed computing environment is not fixed. A two-tiered client/server system is quite common for smaller systems, while three tiers is increasingly preferred for larger ones. In three-tiered systems, the layers are client, server, and host; they are also referred to by function as *presentation, application,* and *database*. The software interactions are variable as well. The category of software that does heavy-duty analysis of transactions goes by the handle OLAP (Online Analytical Processing). OLAP packages are, in effect, applications database software and normally run on systems such as Oracle, DB2, Sybase, Informix, SQL Server, and the like.

Client/Server Type 1: The PC Terminal

Despite the appeal of distributed processing, there is still a need for fairly simple structures. As a result, a fast-growing option in client/server systems is for the client to be only a sophisticated terminal. Unlike a regular terminal, this version of *thin client* provides the user interface (almost always Windows) as well as management of communications. The client appears to be a PC because the part of the OS that handles the presentation of information on the screen executes locally. But it is terminal-like in that the OS boots from the server and application programs run there as well.

The most popular version of the PC as terminal comes from a company called Citrix. Originally known as WinFrame, and now going under a number of names, Citrix's software takes the very creative approach of trapping Windows GDI calls on the server, putting them in communications packets, and sending them out to the terminal. If you'll recall, the GDI is a layer in Windows that translates between an application's graphics calls and the instruction set of the display adapter. What WinFrame does is simply extend this model to a remote rather than a local display. Of course, it's not as easy as all that, but Citrix has quickly taken the software from concept to execution. So fast, in fact, that Microsoft has licensed the server-side software and incorporated it into Windows NT/2000. This gives Redmond a big slice of what could be a very important product in the corporate market. The WinFrame client can run on lots of different platforms, including the Mac. Reasonably speaking, though, it will be used almost entirely on Intel systems—low-end Pentium boxes and up.

THE X-WINDOW SYSTEM

X-Windows refers to a system funded by major computer vendors and developed at MIT that allows one computer to have a window that displays an application running on another computer. X-Windows includes a windowing manager and a system that facilitates client/server communication. It was developed for Unix, and finds almost all its use on this OS, but is also available for other OSs. In order to confuse ordinary people, MIT has reversed the standard terminology in describing X-Windows: the machine with the window is called the server and the one running the application is the client. X-Windows technology was important in the development of distributed computing, but other than this historical role, its current significance is that it is the way in which most Unix servers support clients.

Client/Server Type 2: The Network Computer (NC)

An alternative thin client approach is to not run a true OS at all, but instead to have a microkernel, written for the specific hardware, that boots locally and then invokes Internet browser-type software from the server. The browser in turn provides the interface from which the user runs application programs on the server. This package, known as a Net PC, will typically have somewhat more in the way of CPU and memory than the Windows terminal, but there is still no local hard disk, or if there is, it is used only for cache.

In the most advanced version of the NC approach, the client and the server will use object-based software, written in Java, that will allow the two to share processing tasks dynamically. For example, a database query will trigger a front-end program that resides on the server. The server will download part of the program, in the form of Java applets (or perhaps Active X controls), for execution on the client. But the server will reserve other parts for itself. As an example, the client might be asked to run a program that issues prompts and commands for a database query, but the server would contain and manage information specific to the database, such as the names and types of the data components.

Why bother with an NC instead of the simpler terminal or more complex full PC? The value when compared to the terminal is that, for only a little greater investment, the client can do some real work that relieves pressure on the server. Powerful CPUs, ones that function at levels comparable to workstations of just a few years ago, are extremely cheap. Getting the same computational abilities—equivalent to the sum of all the NCs—on the server will be quite a bit more expensive. Boosting CPU power on the server side quickly runs into problems of scalability. Remember that as multiple CPU systems pass four or so processors, contention for access to memory and I/O requires very expensive hardware designs and much more elaborate (and likely buggier) software. Also, putting ever more of the activity on the server side can put additional stress on LAN bandwidth.

When compared to the full PC client, the NC has the advantage of not wasting money on hard disks or complex client OSs. In many cases, it is actually desirable for the client not to store or manage important information itself. Security is one reason for keeping the client ignorant, but a more important reason is the integrity of distributed systems. In most data systems there is constant updating not only of the data itself, but of the "business logic" that governs their use. Airlines provide a good example. The core database, of course, is constantly changing—the number of flights, the seats available, and so forth. If you have a big database like this, one that is constantly used by a large number of simultaneous users, you need to put it on a central mainframe (or very powerful server cluster) and provide fast, secure, redundant communications links.

But it isn't just the data that changes. Airlines are constantly revising the pricing and other policies that govern use of their databases. For example, on sunny Tuesdays, flights connecting to port cities may sell half of their seats to woman veterans at a discount of 43.7 percent, etc. These are the system's "business rules" (come to think of it, business *logic* doesn't fit here). If the business rules were enforced on the client, the system would have to have a way to download all of the changes to all of the clients (Sabre, the pioneering airline reservation system founded by American Airlines, has about 200,000) all at the same time (e.g., right after the official Tuesday weather forecast). This situation has considerable potential for disaster—what if some of these likely far-flung clients aren't updated on time or at all? You would then have a potentially disastrous inconsistency in fares. Of course, that wouldn't work because people would rebel if they found out that others were paying less than they had for exactly the same thing (the more I think about it, the airline example isn't a good one). Keeping the business rules on a fairly small set of servers is more manageable, even if they are physically distributed.

The NC Morphs into the Information Appliance ▪ The network computer represents an interesting direction in computer development. The first approaches to the idea, coming in the mid- to late 1990s, were advanced by vendors like IBM and Oracle, who wished to challenge Microsoft and Intel's dominance of the desktop market. IBM, for example, wanted a situation in which, if the PowerPC could run a program faster than a Pentium, then the better chip would win. Many people came to believe that with these tools at hand, a new vision of computing, with the potential for dramatic developments in both hardware and software, could emerge. Early iterations were not successful for a variety of reasons: 1) the advent of the sub-$1,000 desktop computer put prices into a dramatic fall, cutting the potential margins on NCs sharply; 2) the software wasn't mature, and in some cases, was proprietary; 3) standard CPU/memory configurations were inadequate; and 4) network connections were too slow.

There are now some important changes. First, of course, is the Web and the standardization it brings to software. Second, the inexorable march of Moore's Law has made it possible to have an enormous amount of computing power and memory for a very small price. Finally, there is the advent of Java as a flexible but powerful programming tool. Java's "write once run everywhere" potential means that the same software can work on many completely different types of computers.

Let's consider the operation of the NC as currently deployed. A client computer, using any of a wide range of CPUs, boots up by loading a minimal OS. The kernel of this OS includes a Java Virtual Machine in addition to basic LAN and TCP/IP communications elements. The OS loads in part from local ROM (no hard disks, please!) and then from the network. The kernel and Java Virtual Machine are the only pieces of software that have to be written specifically for that CPU. Once loaded, the OS can invoke an Internet browser or other OS-like software. Java applications and applets are then downloaded as needed from the local server. The Java applications represent a new category of software because developers can write one program that will work with any CPU for which there is a Java Virtual Machine. This includes, at the same time, the new category of NCs and the entire stock of browser-equipped Windows PCs. There is also a potential bonanza for hardware vendors. Because they only have to worry about one layer of software compatibility (the slimmed down OS), they can begin to compete in a straightforward way on price and performance rather than on how closely their design conforms to the Intel legacy. In such a market, companies that are now mere cloners could become real leaders.

The initial NC effort was led by three companies whose credentials as archenemies of Microsoft are well known: IBM, Sun, and Oracle. IBM saw the NC as a way to return to something very much like the terminal-host environment that it once dominated. The company could again sell an entire two- or three-tier package and would not have to worry about the machinations of Microsoft or Intel. Sun's enthusiasm was based on its link to Java, and its belief that it would be a leading developer of both hardware and software products for the NC market; it too could sell a complete multi-tier package. Sun's Java OS is the first of the JVM-oriented OSs for Network Computers. The benefits to Oracle were initially less clear. The database giant, which has offered its own browser for some time, could expect to extend its reach into the business world with an NC environment. It even took some tentative steps toward getting into the hardware market. But Oracle, like the others, has seen the potential for the NC as extending far beyond the office environment.

While the NC idea was initially pitched to the medium to large business space, most advocates now see a second principal market for the NC as the primary Internet access point for schools and homes. And since the initial NC push failed, the computing industry has again displayed its Orwellian approach to language—the term *network computer* has been replaced by *information appliance* (sometimes *Internet appliance*).

The NC/Information Appliance idea still has a way to go before the vision is realized. NC/IAs will not only have to compete with Windows PCs on the pricey side, but the low end could get much more competitive if Microsoft introduces Windows CE-based terminals that are cheap, efficient, and have functions similar to the NC/IA. The NC cannot be assumed to have a secure market niche. Another barrier to the NC/IA, at least in the short term, is what one could call the "misconvergence" scenario. The capabilities of computer hardware systems are advancing at a ferocious rate, and for the most part, these advances are getting out into the business and consumer worlds with very little delay. Telecommunications is another story. There are very rapid advances in the effective speed of backbone and regional networks, but the "last mile problem," the lack of capacity in the link to homes, schools, and small businesses, is still a major concern. Improvement will occur, but not evenly, and in many cases, not soon. Absent significant improvements in the efficiency of software relationships, the "last mile" bottleneck will make NC/IAs appear slower, and therefore less desirable, than machines that store the OS and applications locally.

Client/Server Type 3: The Network PC (NetPC)

The third approach to the client in client/server is a full-powered PC, with normal (though perhaps not state-of-the-art) CPU and memory, but no hard drive (or, again, only for cache). You can think of this as the not-thin-and-not-fat-but-just-signed-with-Jenny-Craig client. The idea here is that the client needs to have the power to do a lot of work, but should be protected from users messing around with it. To accommodate this market, vendors are selling PCs with sealed cases; they're pretty much like a normal PC except that you can't open the case to add boards. They may or may not have a hard drive. This sounds pretty dumb, doesn't it? Why would someone buy a computer, very likely at a premium, that differs from other machines principally in that it *isn't* flexible? The answer is that many businesses have been frustrated by "improvements" that their employees make to networked PCs. Instead of hanging around the water cooler as in the good old days, the guys and gals add programs that the IS people don't support, they bring in viruses, they modify system settings, and so on.

Moreover, studies show that few computers are actually upgraded (they are passed on to lesser ranking employees who do most of the work, while the newer machines sit as trophies on the desks of perpetually-golfing executives). There is ample evidence that the changes introduced by users cost a lot of money in extra support and, according to the experts, support is more expensive than the machines themselves. A consulting firm, the Gartner Group, was the first to advance the concept of Total Cost of Ownership (TCO) and to show that it is many times greater than the cost of the hardware. So the idea is that a locked box is actually cheaper than one you can upgrade. Once you understand the many reasons for this approach, you will very likely feel, like me, that it's still stupid. I wonder if these same companies insist that their employees only take cabs when they travel, no matter how expensive, because if they rented a car, they might drive in the wrong direction?

NAKED SOLITAIRE

The Total Cost of Ownership analysts may have a point when they factor in the time wasted by PC users. You don't need a study to know that, from earliest days, a lot of microcomputer users have spent a lot of office time playing games on their machines (studies have been done anyway). In addition, the explosive popularity of the Web has made it possible for people to sit at their desks and view pictures of naked people. It seems that quite a few people prefer watching these images to reviewing insurance claims or whatever. The official plan is that the Network Computer will eliminate all this silliness because you can't run programs locally. For sure, servers won't include games. But how will they block access to stuff on the Internet? Expect to see studies documenting how much time workers waste finding ways to evade the software controls managers place on their systems.

We have noted that the three client approaches we have just described are often called *thin clients.* There is also, of course, the *fat client,* which is just like a normal

Table 13.1 **Client/Server Approaches.** These are the general categories as of early 2000. Note, however, that there is considerable potential for flexibility.

Client/Server Approaches

	Local CPU power	Local RAM	Local storage	Operating system	Price (w/out monitor & w/OS)
Thin Clients					
PC Terminal	Minimal/Intel and others	Minimal	None	Boots from network and gets Windows terminal software and apps from there; can also use local OS	~$300–500
Network Computer/Information Appliance	Moderate/Intel and others	Moderate to high	None (or used only as cache)	Loads microkernel, then boots from network to get rest of OS, browser and Java-based apps	~$300–500
Network PC	High/Intel	High	None (or used only as cache)	Regular OS and browser, but boot from network	~$500–800
Fat Client					
Regular PC	Very high/Intel	High	Yes	Regular OS and browser	~$800–2,000

PC except that it does its work in a client/server environment (like most business PCs). Table 13.1 is a summary of what does what; remember, though, that these are illustrative. There a lot of possible variations within and across these categories.

CLIENT/SERVER DATA SYSTEMS . . . .

There is a tremendous and constantly changing variety of client/server data systems. We'll illustrate the possibilities with two examples—the data warehouse and computer telephony integration.

Data Warehouses

The concept of a *data warehouse* is usually attributed to IBM. The idea is that information from all of a company's operations are aggregated into a single central database that can be used for decision support. The data warehouse doesn't replace the other databases; rather, it is a replica of portions of them, organized to create reports that span some defined period of time. An example would be a company with a series of transactional databases that are constantly working hard selling airline tickets or whatever. At least daily, perhaps more often, managers want to know what's selling and what's not. It would be very inefficient, perhaps dangerously so, to run queries against these transactional databases. Instead, at regular intervals their data is copied over to the data warehouse. Queries run against the warehouse don't provide up-to-the-minute data, but they don't need to. The purpose is to understand trends, not sell seats. Figure 13.1 illustrates a data warehouse.

The extra dimension of a data warehouse comes into play when the managers want to make changes as a result of their analyses. Airlines have lots of other databases—plane and crew scheduling, gate availability, fuel and maintenance, and so forth. If these are also integrated into the data warehouse (via regular copying), it will be possible for the managers to do dynamic "what if" scenarios about changes to routes or crew scheduling. Once decisions have been made in this comparatively secure environment, changes can be made to the main business system.

Computer Telephony Integration

There are two general ways in which systems developers are planning to integrate telephones and computers. The first is to combine the PC and the telephone on the desktop. In this scenario, your network connection would handle voice as well as data, and the PC would be able to assume the functions of a very sophisticated an-

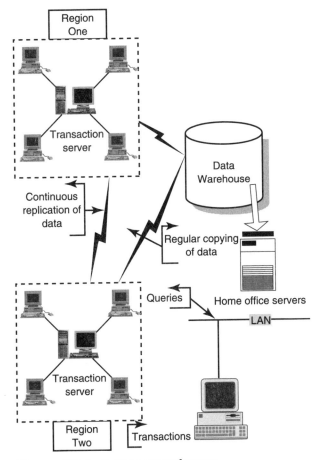

Figure 13.1 A data warehouse.

swering machine. On the server side, things would be simplified because one machine (or cluster of machines) would be both network server and office telephone switching system (private branch exchange, or PBX).

This approach has a lot of promise, but is not yet widely used. The major barrier is that LAN technology doesn't handle voice well. Neither Ethernet nor Token Ring networks, which comprise all but a small percentage of LANs, can handle time-dependent communications. While packets that get there when they feel like it are OK for normal data connections, they make telephone conversations jerky and awkward. There is some progress in improving existing protocols; for example, there is a form of Ethernet (called *isochronous* Ethernet) that is designed to prevent latency, but the real transition to combined voice/data LANs will have to wait for improved LAN switching or for ATM to be cheap enough for the desktop (some standards work needs to be done as well). So expect to wait a few years to see this technology widely available and, more important, widely adopted. One the other hand, it could be cheaper and more effective to keep the two separate, especially if ATM fails in its move to the LAN.

The second kind of telephone/computer integration is connecting phones to databases. Given its tremendous business potential, this still immature technology is quite popular with small, medium, and large companies. A major reason for progress is the availability of the TAPI (Telephony API) protocol for Windows NT/2000. TAPI defines a set of APIs that programmers can use to connect digital telephones and telephone systems (PBXs) to network servers. For some time now, there has been a similar protocol (TSAPI) for Unix systems, but it has suffered from the usual Unix problems; it isn't really standard and many smaller businesses are reluctant to undertake the software maintenance associated with Unix—they don't want to have to hire one of those weirdo "wizards" to make it all work. By contrast, Windows NT/2000 is perceived to be much simpler because it has the familiar Windows interface.

To illustrate what telephone/computer database integration can mean to a small operation, we'll give you three examples, one *before* and two *afters*.

Before

Mrs. Jones calls RX Pharmacy to see if her prescription has been filled and is ready to pick up. After a few rings, the phone is answered by a clerk or the pharmacist. Mrs. Jones asks her question and the employee goes to look through the stack of filled prescriptions, then returns to the phone to say, "Yes, it's ready," or "No, it isn't." A very inefficient process no matter how you look at it.

Automated Option 1

Mrs. Jones gave her home phone number when she left the prescription and was told that if she called from that number, she could get an immediate response about her prescription's status. When she calls, the digital telephone uses caller ID to associate the number with a name—this is usually accomplished by the telephone device, but for a large business, an attached computer would have to do it. This takes just a few seconds and is done when the phone is picked up. A prerecorded voice says, "Good evening, Mrs. Jones. We're checking on the status of your prescription." The pharmacist earlier gave the prescription a number and entered it in the computer (something that all modern pharmacies have to do, in any case) and the computer printed a bar code to attach to the label; when it was filled, the pharmacist simply passed the package by a scanner and the computer knew it was filled (the computer could also know exactly what the prescription was and how much it cost). After, at most, a second or two, Mrs. Jones is told by the recorded voice that the prescription is ready and can be picked up at any time. It might also offer an option for her to listen to a description of precautions associated with the medication. Computer assistance of this kind is simple, effective, and efficient; it will make it much easier for businesses to keep staffing levels low and/or provide better personal customer service when needed.

Automated Option 2

In this approach, the pharmacy (or any business) is more interested in selling additional stuff to the customer than in saving staff time, so a real person answers the phone and looks at the computer terminal to find the status of the prescription. While this is going on, the local computer is querying a remote system, a data warehouse that includes information from all of the chain's pharmacies in the city, the region, and perhaps the nation. The query from the local computer takes information about Mrs. Jones and asks the data warehouse for information about preferences, recent purchases, and so forth. This information is also flashed on the screen so that the real person talking to the customer can say something like, "By the way, Mrs. Jones, I see that you've tried just about every weight loss formula ever made—presumably with no success. You might want to know that we carry some new products that are even more expensive than the old ones. Can I add some to your package?"

Businesses believe that this kind of selling, because it connects to an individual customers' preferences, can be very effective. Of course, our pharmacy could use both—Option 1 when they were busy and Option 2 when they weren't. Needless to say, there are a lot of variations that will be used—perhaps including employee training.

While most people don't like automated voices and telephone systems that present them with a baffling series of requests to push different numbers, reasonable people appreciate that it saves a lot of time. Think about the old days of calling an airline to find out if a flight was on time. In effect, you're waiting for someone to punch a few keys on a computer terminal and tell you what it says. If you can cut out the middleman, everyone will be happier (including the clerks, who would almost certainly prefer other employment).

DISTRIBUTED DATA VS.
DISTRIBUTED PROCESSING . . . .

The examples we have shown so far are mostly of distributed processing rather than distributed data. The data in these examples (e.g., information on flights and seats available) sits in one place and is accessed by many users simultaneously. You can well imagine that having one single repository of data with a huge number of concurrent users, but also strict limits on access, is very difficult to do. IBM, which developed the first airline reservation system, Sabre, for American Airlines, would agree, and expects to be well-compensated for its hardware, software, and organizational expertise. Of course, the Sabre system, which is as complex as anything around, isn't just one machine—there are local and remote backup sites with machines in "failover" mode (if the primary machine fails, they automatically take over).

One very expensive aspect of centralized data systems is that they have to have very complex, very high-capacity communications links. Actually, they have to have at least two of them for redundancy, since construction crews and others who like to dig have a tendency to cut even deeply buried cables. Couldn't you simplify this situation by distributing the data as well as the processing? The answer is yes, depending on what kind of data you have. If, like the airlines, you have a database with multiple seekers of a unique item, you have to have a single data source or else you could sell the same thing twice (aargh! the airline example fails *again!*).

A TRAVELING SALESMAN JOKE

There was this traveling salesman, and he had only one laptop. One day. . . . Sorry, no prurience here. The point of this sidebar is cautionary. Having owned a lot of laptops, I can tell you that I would want at least one backup all the time if my job depended on it. To say they are fragile is an understatement. Of the seven or so I've had, every one has had some kind of major mechanical problem.

A feasible sort of database for distributed data would be one in which you have multiple copies of an item being sought, and while you don't expect to run out of it, you want to keep a pretty tight grip on demand and supply so you can reorder when needed. In the case of a tool salesman traveling with his laptop to hardware stores, you would have a local database on the hard drive showing inventory. As you went to make a sale, you would link to a network and log the sale to the regional database. It would then download any changes to inventory that had occurred since you last connected (and perhaps also some sales advisory information, including new pricing). The regional database would give you the national picture, but because it would only connect to the national system every hour or so, it would not necessarily be valid as of the moment you got it. Instead of real-time validity, the regional database in this system would be updated upward (information about new sales) and downward (revised inventory) at regular intervals, rather than continuously.

The process of moving data records to synchronize disparate databases is called *replication*. Replication will work well in our hardware sales example. It's going to be very unusual that the salesman will mislead the customer about supply. In return

Groupware: Lotus Notes and Others

When LANs first appeared, users were thrilled by the ability to share files directly—no more having to circulate diskettes or (worse) printed documents for comment, revision, etc. The thrill faded, though, as people discovered the horrendous difficulty of keeping information on the LAN organized in anything like a coherent way. Lotus Notes was the first answer to this problem. Notes is essentially a database program that works with documents rather than records. People working on a project or task can create a Notes database that allows them to (among other things) track revisions, maintain security, and develop an indexing system for quick retrieval. Document movement is facilitated by integration of the program with e-mail (this explains why Notes and similar programs are often styled as "workflow" software). Notes' power is enhanced by the fact that it is programmable—groups can customize their databases, electronic forms can be created for online circulation, and so on. Notes sold quite poorly for a while because a) Lotus couldn't really explain what the software did, and b) they charged a huge amount of money per seat, anyway. IBM has improved Notes' marketing; indeed, Notes was the major reason that IBM bought Lotus. The product has also been greatly refined and, of course, integrated into IBM mainframe environments. Direct competitors have been kept at bay, but that doesn't mean that Lotus has the market to itself. Instead, the opposition is executing a flanking move, developing applications that do the same thing except that they are based on Internet browsers rather than on an equivalent of Notes' proprietary client software.

Web Integration

The Web has changed much of the logic behind programs like Notes. One of the purposes of the original family of groupware programs was to provide a common, seamless interface to documents used over the network. This, by definition, is what a Web browser does. Extending the browser concept to the browser as the center for collaborative document management is not a huge step. The two major suite vendors, Microsoft and Corel, are pursuing this, as is Lotus, which has done a good job of integrating Notes with the Web (Lotus Domino). Netscape has pretensions in this area as well. Despite all the activity, most desktop users still see an electronic Tower of Babel when they try to do anything complicated. There is a great deal of work yet to be done before people can sit down to a simple, easy-to-use interface and work naturally with material scattered over local and wide area networks.

Agent Software

One really exciting application that is appearing in the wake of the Internet's dominance is agent software. The idea here is simple. Let's say you want to take a winter vacation to the Caribbean, but are having a hard time sorting out the options and prices. You program a piece of software on your local machine with an array of variables—length of trip, which time period (perhaps specifying weekends and excluding certain days), which class of hotel, departure airport, total price range, and likely a lot more factors. The original idea was that you would then launch the agent on to the Internet with instructions to attach itself to the servers of a certain group of travel agents whose ads you like (at some point in the future, there may be a travel agent "class" on the Web so that you won't have to select any single company or companies—the agent will recognize them by their class IDs). The agent would then multiply and sit on the servers, like remoras on a shark, monitoring travel packages as they appear. You could program the agents to send reports at regular intervals or to send urgent e-mail if something really close to your specifications appeared. The big problem with this scenario, of course, is security. An agent (sometimes called a *bot,* which is short for *software robot*) that could monitor a server could likely crash it. Or, diabolically altered by some rogue out there in the galaxy, they could come back and crash *your* machine.

There are two more secure alternatives to this approach. One is simply to have the agent stay on your local desktop or server, and then query the travel servers on a regular basis. Another, and the one that is becoming the most common, is that you simply register with one or more brokers who do the checking for you. They have secure arrangements with the various service providers. Both of these approaches have some tradeoffs—leaving the query software on your machine will likely make for slower updates, and the brokers may not survey providers they don't like (I'll bet you can think of reasons for this). Expect many innovations in this extremely important approach to dealing with distributed data.

CONCLUSION ·

Computing has evolved from the highly centralized early days of the terminal-host system to today's client/server environment. Though the term is widely used without qualification, *client/server* can mean a lot of different things. In the original version, the client-file server approach, the server has little intelligence (processing power, memory, storage); it's just a data repository. This model, however, has in turn given way to approaches in which the server and the client are both intelligent and share in the execution of tasks. There are many ways to distribute intelligence, however, and it is likely that an array of different strategies will coexist for some time to come. Interestingly, the most radical and most promising change is one that most resembles the original terminal-host world; the use of the Network Computer (also known as the Information Appliance) is a strategy that gives the client some intelligence but recognizes that both application programs and the information they act on will come from somewhere on a network.

The advent of pervasive computing has progressed from rearranging the pieces in the network to changing the way people think about data and applications. Client/server approaches support new structures like the data warehouse and new connections such as computer telephony integration. As new concepts like these develop, it's tempting for systems managers to distribute data as well as processing. Moving data from the center to the periphery of the network presents new challenges, however, and there is increasing attention to the problem of how software objects can work together across network connections. Finally, pervasive computing is spawning a whole new class of software—e-mail, groupware, agent or *bot* software—that didn't exist before. While most observers now agree that the client/server environment is responsible for a large part of the increased productivity that has fueled the economic growth that began in the mid-1990s, there is also broad agreement that much remains to be done before users really have the much-predicted "seamless" access to information.

As with other elements of computing, there is no reason to believe that the current ideas about networks and systems will hold for long. In the short term, the big issue is likely to be where to keep the information and applications. Most theories say that as much as possible should be kept on the network; thus, users will always get what is most current and will only be charged for what they need. The incredible surges in the capacity of fiber optics, resulting in bandwidth that some say will be "too cheap to meter," lends credence to this approach. Unfortunately, the "last mile" problem still presents a barrier to high speed access for home and small business users. Since a new age of electronic commerce depends on easy, high-speed access to consumers, meeting this challenge will likely be the source of a disproportionate level of technology development and investment. We turn next to the current state of the Internet and to the major challenge to e-commerce, network security.

TEST YOUR UNDERSTANDING . . . .

1. What is the difference between a terminal-host system and a client-file server system?

2. How does client/server differ from client-file server?

3. What are the advantages and disadvantages of the different types of client/server computing?

4. How have developments in the traditional desktop PC challenged the economic assumptions of the *network computer?*

5. Why is network bandwidth a problem for systems that use the *network computer* (or *information appliance*)?

6. Why create a separate data warehouse when it is possible to query transactional systems directly?

7. What are some dangers of distributed data?

8. What are some key issues in the movement toward distributed objects?

9. Assuming that high bandwidth access to the Internet is available and inexpensive, what are some ideas for networked applications that might be implemented in the future?

14 The Internet and Network Security

The Internet is driving today's economy and even its culture. This chapter will take a brief look at its origins, then proceed to describe how the Internet functions by tracing the flow of data out of a desktop computer and up through the various levels to the high-speed backbone and switching centers at its core. This chapter also describes the Internet's economic model and characterizes the tools that are being used to make it the world's principal venue for commercial activity. The final section takes a look at the critical issue of network security—if the Internet is really to be used for the bulk of business transactions, how can we be sure that these exchanges are secure?

By the end of this chapter you should understand

- How the Internet was started and why it was successful
- Why the Internet's economic model is so different from that of other networks
- What the operating levels of the Internet are and what they do
- The principal elements of data security, including encryption, digital signatures, and related concepts

ORIGINS OF THE INTERNET ......

An extended description of the history and operation of the Internet would take more space than is available. If you've read this far, you know the general technological principles. This section aims only to describe those elements of the Internet that are unique or unusual by comparison to basic network operations.

From DARPA to ARPA

The Internet was created by the Defense Advanced Research Projects Agency (DARPA) all the way back in 1969. It was the first implementation of a packet-switched network, and DARPA funded it both for basic research purposes and as a way of connecting universities and government laboratories that were doing other work it was paying for. The connection to universities was important because the presence of the network on campus got a lot of bright young people involved in network R&D. You will recall that it was a team at Berkeley that integrated the Internet's TCP/IP protocol into Unix, thus creating an extraordinarily productive relationship. Though DARPA continued to provide funding for many years, a great deal of the development of the Internet was provided free by creative university faculty and students at such places as Stanford, Berkeley, MIT, and Carnegie Mellon. Later, most of the major research universities in the U.S. were involved in one way or another in extending and/or scaling the Internet.

Early Uses

The Internet grew as it did because TCP/IP was cheap and effective, and because it integrated smoothly with Unix. The latter point is important—every Unix machine, off-the-shelf, could function as a router. So when a college or university wanted to connect to the Internet, all it had to do was run a line (i.e., a leased analog telephone line or maybe just a dial-up connection) to the nearest Internet-backbone connected university or institution. Of course the backbone-connected institution had to agree, but acquiescence wasn't hard to get. Part of the reason is the culture of universities in general and scientists in particular; cooperative work and resource sharing are a part of their way of life (and nationalism isn't—the Internet swiftly expanded to include universities and laboratories around the world). Another reason is that costs to the backbone-connected institution weren't high, at least not in those early days. The feds were paying for the backbone, so there weren't additional costs there. Nor were local costs a big deal in the earliest days. A server functioning as a router and linking another server to the Internet typically did only some simple stuff like forwarding e-mail and brokering occasional file transfers and remote terminal connections. For these chores, it only required adding a little bit of memory for the server's owners to not know the difference.

Internet Scale-up

So most of the cost of expanding the Internet went to those who were joining. This led to an interesting dynamic. If the original interest in the Internet came from the physics department at Solid State U, it would be their budget that would bear the entire cost of the line to the connected institution. Obviously, it was in the interests of the physicists to find some other departments that wanted to connect as well. That way, costs could be shared. So the electrical engineers and the computer scientists signed up. Soon, everybody wanted a faster line. One way to do that was to get their friends at the state college down the line to join them. The state college folks were asked to pay for their line to Solid State *and* a share of the cost of Solid State's line to the institution that was in turn connected to the Internet backbone. Solid State thus became an Internet Service Provider. Internet growth was facilitated as informal arrangements grew into formal consortia; for example, Solid State and its partners could form an organization and share the costs of getting their own direct backbone connection. The National Science Foundation (NSF) accelerated all this with programs that provided grants to connect smaller colleges and universities.

The Internet scaled well both politically and technically. As traffic increased, the software architecture allowed vendors to design special purpose computers that did nothing but handle the movement of packets. These machines, which became what we now call routers, relieved the local servers of network responsibilities. Because routers could deal with multiple alternate paths through the network, Internet users could build multiple links to the backbone, so Solid State would lease a second line and connect to the backbone through a different point. This made it possible to balance the traffic load (e.g., splitting eastbound and westbound flows) and also provided for redundancy in case there were problems with lines or routers. Routing did become more complex, as we've discussed earlier, but problems were dealt with by standards organizations (IETF) in which key vendors like Cisco (developers of the first routers) were active participants.

Tech Talk

IETF: The Internet Engineering Task Force (IETF) is responsible for setting many Internet-related standards, for example, the new version of the Internet Protocol, IPv6.

The NSF, which took over management of the backbone from the Department of Defense, over time spun it off to the long-distance carriers from whom the lines were leased. The Internet backbone today is provided predominantly by WorldCom (including the former UUnet, CompuServe, and Sprint networks), GTE, and Cable and Wireless (most of the former MCI system).

The Internet was principally a higher education/federal government service until the late 1980s. Large corporations at that time used private networks, based usually on IBM or DEC software, that provided e-mail and remote terminal connections. There was a growing cadre of individuals and small organizations that used proprietary carriers like CompuServe and America OnLine (AOL) for e-mail and information services. The explosion of the installed base of PCs and LANs drove increased demand for wide area connectivity. Services like CompuServe, which had per-minute connect time charges that could quickly add up to big dollars, were too expensive for most organizations. The Internet, on the other hand, was essentially free. We need a short digression to explain why this is so.

The Internet vs. Proprietary Networks

Proprietary networks like those pioneered by CompuServe (now a division of AOL) were built on a star topology. Before its remaking as an Internet Service Provider (ISP), CompuServe's only computers were in Columbus, Ohio. The company provided national access by leasing long-distance lines that connected Columbus with local telephone company exchanges. At each exchange, CompuServe had dedicated local telephone numbers that connected to these leased lines. In effect, this was a private long-distance telephone system. There are economies of scale in this—CompuServe offered connections that were cheaper to the user than either of the other options: a long-distance call billed directly to the customer or access via a toll-free number. Also, national usage was more attractive since CompuServe averaged the network costs. This meant that a user in Los Angeles paid the same amount for connect time as one in Columbus. In any case, though, there were long-distance charges and they had to be billed back to the user. In addition, CompuServe had to size its computers proportionally (we're talking mainframes here) to accommodate simultaneous users and information stored on its disk drives. Then there was the cost of billing and administration. Finally, of course, they had to add profit. Add this up and the user had to pay for every minute of connection time.

The Internet is very different. First, there is no center, no equivalent of CompuServe's Columbus headquarters. Among other things, this means there is no central point that can handle billing. Indeed, as you think about how the Internet is organized, you will understand that it would take a total reorganization and consolidation to have any centralized, distance-based billing. Instead, we have flat-rate access costs that are charged at the network periphery by the Internet Service Provider (ISP). Originally, these were just the costs of the physical connection, including a line or lines and a router. However, as traffic increased and NSF got out of the backbone business, there was also a need for some kind of charge-back process. As the backbone moved from T-1 to T-3 to OC-3 and up, and as more and more powerful routers were needed, someone had to pay for it. The result has been a cascading economic model. Those connected directly to the backbone are charged for access by the backbone provider. They then charge those who connect through them, and so on. So, as Solid State had to pay more to MCI, it increased the charges both to its departments and to the universities and other organizations that used Solid State as their access point. This was OK for everyone because, although they were paying more, they were also using the network more.

Tech Talk

ISP: An Internet Service Provider (ISP) provides the link from a residence or business to the regional or backbone levels of the Internet. ISPs range from small mom-and-pop operations to giant companies like AT&T.

Organization

The Internet has no definable physical topology. Indeed, no one knows how many servers, let alone how many nodes, are connected and active at any given time. As noted, the Internet was managed for a time by DARPA, and later by the National Science Foundation. But "manage," in this context, is deceptive. Once the Internet expanded beyond the initial handful of nodes, there was no way to control its far-flung activities. Instead, DARPA, and later NSF, took responsibility for the backbone. Initially, this meant ensuring capacity and paying for it. Later, as growth made it all but impossible to distinguish NSF's part of the backbone from the amazing proliferation of other high-speed links, and as the ascent of commercial use made subsidization inappropriate, the Internet was left to its own devices. Two organizations have a role in keeping it going. One, the Internet Engineering Task Force, an international standards group, deals with advances in technology, most importantly, addressing and routing. Another, Network Solutions, Inc., was initially responsible for the allocation of domain names (this function has since been privatized). Various academic groups, working with NSF and other government agencies, are actively developing the next-generation Internet, variously known as Internet2, and the NGI (Next Generation Internet). The basic idea behind Internet2 is to build a separate network, employing the same protocols but using very high speed lines and routers or switches.

Current Architecture

There is a standard architectural description of the Internet that uses four levels. This discussion approaches these from the bottom up, beginning with Level 4. We'll describe each level as a discrete entity, but remember that real-world companies span these categories in a variety of ways. Some companies, like WorldCom's Sprint subsidiary, exist at all four levels. Others, like some of the old telephone companies, span two or three of the levels. In fact, there has been considerable consolidation and this trend is likely to accelerate.

Level 4: Internet Service Providers • Level 4 is the Internet Service Provider, usually called the ISP. An ISP is the business that connects directly with the user. ISPs come in a variety of sizes, from a couple of teenagers with some gear in the garage to huge, multinational corporations. There are about 4,500 in the U.S. at the moment, with a typical size being about 3,000 subscribers. We'll focus on the small side for our example. Think of Pete's Texaco, Video Rental, and Internet Service and his 500 customers (there really are a lot of companies of this kind still out there). This typical small ISP will have a telephone number that its customers use. The customers' modems dial the ISP through the telephone network as if making a regular call. At the ISP's place of business, the call is answered by a modem. The modem is connected not to a computer, but to a router (remember that a router is a special kind of computer). The router's very straightforward job is to take the IP packets and, except for the rare case when they are directed to one of Pete's other customers, to put them on an outgoing line to the next layer of the Internet, Level 3, or the Regional Network (see Figure 14.1). The router doesn't have to be running a very sophisticated routing protocol, nor does it need a very fast CPU or a lot of memory.

Before we go on to Level 3, some notes about the ISP. Access doesn't have to be exclusively by regular phone line and modem. In some cases, the customer will have an ISDN or Frame Relay connection, or a leased line through the telephone network, to the ISP. Also, the ISP may make an arrangement with the phone company (or companies) so that a call from the customer to the ISP appears to the caller to be a free local call, even if the ISP is in a different telephone service area.

The ISP's office may also have a number of arrangements to handle incoming calls more effectively. It likely has set up a "hunt group" with the phone company. This simply means that a call to the main number, for example 481-3425, is automatically rolled over to the ISP's other lines if that number is busy. This way, the ISP can give out one number, but have a dozen or more actual connections to the telephone system. The ISP will also likely need a terminal server once the number of modems exceeds two or three. A terminal server is a device that connects an array of serial devices (modems in this case) to the router. The terminal server multiplexes the incoming lines into one high-speed connection. There are a variety of other electronic devices and software systems that an ISP will need as business grows. For example, there must be a way to manage billing and other business functions.

Level 3: Regional Networks • The connection from our small ISP at Level 4 to the Regional Network at Level 3 (see Figure 14.2) is almost certainly a leased line,

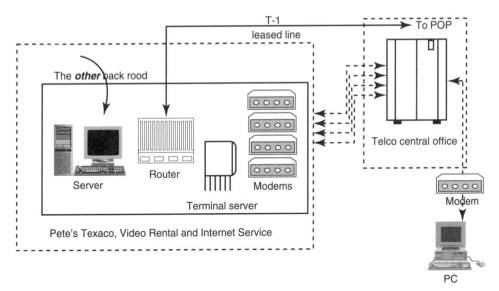

Figure 14.1 The Internet service provider level.

1. In the first stage of our packet's journey across the Internet, it gets sent from the user's modem to the ISP. The packet is sent under TCP/IP, but the protocol is not used for this leg. The link here is through the public switched telephone network (PSTN), which means that it is circuit-switched (and also that it is *slow*).

2. When the packet reaches the ISP, a modem answers the call and sends the packet to the terminal server, which interleaves it with packets coming in from other modems and sends it to the router. The server manages accounts, billing, etc.

3. Since Pete's ISP is at the bottom tier of the Internet, the router, which works only with TCP/IP, has a small, straightforward routing table. Packets coming in from the terminal server are almost always sent out to the regional network provider, which means that they are addressed for the router's T-1 port. For packets arriving from the Internet, the number of choices is equal to the direct subscribers to Pete's ISP. Thus, both incoming and outgoing addresses can be entered manually into the routing table; there is no need for dynamic routing.

probably one or more T-1s. T-3s are pretty much limited to the big boys. Let's digress (again) to talk about the size of this line. You'll recall that a T-1 equals 24 digital phone lines, so you would think that our ISP will need about 20 T-1s for his 500 customers. No way. First, all of them won't be using the net at the same time, and the first limiting factor is the number of lines and modems for incoming calls. If there are 48 modems for 500 customers (about the 1 to 10 ratio that is the ISP rule of thumb),

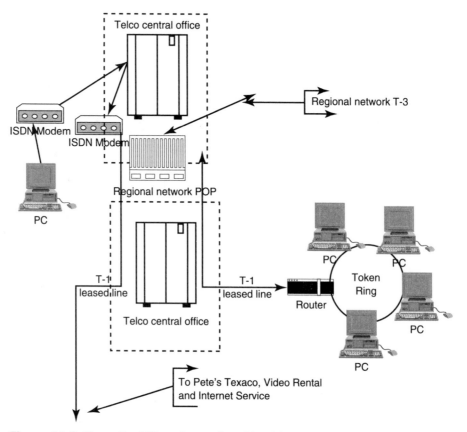

Figure 14.2 From the ISP to the regional backbone.

1. When our packet leaves Pete's place, it goes to the local telephone company central office on the T-1 he has leased. Unfortunately, since Pete's regional network provider doesn't have a point of presence (POP) at this office, Pete has to pay for the T-1 to continue from there to another, more distant central office which is co-located with a POP (or has one very close). Remember that the T-1 is a point-to-point circuit-switched link; it goes through the central office, but is not switched there. POPs are small, perhaps a corner of a switching office or maybe a small building nearby. One *sine qua non* of a POP is an independent, backup power supply, likely provided by a diesel generator.

2. At the POP, our packet is routed onto the regional network provider's T-3. The router here is heavy-duty in the sense that it handles a lot of packets. It has only one upstream connection (to the T-3), but there are multiple routes for downstream packets coming in from the Internet to the ISPs and businesses who are connected through this network. Still, there are a fixed number of destinations and paths in both directions, so static routing is adequate.

3. Note that the regional network provider has some customers who don't go through Level 4 ISPs like Pete. Shown here is a large business that has a T-1 from its LAN directly to the regional network's POP. Another example is a small business that has an ISDN connection through the local central office to the POP (which has ports for ISDN as well as T-1 lines).

then only two T-1s would be needed to accommodate all at once. In fact, even that would be too much. It's very unlikely that all 48 modems could saturate one outgoing T-1. The reason is that computer traffic is bursty and that the connection is packet-switched. If 48 connections are active, it's still probable that fewer than half are then actually sending or receiving packets at any particular second. And, even for that unusual fraction of a second when the circuit is oversubscribed, it's in the nature of packet-switching to just put the packets in buffers and wait until the capacity becomes available. As we've mentioned on a number of occasions, this waiting for a second or so can be a big problem for voice or video, but doesn't trouble normal data transfers like requesting Web pages or other data. Needless to say, ISPs have to think constantly about how to size their systems, especially about such key factors as how many incoming lines and modems, how much router processing power and memory, and how much bandwidth to the Regional Network are needed.

The Regional Network is owned by a good sized business or organization. No more amateurs. The Regional Network is a collection of leased lines and routers/switches (see Figure 14.3). On one end, they connect to ISPs; on the other they are attached, at one or more points, to the Internet Backbone. The Regional Network could be a telephone company, it could be one of the university consortia that developed in the NSF days, or it could be a specialized business. In any case, the lines are almost certainly leased—from one or more telephone companies, from one of the emerging nontelephone fiber optic bandwidth providers, or from some combination of both. The Regional Network doesn't actually use the switched part of the public telephone system, however. Instead, it exists as leased lines tied together with IP routers or (perhaps) ATM switches. The physical place at which an external entity like an ISP connects to this private network is known as a *POP* (for *point of presence*), a term that comes from telephone company jargon. In the telco world, a POP is the point where a local telephone system connects to a long-distance carrier.

Tech Talk

Point of Presence (POP): A *point of presence* (POP) is the location where one network touches another. The term is borrowed from telephone company jargon, in which a POP is the place where the local network connects to the long-distance system.

The Regional Network normally bills its customers (the ISPs) according to the speed (capacity) of their connections to it. Often, however, the simple size-of-the-pipe charge is modified by some traffic-based considerations. For example, a carrier may offer T-3 service, then sample the traffic at regular intervals (e.g., every 15 minutes). The average of these samples would then be the basis for the monthly charge. Fractional T-1 and T-3 connections are also offered, but remember that the available

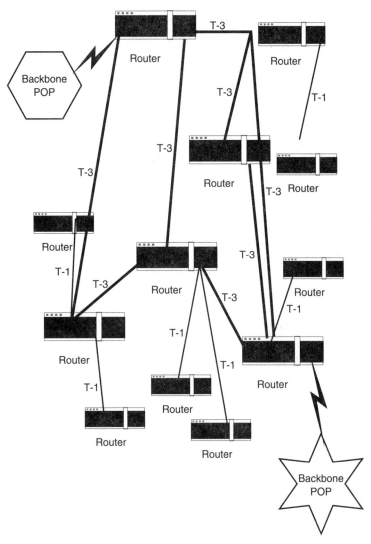

Figure 14.3 A regional Internet network provider.

1. The regional network is a collection of routers and high speed lines. It has its own backbone, comprising T-3s and a few T-1s as tributaries. Each router represents a city, with T-3s in the large ones and T-1s in smaller centers. Of course, there might be cities with more than one router.

2. In this example the backbone is meshed, but not fully meshed. This means that there are multiple connections, but that there isn't a direct path from every node to every other node.

3. A regional network provider probably leases the circuits from a telco (either a local or long-distance carrier, or both), but provides its own routers. More likely than not, the T-3s are not individual lines, but circuits on a SONET ring.

4. Our regional network has two connections to the Internet backbone, using two different providers. This allows for redundancy and load balancing.

5. At this level of the network, it is easy to see that there are many potential paths that our packet might take, and that the routers have to be able to both evaluate options very quickly and handle a heavy packet load. Thus, the routers use dynamic protocols based on continuous router-to-router communications.

bandwidth depends on the electronics. If the router at the network POP can't handle more than, for example, half of a T-3, it doesn't matter that the line itself will accommodate T-3. To get the higher bandwidth, you have to upgrade the electronics.

The table below shows the charges from Sprint to its customers as of 1997. You'll see that there are substantial discounts for volume, but that none of the connections are cheap. Note that these rates are for access to the network at one of Sprint's POPs. The cost of a line from the customer's place of business to the POP is additional. Connections could be directly from end users as well as from ISPs, since a company like Sprint is at once an ISP, a regional network provider, and a backbone carrier.

The Cost of Connecting to the Backbone

Size of pipe	Monthly
T-3	$20,620
12 Mbps (8xT-1; Fractional T-3)	$13,839
T-1	$2,216
128 Kbps (Fractional T-1)	$986

Source: Boardwatch Magazine *Web site.*

Routers in Regional Networks don't have the simple gateway responsibility that an ISP's routers have. At this level, thousands of user connections are aggregated. Traffic can go in a number of different directions, and the routers have to use the more sophisticated exterior protocols, such as Border Gateway Protocol, to manage links.

Regional Networks obviously need very fast connections to Level 2, the Internet Backbone. As the Internet has grown in size and complexity, it is common for these Level 3-to-Level 2 connections to exist at more than one point. The reasons for multiplicity, called *multihoming,* include redundancy in the event of outages as well as the ability to balance traffic—something that itself helps to prevent Internet outages or their increasingly common little brothers, "Internet brownouts."

Tech Talk

Multihoming: A network or computer that has two or more connections to the Internet or other wide area network is said to be *multihomed.*

Level 2: The Backbone • Internet Backbone providers are all large businesses. MCI, now part of WorldCom, is the long-time leader. Others are Sprint and GTE. A company like MCI/WorldCom is a full service provider; it owns not only switches and routers, but also the fiber that connects them. In other cases, companies own routers but lease fiber, or vice versa. The highest speed backbone links, which are typically ATM over SONET, have now reached 2.48 Gbps. They will quickly scale beyond that. Figure 14.4 illustrates a backbone.

Level 1: The Network Access Point • What could be higher than the backbone? Well, actually nothing, but remember that there is now more than one backbone provider. If packets are to cross from one to another of these super-capacity lines, they have to connect. This happens at Level One, Network Access Points (NAPs). These were initially set up on contract basis by NSF. The locations of the original four are San Francisco, Chicago, New York, and Washington, D.C. It's not that simple, of course. There were already other such connection points when NSF launched the NAPs, and these continue to exist. One example is the so-called MAEs, Metropolitan Area Ethernets. These are links provided by telephone companies or Competitive Access Providers (CAPs) to serve high-volume data needs for businesses. Backbone providers realized that these Ethernets would provide a cheap and easy way of exchanging traffic; instead of sending packets to Chicago, you could swap them right there in Houston. In the grand tradition of cutesy naming, these MAEs have handles like MAE West. In fact, most of the exchange of backbone data now occurs at private peering points, which are NAP-like, large-scale, high-speed interchanges. In addition, since Regional Networks often have links to two or more of the backbone networks, routes through these networks provide numerous *de facto* alternatives to the NAPs. When you put all the possibilities together, you will understand why routing at the backbone and regional levels is a daunting task.

Other Architectural Issues • Before we move on from Internet architecture, we need to mention two issues: *peering* and the idea of a Level 5. First, peering. Back when NSF ran the backbone, it was all one happy family and packets flowed without passports. Now, with businesses operating backbones for profit, the question of who pays for what becomes of acute importance to the bottom line. Backbone providers charge Regional Networks the same way the regionals charge ISPs—according to the speed of the connection. But this logic loses its value at the backbone level. If MCI and Sprint connect to each other at 622 Mbps at a NAP, do they exchange bills for the service? No. The obvious answer is to call it a wash; that's what peering means.

The problem comes when a littler guy wants to connect under the same rules. MCI and Sprint can reasonably wonder if they are really peers with the small fry. Probably not—the company with the greater capacity is likely giving something away to the one with less bandwidth. The idea that someone would refuse to peer is shock-

it can include commands for manipulation—for example, linking to a database. The hope is that with XML, those who want to do really complicated documents will be able to do so, but those who only want to publish basic information will not have a more complicated task than they now have with HTML. This is a logical approach. Together with revised versions of HTML proper, and such extensions as Dynamic HTML (see below), XML should allow a more responsive and flexible Web.

Tech Talk

XML: The eXtensible Markup Language (XML) offers the possibility of creating Web documents that are far more powerful and flexible than HTML. XML documents can provide specialized commands that ease the manipulation of data sets.

Tech Talk

DTD: XML uses a Data Type Definition (DTD) to allow one Web source to tell another how to read and work with specialized information.

HTML Compared to XML

The difference between these two seems subtle to most people, and to some extent it is, but the impact of implementing XML will be far from trivial.

Think of HTML as a fairly simple language that everyone has learned—in this case, *everyone* refers to Web browsing software. If you, as the originator of an HTML document, restrict yourself to the commands of that language, you know that the machine at the other end will be able to understand it. The problem is that HTML is simple. It doesn't, for example, describe how to manage a document that in turn connects to a database—a key function of e-commerce. How to solve this? One approach would be to replace HTML with a huge, complex language that could satisfy everyone's needs. This presents several problems, however. One is that the new language would cause the browser to use enormous amounts of storage and memory, making it difficult to deploy on the increasingly popular smaller devices. Second, no matter how big the vocabulary became, there would always be additions as systems evolved. Keeping everything up-to-date would be a tremendous challenge.

Essentially, what XML does is equip every browser with the ability to learn not so much a new language as a new dialect that is based on some general rules. The new dialect, which is communicated in the Document Type Definition (DTD) when a Web page is accessed, then becomes the basis for efficient, specialized communication. When the new dialect is no longer needed on the receiving computer, it can be dumped (or stored if it is required frequently). Java can do the same things as XML, but the consensus at the moment is that XML is more efficient for e-commerce kinds of applications.

Making the Web Go Faster

The accelerating popularity of the Web has resulted in cynical comments about the "world wide wait." Now that the Web is perceived to be the mechanism on which an entire new generation of entertainment and commercial activities will be built, speeding it up has become a major societal undertaking. The most important factor in a faster Web, of course, is faster communications links. At the top end of the Net, a continuing stream of improvements has allowed systems to stay up with, and in some cases move ahead of, the increasing traffic. Technologies such as ATM switches, ASIC-based routers, and dense and ultra-dense wave division multiplexing are driving enormous increases in backbone and regional network capacity. Cable modems, xDSL loops, and various wireless strategies offer the promise of better home and business access to this speedy network core. Unfortunately, most of these improvements are irrelevant to the average user with a 33.6 dial-up modem. For the vast majority of Web surfers, this will be the fastest they can go for at least the next few years. What can we do about making bits move faster over a slow line?

One way to speed things up, of course, is to improve compression so that less is actually transmitted. Web browsers have been pretty good at compression from the beginning, but more can be done. Currently, HTML graphics are usually in GIF (Graphics Image File) format, a bitmap structure that provides an excellent compression ratio. But, because the average computer now has processing power to spare, a move to vector images should occur quickly. These will not only be smaller and therefore faster to transmit, they will also allow for better quality at varying resolutions. Newer compression techniques, such as *wavelets,* will allow even better graphics in less time. There are some significant barriers here, though. Since wavelets are very computationally-intensive even for decompressing, better algorithms and faster hardware will be important.

Tech Talk

Wavelets: A very powerful approach to compressing graphical images uses a technique called *wavelets*. Wavelet-based compression builds on a complex mathematical technique originally applied to the analysis of music.

An especially promising way of making the Web go faster in the short term is the use of more intelligent software methods. The current HTML page over HTTP approach is amenable to lots of improvements. First, consider that getting one Web page often requires more than one TCP connection (end-to-end negotiation). The page itself needs a connection, as does each graphic embedded in the page. This makes for a lot of network overhead. In the long run, improvements to the network architecture, such as label switching, will minimize this busy work. In the interim, though, simple caching can provide tremendous benefits. In Web caching, your ISP will retain many frequently used pages in the disk cache of its local servers. If you use Netscape as your home page (millions do, and Netscape and its owner, AOL, reap big advertising bucks as a result), you will get the page not from Netscape but from your ISP's server. The local server, called a *proxy server,* gets updates from Netscape as needed, so what you see will (almost) always be current. The proxy can also do the kind of read-ahead caching that CPUs and other hardware systems do. Given the appropriate software at both ends, the proxy can guess what a client's next request will be and pull it into its cache while the previous page is being read.

Tech Talk

Proxy server: A server that functions in place of another is called a *proxy server.* They can have many functions, including security and serving as a network cache.

Even better than compression and caching is not to send information at all. This idea animates much of the popularity of Java applets, Active X controls, XML, and similar extensions to HTML (sometimes generically referred to as *Dynamic HTML,* or DHTML). To illustrate, consider Web servers used for database access. In the early days of the Web, when you looked up something on a Web database, for example, a catalog of music CDs, this is what happened when you sent a query to the server: First, the Web server software intercepted the query and sent it to a program using a scripting language running on the server (e.g., Perl). This program then used a protocol, called the Common Gateway Interface, to send a request to the database program. Once the database had looked up the information and returned it to the program, a new Web page was created by the Web server software and sent to the client. This process was slow on the server (it created lots of additional processes and/or threads) and resulted in a great deal of HTTP and TCP/IP traffic.

Tech Talk

Dynamic HTML: A variation of HTML, Dynamic HTML, allows designers considerable additional flexibility in page layout as well as the opportunity to add things like animation.

In its simplest form, Dynamic HTML is a way of getting around the limitations of HTML. Let's say you have a Web site and want to do something cool, like animation on your customers' computers. Doing it with HTML means that you will need to send a long string of verbose instructions requiring a lot of TCP/IP activity. DHTML, on the other hand, is similar to XML in that you now send a compact set of instructions to your DHTML-aware browser and it uses these to do the animation.

The new approach works by sending a Java applet (or an Active X control) to the client when a database page is first requested. This makes the beginning of the session slower as the extra code is pulled over the wire. Once downloaded, however, things proceed differently. A database request now goes first to the client side of the Java applet, which formats it for greatest efficiency. Once on the server, the server side of the Java application uses a driver to talk directly to the database. The report is then sent out to the client. It isn't necessary to create an entirely new page on the server and send it through a bunch of HTTP and TCP/IP connections. Instead, the client side of the Java applet takes the incoming data and generates or revises the page as needed. This process can be even more powerful with distributed objects. The client side of the Java applet can grow and extend itself by simply pulling in a few remote objects (Java "beans"). If the Java applet is cached on the client hard disk, then using the same or similar database again later would mean that a substantial amount of information could be retrieved with very little use of network bandwidth.

Virtual Private Networks, Firewalls, and the Concept of an Intranet

Two terms that have cropped up since the Internet explosion to add to the general linguistic fog are *intranet* and *virtual private network*. The first simply refers to a network, normally one used by a business, that employs all of the Internet standards (TCP/IP), but that either is not physically a part of the Internet or is isolated from it in some way. A linked collection of TCP/IP-based LANs on a corporate campus would be an intranet. Given the explosion of inexpensive and well understood TCP/IP-based software and hardware that has followed the success of the Internet, it makes a lot more sense for a business to organize its network in this way rather than with proprietary protocols like SNA, DECnet, or Novell's IPX/SPX.

Tech Talk

Intranet: A private network, separate from the Internet, but that uses the Internet's TCP/IP structure, is called an *intranet*. This term is used very loosely.

One approach to keeping an intranet separate from the Internet is to use a *firewall*. A firewall is simply a router that will only pass certain kinds of packets. The most common use of a firewall is to hide IP addresses. For example, when a node on

I'll bet you now have two questions: 1) how do you make sure that the whole transmission, including the text itself, is secure? and 2) how do you really know that the public key came from Joe Smith and not someone else pretending to be him? The answers are digital envelopes and digital certificates.

Digital Envelopes

In practice, the entire communication, including digital signature and full text, will be included in an encrypted package. This is called a digital envelope. To minimize the amount of work that a system has to do with the hard-to-decipher public key codes, the envelope will use a PGP-like approach—it will be preceded by a secret key that is encrypted with a private/public key. The rest of the message is then read using the secret key, which puts much less strain on the CPU. When the session is over, the secret key is thrown away, making it what intelligence people call a *one-time pad.*

> **Tech Talk**
>
> **Digital envelope:** A *digital envelope* uses a secret key to encode a message, then uses a public key to carry the secret key. This is more efficient than using a public key for everything.

Digital Certificates/Digital IDs

We've focused on the technology here, but in fact, much of the secure exchange of information depends on people knowing who they are talking to. If you think your message is being sent to Joe Smith but it's really going to Joe Mafioso pretending to be Joe Smith, it won't cheer you up to find out that no one could read it en route. Enter the digital certificate, a.k.a. the digital ID.

> **Tech Talk**
>
> **Digital certificate:** A *digital certificate* is a means of verifying that a digital signature belongs to a specific person or organization. Digital certificates are maintained by Certifying Authorities (CAs).

A digital certificate is a way of verifying the identity of a sender. Digital certificates also depend on the fact that the public/private key approach works both ways. A digital certificate contains the name, address, and public key of the owner, and carries the digital signature of the certifying authority (CA). The recipient decrypts it using the certifying authority's public key, which is published on the Internet (or, if you're somebody really picky, perhaps a financial institution, you can get it physically). Once this is done, the enclosed public key can be used to read the rest of the message (open the digital envelope and verify the digital signature). Are you dizzy yet?

OK, let's simplify. A digital certificate uses the same approach as a digital signature. The difference is that instead of getting the public key from the sender of the message, you get it from a certifying authority. For example, you receive a digitally signed message from Company X, which you could verify using the company's public key (sent in a previous message or even in the current one), but you want to be sure that Company X is actually the sender. You do this by going to a certifying authority's Web site and getting Company X's public key from there.

To get a digital certificate, you need to contact a certifying authority (a company called VeriSign started and leads the market). There are various classes. The lowest, Classes 1 and 2, are issued over the Internet and therefore have some limited potential to be abused since the certifying authority doesn't actually meet with the individual or entity requesting the certificate. The difference between Class 1 and Class 2 is that in the latter, the issuer will try to verify the requestor's identity by checking an online database. In Classes 3 and 4, the owner is more carefully identified, directly and personally.

Class 3 and 4 certificates provide a very high level of security; they are described as non-repudiable, since I won't be able to say that someone else faked my certificate. Equally important, the receiver of a certificate doesn't have to worry about someone breaking into its machine and stealing the digital certificates since they must be secured directly from the CA to be valid. The only apparent danger to the digital certificate system would come if someone stole the certifying authority's private key and used it to send out phony certificates. Of course, in the fast-emerging PKI (public key infrastructure) world, losing control of any private key is dangerous. This is one reason that certificates are usually time-stamped with a limited period of validity.

By the way, if all this overlapping digital coding doesn't make sense to you, skip ahead to the section "Summary on Digital Security" for a surefire way to understand it. Well, sort of.

Digital Birthmarks

There is a whole class of security that depends on something known as *biometrics*. People can be identified by digitized versions of finger or palm prints, by a reading of the patterns in the retina, by voice patterns, by facial patterns and, who knows, likely someday by smell. Devices that read fingerprints are already fairly cheap, and prices for all types of biometrics are sure to continue to fall dramatically. There is a considerable danger in these devices, though. To illustrate the problem, a few years ago some very bold thieves stole an ATM machine, then arranged to have it set up in a shopping center. The ATM actually dispensed cash to a few customers, though it mostly "malfunctioned" right after it received both the credit card and the PIN (personal identification number). When they serviced the machine, the thieves pulled off a nice database of card numbers and PINs. If bad guys could do something analogous, capture the digital version of your fingerprint as it left a reader, they could have access to everything you own. That's why, even with something as secure as biometrics, encryption of the output is still a critical issue.

Tech Talk

Biometrics: The processing of using some element of human anatomy—a fingerprint or voice pattern, for example—to identify a person is called *biometrics*.

CRACKING CODES . . . .

The following is a very brief introduction to a particularly complex topic. Also, although the technology behind code breaking is fairly stable, the very important legal environment is subject to extreme stress and could change significantly.

Methodology

The easiest way to crack a code is to physically steal the key—e.g., copy it from a screen. Don't laugh, it happens all the time. Next easiest is to have some clue as to what it is. A simple way to get a password is to try people's names, addresses, phone numbers, etc. Another way is to check "welcome," or whatever the default for that system is, since many people never change it. The prevalence of this kind of cracking is why system security people insist (and sometimes software requires) that passwords not be English words (or whatever language), that they include both letters and numbers, that passwords expire after a given period of time, and so forth.

When code crackers don't have a clue and can't steal one, they rely on some form or another of brute force. This simply means using the speed of a computer to examine all possible alternatives. Comparing a password to a dictionary is a form of brute force; even a garden variety PC can do this *real* fast. Of course, most codes are quite complex and cracking is harder than simply comparing a string of characters to a list. However, crackers usually have some idea of how to start. Someone trying to decipher a code like DES will know generally how the encoding works and will be able to design a cracking algorithm specifically for that code. The quality of the cracking algorithm matters a lot. A poorly designed one will never get close; a brilliant one greatly maximizes the chances of success. After the algorithm is designed, the speed of the computers takes over. University students (and other people with a lot of time on their hands) have attacked DES in a massively parallel fashion, using coordinated processing by machines and groups of machines around the world. Remember when students liked to play bridge?

Cryptography is a complex (and fascinating) subject that we can't really deal with here. It's important to know, however, that a critical element in making a code invulnerable to attack is the length of the key. Described in the simplest possible way, the longer in bits the key is, the more possible keys there are and the harder it will be to crack it.

The Role of the U.S. Government

The U.S. government has developed extraordinary expertise in the area of data encryption. The National Security Agency, a.k.a. the Puzzle Palace, is probably (only a few people really know) the biggest purchaser of high-end computers in the world. Throw in some of the smartest people anywhere, and pretty much unlimited amounts of cash, and citizens of the U.S. have a government that can read other governments' mail. Civilian and military leaders in Washington like it that way, and have done everything possible to preserve their special power because they perceive it to be of direct value to national security. As a result, laws have been passed that restrict what kinds of encryption can be sold. So, for example, IBM originally wanted DES to have a 128-bit key, but the U.S. forced a reduction to 64 bits. The U.S. has long attempted to maintain export controls that prohibit U.S. companies from selling encryption software that the NSA can't easily break.

Unfortunately, this generally means that the key is pretty weak and that others (e.g., bored college students) can break it as well. In recognition of this, the feds developed an alternative approach. Companies could market software with a more powerful key, but it had to include a *trapdoor* that the folks at the NSA could use to break the code if they needed to. The trapdoor is, in effect, a secret key that is known only to the government. In response to concerns about citizens' privacy, the law requires that the trapdoor key not be used except by court order. This type of approach is also called *key escrow*.

A reasonable person (to be more precise, just a reasonable American citizen) might conclude that the U.S. approach is a fair response to a valid concern. The problem is that in reality, export controls don't prevent people in other countries from getting access to and using very powerful keys—ones that the U.S. won't allow to be exported. There are many companies outside of the U.S. that, in the absence of American competition, are thriving in the software security market. As a result, the U.S. has substantially eased its position.

One reason that the U.S. government has fought so hard to control the kinds of encryption that can be used is that its concern goes beyond the security of data. Per-

Now that you've dealt with the network side, let's go back to your garage. You can now use all that extra space for the programmers, Web page designers, secretaries, and other folk who will claim to have been with you from Day One when you get to the IPO. What kinds of computers do you get these people? Well, they're going to be linked to one or more servers so that they can share files (you can never get rid of all the servers), so maybe you can get them cheap network computers and let the server do all the work. This might be acceptable for the clerks; their applications don't require much processing power, and your Fast Ethernet network will give them enough bandwidth so that they can pull applications from the server. A "thin client" approach would work for these people also. But the programmers and Web page designers will be doing a lot of CPU-intensive work on their local machines and, at least today, it's cheaper to do that work locally rather than move it to the server. A logical thing also would be to hang a modem on the server and have it connected to a PC somewhere. That way, you can test the speed of access for people who have only dial-up connections. You'll be especially concerned to see how fast your complex graphics and Java applets download and execute.

The final point is, of course, security. You have done the basic protection of your site with the firewall. Think of it as child-proofing your house. But you will also need to do your utmost to see that the actual transactions are secure. This means some kind of encryption such as the variations on public key cryptography. You'll never stop worrying about security. Even as you lie in bed at night calculating how much stock you should sell in order to buy this year's Ferrari, you'll be well advised to remember that the easiest way to let things go down the tubes would be to stop being vigilant about protecting your site and your transactions.

Conclusion: The Next Stages of Computing

The purpose of this book is to provide the reader with the foundation needed to follow developments in computing and related technologies. Given the rapid changes that continue to occur, the traditional type of conclusion, one that describes what the future holds, is doomed to failure. Still, speculation is fun (and in some cases, profitable). If you've read all the way through the book, and thought about the rate of change to date, you should not only understand these views, but very likely disagree with some of them.

THE STATE OF THE FOUNDATION . . . .

Before moving on to talk about some of the key new technologies and the major challenges facing computing, let's quickly do a review of where we are with hardware, software, and networks.

- **Hardware**

  Hardware is the great enabler. It is Moore's Law that has made possible the enormous advances in computing that have transformed society in the last few decades. Leaders in the software world point out that much of the improvement in the efficiency of today's computers comes from improved software—more efficient algorithms, more effective structures. This is all true, but the simple fact is that, absent the advances

451

in hardware, this more efficient and more effective software wouldn't have had sufficient machine resources to run even the first time. Today's CPUs and storage make possible software that designers found hard to imagine just a decade earlier

We should expect that we are only at the beginning of the Golden Age of Hardware. All of the key technologies—lithography in chipmaking, increases in areal density in magnetic and optical drives, higher resolution and better performing displays, are a decade or more from their peak if we think in terms of existing technology. And, even in the unlikely event that progress stalls in the period 2010–15 as some predict, devices using these technologies will by then be orders of magnitude faster, smaller, cheaper, and just plain better than they are today.

- **Software**

  One could take an optimistic or a pessimistic view of the state of software. On the positive side, the concerns about software becoming so complex to develop that no one would be able to do it have been alleviated. Windows 2000, with its circa 35 million lines of code, should address skepticism about the feasibility of large software projects. Further, object-oriented technology, which is just entering widespread use, offers the possibility of software modules that interact not just locally on one computer, but worldwide. This modular strategy will surely increase the productivity of software development even as applications become more complex. The pessimistic view is simple—things are going OK only because we haven't yet reached the threshold of chaos. The magic number is unknown—perhaps 50 million lines of code or its equivalent in interacting programs—but when it is reached things will start to go haywire. Negative views of this kind are, of course, impossible to refute. It's like "the world will end in 1999" gang; prove them wrong and they just move the number further out.

- **Networks**

  There is a certain irony in the development of networking, as computing began with networks, then moved away, then moved back. Some even argue that we have come full circle, that we are now returning to the terminal-host model that obtained when computing began. Such a view is surely wrong. While current computing is clearly network-centric, with desktop machines dependent on external servers for information and services, even the dumbest of contemporary clients are quite intelligent by comparison to the first mainframes. And, while there is reason to believe that it will soon be common for computers to get not only data but even application programs from the network, there are also strong counter trends in which networks of powerful computers are being used to tackle problems of exceptional difficulty. Whatever your view of the role of net-

ensued, the analog solutions fell by the wayside (and the Japanese system with them) in favor a full digital and packet-based approach. As a result, beginning in 1999, television stations began to use newly available channels to broadcast digital data at 19.3 Mbps. I say "data," because it doesn't all have to be TV. In the event that the entire channel is used for high definition television, it will take all that bandwidth. But, it will use all of it only at peak times. If a company's logo stays on the screen for 10 seconds, only a tiny bit of the bandwidth will be needed for the logo—the rest can be used to deliver 180 Mbits or so of data. That's some 22 Mbytes, or enough to deliver that morning's animated Victoria's Secret catalog. Of course, if the television station opts to show a channel at lower than high definition, it can show a bunch of channels in its 6 MHz, or some mixture of channels and data. Since the FCC has mandated that stations will switch to digital by 2006 (people with older televisions will be able to buy inexpensive set-top convertor boxes), the impact of all this, as well as the similar migration of broadcast radio to digital, will be enormous.

- **Piconets**

The first three topics in this section cover the transition of some existing technologies—cell phones, the telephone, and TV/radio—to new, digital formats. The category of the piconet, however, is new. The term "piconet," meaning very small network, builds on the prefix "pico," which in scientific terms is a trillionth—a "picosecond" is one trillionth of a second. Piconets are designed to allow small devices—cell phones, PDAs, etc.—to communicate smoothly and easily without wires. In many respects, therefore, piconets comprise the final stitches in the fabric of pervasive computing.

The challenges in building piconets are significant. Designers will have to find easy ways to use (and reuse) frequencies, as well as an effective and efficient method for devices to recognize each other and determine if they have been properly introduced so that they can exchange information. The effort here is being led by the "Bluetooth Consortium" comprising 3Com, Ericsson, IBM, Intel, Lucent, Microsoft, Motorola, Nokia, and Toshiba—about as heavyweight an industry group as you can get. They plan to use the unlicensed 2.4GHz frequency band, and have already developed algorithms for the ways devices identify each other and know whether it is safe to communicate. There will likely be competition to Bluetooth—critics say that the appeal of the 2.4Ghz band, the fact that it can be used by any device, also makes it too noisy—but in any case the process of creating piconets is well launched.

SEVEN CHALLENGES TO THE PERVASIVE FUTURE

Conceptually, pervasive computing is well on its way to implementation. Engineers and others are now actively engaged in envisioning the kinds of services and systems that will cause pervasive computing to transform the world. But, the environment of ultra-intelligent, totally networked devices isn't here yet. The following section describes, very briefly, seven challenges that will have to be met before "my machine will call your machine" is more than a joke.

- **Lithography**

  How long will existing optical lithography be able to sustain Moore's Law? When this technology ceases to be productive—something that we know will happen—what will replace it? Will the new technology be able to maintain optical's amazing ability to double the number of transistors on a chip every eighteen months while dropping prices about fifty percent? These are big questions. If hardware is the enabler of pervasive computing, then lithography has been the enabler of hardware. At the moment things look good. Optical seems to be able to go to at least 0.10 microns and likely below, and alternative technologies appear to be ready to take over when it falters. If any glitches develop in this scenario, however, expect enormously negative consequences for computing.

- **Portable power**

  Portable devices are central to the concept of pervasive computing. The first generation of portable computers, back in the 1980s, had no batteries because they used too much power. Though machines with batteries followed not long after, they were not very powerful and could rarely last an hour without recharging. Today we have very powerful computers with color displays, capacious hard drives, and lots of peripheral gadgets like speakers, that get three hours or so on a battery charge. The principal reasons for these advances are: 1) CPUs and other chips have become dramatically more power efficient as their transistors and traces get smaller; and 2) operating software now includes sophisticated power management tools that shut or slow down subsystems when they're not needed. While improved batteries have contributed some to this progress, their role has been far less than has been desired or will be needed if improvements are to continue. The good news here is that many of the new devices such as PDAs and cell phones are sufficiently small that they don't need tremendous amounts of battery power. But as more and more functions get stuffed into these gadgets, and as people become ever more dependent on them, lack of battery life will become a real problem. Ideally, we want de-

gines should function. And don't try to make long-term decisions. The relationship between standards and innovation will continue to be dynamic.

- **Human factors**

The single biggest challenge to pervasive computing comes in presenting the technologies to the user in a way that makes them truly useful. To be candid, much of what is available now is not useful. The market is driven to a remarkable extent by companies that decide to offer products because they are both cool and possible. The fact that what is cool is not always what is needed escapes these vendors, often small producers who lack the resources for vision. Another aspect of the human factors problem is that cool products may in fact become useful—but only if combined with other products. Since the developers lack the ability and/ or the resources to make the needed connections, cool quickly becomes curiosity.

To illustrate the need for improved human factors, consider that my son and his college roommates have linked an X-10 household switching system to a Linux-based server that is attached to an always-on cable modem (the computer is one of the eight operating on a LAN in this three-person apartment). Now, observes my son, they can "turn their lights on and off from anywhere in the world." It's cool. But useful?

Let's extend the point—technology will soon make possible the appearance of cheap, high quality video cameras based on single chip sensor/ processors. Such cameras will lead to increases in security (and perhaps insecurity if we think of them in the Big Brother context), but much more than that. If you pair these cameras with a group of fast processors, a terabyte or so of storage, high speed wireless network connections, and a few garden variety electric motors, you have (among other things) a pretty sophisticated robot. Such devices, however, will be more disaster than benefit if we don't pay attention to human factors. A great deal of effort, perhaps more than in the actual system design, will need to go into how to use these sophisticated creations in safe and practical manner.

A FINAL COMMENT . . . .

Historians are known for their reluctance to use the past to predict the future. It's often possible to predict change a few years forward, but after that new developments start to interact, and even the most informed person can't speculate past these events with any hope of accuracy. However, historians do argue that, while the past can't predict, it does provide an "essential guide" to understanding the future. I hope this book helps as you watch and participate in the rapid changes in technology and the social and economic developments they produce.

Glossary

Address   Computers use addresses to keep track of information in much the same way as the post office uses them to find residences and businesses. The bigger the number in an address, the more locations it can refer to. Most current computers use a 32-bit "address space" for memory, which means that there can be over four billion separate locations to hold information. See Chapter 5 for more about addresses.

AGP   In an Intel system, the Advanced Graphics Port is a high speed bus that connects the graphics processor to the CPU/memory system.

Algorithm   An algorithm is another word for "formula." It is a set of rules and/or computations that is intended to be used over and over, like a recipe.

Analog   An analog system uses a representation of information, rather than a numerical version, in its processing. For example, traditional radio sends and receives sound with an electronic wave that is an analog of the voice, music, or noise waves that enter a microphone. Analog systems are well suited to carrying information, but not to modifying it.

Applet   In Java programming, an "applet" is a small special purpose application program that is designed to be downloaded over a network for use on a client machine.

Application program   A program that is at the command of a user is normally called an "application." By contrast, the operating system and other programs are usually known as "systems software."

Areal density   The number of bits that a disk drive can hold in a given space. The first generation of drives used in microcomputers had an areal density of 15 megabits per square inch; current drives have about 5,000–10,000 megabits per square inch (5–10 Gigabits).

ASCII   ASCII stands for "American Standard Code for Information Interchange." It uses 7 bits to reference 128 character letters, numbers, punctuation marks and some symbols used for system control. A version using 8 bits, "Extended ASCII," provides the same 128 plus another 128 special characters.

ATM   Asynchronous Transfer Mode (ATM) is a protocol stack developed as an international standard by the telephone companies. It uses packet switching technology (it's packets are called "cells"), but also creates virtual circuits that are effective in supporting streaming data. The small size of its cells is good for reducing jitter in voice and video, but inefficient for data.

Bandwidth   The capacity of a communications channel is its bandwidth. In computers, this is measured in bits per second. See also Chapter 10 for a primer on digital communications.

Batch processing   means that a program runs until it is complete with no user interaction. Also known as "batch mode."

Binary   Binary mathematics is a form that uses only two digits vs. the ten in our normal decimal system. Binary numbers are used in computing because they conform very well to the "on" and "off" states of electronic devices.

Biometrics   The processing of using some element of human anatomy—a fingerprint, voice pattern, etc.—to identify a person is called biometrics.

BIOS   The Basic Input/Output System (BIOS) refers to a chip in some types of microcomputers, especially those that use Microsoft operating systems. The BIOS, which can be thought of as an extension of the operating system, holds information about attached devices such as disk drives, external buses, etc. The BIOS also helps systems boot up. See Chapter 7 for more detail.

Bitmap   Bitmap has two meanings. In one, it simply refers to an image that comprises a pattern of dots. Using this definition, essentially all computer graphics—monitor or printer—are bitmaps. In the other definition, bitmap refers to how an image is made. A bitmapped image is created dot by dot for a specific size and resolution. Contrast with "vector."

BLOB   A Binary Large Object (BLOB) refers to a collection of data, usually video or sound information, that a relational database is able to access but not manipulate.

Booting   Computers are described as "booting up" after the observation of early designers that the system should "pull itself up by its bootstraps."

Border gateway protocol   Used in wide area networks, BGP is a router to router protocol that allows exterior routers to communicate with each other. More efficient than its predecessor, Exterior Gateway Protocol (EGP), because routers exchange only changes to their tables, not the entire table.

Branch   A point in a program where the CPU may have to switch to a different stream of instructions. A conditional branch is where the stream chosen depends on the result of some computation.

Garbage collection   Garbage collection refers to the need for a programmer to make sure that code that has been loaded into memory is removed when no longer needed. If this isn't done, the "garbage" will soak up memory and possibly cause conflicts. Software tool kits for developers provide code and techniques for dealing with this problem, but some programmers manage to leave garbage behind anyway.

Geometry   In 3D graphics, "geometry" refers to the work the CPU does in calculating the size and place of objects that are themselves made up of many polygons.

Grayscale   Refers to an image that can show shades of black (gray), though the term is also used for color. In a true grayscale image, each dot can be a number of different shades. Most printing approaches simulate this with "halftoning" or "dithering." A color (including black) that can be shown in 256 shades has "256 grayscale definition" and requires 8 bits of memory.

Halftoning   Refers to the process in printing of mixing white areas in with color to get different shades. Also called "dithering." In effect, this approach simulates grayscaling.

Hardware abstraction layer   The HAL (Hardware Abstraction Layer) is the equivalent of the microkernel in Microsoft's Windows NT/ 2000. Its principal purpose is to make it easier to port the OS to a variety of CPUs/ hardware platforms.

Hertz   The term "Hertz" (abbreviated Hz) is a measure used to describe the number of cycles per second in an activity. Examples: the CPU's clock speed is given in millions (MHz) or billions (GHz) of Hertz; the number of times a monitor image is redisplayed is described in Hz, etc. Also, the frequency of electromagnetic waves, the number of wave crests passing a point in a second, is given in Hz. For example, the frequency used by digital cellular telephones is 1.9 GHz (see Chapter 10).

HTML   The Hyper Text Markup Language (HTML) is the programming language used to create Web documents. HTML uses as system of tags (visible in most browsers by clicking on something like View-Page Source on the menu bar), that define a page's layout.

HTTP   The Hypertext Text Transfer Protocol (HTTP) is responsible for moving documents across the Web. The Universal Resource Locater (URL) in your Web browser, e.g. www.prenhall.com, is part of HTTP.

Hub   A hub is a network device that receives a signal from an attached computer and sends it on to other attached machines. A hub is a relatively unsophisticated device.

I/O   The term "input/output" (I/O) refers generally to movement into and out of the computer's CPU/memory system. Since this is frequently to and from disks, it is often called "disk I/O," although I/O can also refer to printers, to network connections, etc.

IEEE   The Institute of Electrical and Electronics Engineers sets international standards for many of the devices used in computing.

IETF   The Internet Engineering Task Force (IETF) is responsible for setting many Internet-related standards, for example the new version of the Internet Protocol, IPv6.

Inheritance   One way in which Object-Oriented Technology simplifies program development is through "inheritance." This simply means that, in creating a sub-class of a larger class, a programmer can have the sub-class inherit some of the characteristics of the class rather than restating them. This saves time and reduces the possibility of error.

Instance In Object-Oriented Technology, an "instance" is an individual object within a specific class.

Instruction set The instruction set refers to both the instructions that a CPU can execute and the way in which they are organized. CPUs from different vendors have different instruction sets—unless one is a "clone" of the other.

Interpreted language A programming language that uses a program, called an interpreter, to create machine language only while the interpreter is running on the computer, is called "interpreted." Contrast with "compiled."

Intranet A private network (separated from the Internet) that uses the Internet's TCP/IP structure, is called an Intranet. This term is used very loosely.

IP The Internet Protocol, IP, is a Layer 3 routable protocol that can deal with very large networks. It carries either TCP or UDP and can ride on a range of lower level protocols.

IPv6 The current version of the Internet Protocol (IP) is version 4, written IPv4. The next generation, now being introduced, is IPv6. IPv6 has many advantages, including the capacity for far more separate numbers, and the ability to maintain quality of service (QoS).

ISP An Internet Service Provider (ISP) provides the link from a residence or business to the regional or backbone levels of the Internet. ISPs range from small mom and pop operations to giant companies like AT&T.

Kernel The kernel is the component ("layer") of the operating system that works directly with the hardware (especially the CPU and memory).

Label switching An effort to combine the speed of switching with the flexibility of routing is know as label switching. The idea is that, once a routing decision is made, packets can flow through a switched virtual circuit instead of requiring continual packet by packet routing decisions.

LAN A local area network (LAN) usually connects up to around 50 or so computers within a limited physical space—such as a small building or a floor of a larger one. The computers on a LAN are connected through a hub or a switch. LAN protocols, almost always Ethernet or Token Ring, operate at layer 2 of the protocol stack.

Latency In communications, latency refers to delay in transmission of packets. While data connections can normally tolerate a fair amount of latency, anything more than a very small quantity will degrade the quality of voice and video connections.

Leased line A connection, sometimes a physical wire but more often a channel in a wire or cable, that a telephone company makes available on a rental basis for data communications.

Logic gate A logic gate is a series of transistors, connected in a way that allows it to carry out a mathematical or logical operation such as addition. Logic gates are grouped into electrical circuits that execute the CPU's instructions such as to "add" two numbers or "compare" two values.

Loop In programming, a loop is code that performs some repetitive chore, repeating a computation until a specific event occurs. For example, a loop might go through a list of a company's sales staff, calculating bonuses according to sales information. The loop would end when the entire list had been evaluated. Writing efficient loops is a central part of programming.

Lossy compression A compression technique that can't precisely recreate the original is called lossy. These approaches are obviously not used for sending spreadsheets or other computer data, but are widely employed for the transmission of voice and video. In many cases, a great deal of such information can be "lost" without humans being able to discern the difference between the source and the copy.

lpi Printers measure the quality of graphics output in lines per inch (lpi). This takes into account the clusters of dots needed to simulate grayscaling.

Memory pages memory is organized into blocks called "pages" that are typically 2–4 Kb in size. Rather than move an individual word from disk to memory (or vice versa), the entire page is moved.

Method In Object-Oriented Technology, a "method" is program logic that is a part of an object and acts on its data.

Microkernel The microkernel is a subset of an operating system's kernel that contains only those elements that interact directly with the local hardware. Separating these parts from the rest of the kernel simplifies "porting" the OS from one CPU/hardware platform to another.

Mission critical The term "mission critical," borrowed from NASA and with obvious meaning, is used to refer to database systems that, should they fail, would bring the business or organization down with them.

Modular programming A hot idea in programming is to segregate code into discrete units or modules, each of which maintains responsibility for specific functions. The approach is really a more structured extension of earlier ideas; object-oriented technology is inherently modular.

Modulation The process of modifying a wave so that it can carry information is known as modulation. There are three ways of modulating a wave: changing its amplitude, frequency, or phase.

Moore's Law Intel pioneer Gordon Moore stated that the number of transistors on a chip would double every eighteen months, and that their cost would fall by 50% during the same time.

MPEG The Motion Picture Experts Group (MPEG) has developed a series of techniques for compressing streaming digital information so that it can be used more efficiently—employing less bandwidth in transmission or less capacity on a disk (DVD disks use MPEG coding). MPEG-1, which can deal with low to medium resolution video, has been replaced in most uses by MPEG-2, which can accommodate the original standards for high definition television. The most recent standard, MPEG-4, is being designed to get even greater efficiency through the use of vector graphics.

ms   A millisecond, abbreviated "ms," is one-thousandth of a second. The speed of access to data on disk drives is normally measured in milliseconds.

Multicasting   Sending a single stream of data to multiple receivers is called multicasting. The objective is to conserve network bandwidth by waiting until the last possible link to create a duplicate stream.

Multihoming   A network or computer that has two or more connections to the Internet or other wide area network is said to be "multihomed."

Network "pipe"   Network terminology often refers to wires or wireless channels as "pipes" because the concept of a pipe, with the size of its diameter regulating flow, is so easy to understand. Broadband access, usually meaning anything over about 1.5 MB/s, is often called a "fat pipe."

Network loop   To illustrate a network loop, consider the case of router A sending a packet to router B, thinking that it is on the path to network node C. But router B has a damaged routing table, which tells it that the way to get to C is through A. So it sends the packet to A, which consults its routing table again and sends it to B. . . .

Object   In Object-Oriented Technology (OOT), an object is an element that includes both program logic (a "method") and data in a consistently structured way.

OLE   Microsoft's Object Linking and Embedding (OLE) allows a user to create an object (e.g. a table or a graphic) and embed it in another. For example, a table in Word could actually be a section of a spreadsheet created in Excel.

Open GL   A 3D graphics language that is available for a variety of hardware and software platforms. One advantage of the language is that it allows programmers to write software that is independent of the hardware. Open GL adapts the program to the capabilities of the system.

Open shortest path first (OSPF)   The most popular router to router communication protocol for interior networks. OSPF, which uses a link/state algorithm, is more efficient than the older RIP (Routing Information Protocol) because routers exchange only a subset, the active links, of their tables.

Overhead   In communications, everything that is sent that is not a part of the original data is overhead. ED/C adds to overhead, as does the various control information that goes with the use of packets (see Chapter 11).

Packet   In communications terms, a packet is a discrete collection of information that includes user data plus protocol information such as destination and source addresses, and controls for error detection/correction, sequencing, flow control, etc.

Parity checking   The simplest form of error detection is called parity checking. In this approach, the bits in a byte are summed—if the result is even, a "0" bit is added to the byte and if it is odd a "1" bit is added. Parity checking is used in the relatively interference free inside of computers, but not beyond that—it is prone to errors in high interference environments and adds a lot of overhead (12.5% more bits are required)

PGP   Pretty Good Privacy (PGP) combines public key and secret key cryptography.

Photolithography   The process of creating patterns on a wafer is known as photolithography. The technology is very similar to that employed in a photographic enlarger. Current processes use visible light, but alternative approaches, using x-rays or electron beams, are in development.

Physical Memory   is the amount of memory that can be directly addressed by a computer's hardware. It is limited by the maximum size and number of DRAM chips that can be accommodated in the system.

Pipeline   Engineers describe the path that instructions follow through a CPU—"fetch," "decode," "execute," "store," and variations—as its "pipeline." In a "pipelined" processor, every stage of the pipeline is doing work on every clock cycle.

Point of Presence (POP)   A point of presence (POP) is the location where one network touches another. The term is borrowed from telephone company jargon, in which a POP is the place where the local network connects to the long distance system.

Port   A port is a place where data can enter or leave the computer through some attached device. The term "port" is used to refer to both physical connections and their software address. The OS manages the use of ports.

Port cost   Devices such as switches and routers come with physical ports that are used for external connections (the points where cables snap in or screw on). As a way of providing consistent comparison, the cost of the various technologies is often given as the cost "per port."

Postscript   A page description language that describes how objects should be located on a printed page and how they should be scaled. Postscript uses vectors to create images and fonts and for layout commands.

Predicted frame   In a coding scheme like MPEG, some frames shown by the computer or television are created by the receiver based on information from a previously received frame. This saves a huge amount of bandwidth.

Private key   In public key cryptography, the private key is the part of the key pair that is not published but used to decrypt data encoded with the public key.

Protocol   A protocol is an agreed upon set of rules for the transmission of data. In packet networks, protocols usually have a variety of layers—"stacks."

Proxy server   A server that functions in place of another is called a proxy server. They can have many functions, including security and serving as a network cache.

Public key   In the public key approach to encryption, the public key is the part of a key pair that is given to others to use to encrypt data. The other part of the pair, the private key, is used for decryption.

QoS   While most data connections can tolerate a fair amount of latency, voice and video cannot. Quality of Service, QoS, refers to the process of providing bandwidth guarantees that keep latency within the limits specified for voice and video.

Rapid application development   An approach to programming that builds on a series of prototypes is called Rapid Application Development (RAD).

Raster   The term "raster," as in "raster image," is sometimes used as a synonym for any kind of bitmap. But "rasterization" also has the more specific meaning of using a scanning motion to create a pattern of dots—whether the original is a bitmap or vector based.

Ray casting   Since ray tracing is so computationally intensive that it can rarely be done in real time, most games employ a subset, called "ray casting." Instead of tracing lighting relationships for every pixel, ray casting does calculations for only a subset and typically limits the kinds of changes that are to be considered. The quality of the image is normally quite a bit lower as a result. Think of ray casting as the lite version of ray tracing.

Ray tracing   Ray tracing calculates the effects of light sources on objects in a 3D image.

Register   A register is an on-CPU storage space where instructions and data can be transferred and held temporarily for fast retrieval.

Relational database (RDBMS)   A relational database is one in which separate tables (usually in separate files), can be linked through common fields. Keeping information in separate, logically related groups most of the time, while retaining the ability to create multiple links when needed, provides a great deal of flexibility.

Rendering   The process of converting 3D information to a 2D screen image is called rendering. It is normally done by the graphics processor.

RGB   Color pixels in most types of monitors and televisions are built from the three primary colors of red, green, and blue. Displays using this approach are called "RGB."

RISC   "RISC" stands for "reduced instruction set computer" and refers to a CPU that is structured to gain efficiency through circuits designed to execute relatively few instructions at high speed.

ROM [vs. RAM]   Read Only Memory (ROM) is a kind of chip that has information permanently burned into it. Since ROM is non-volatile, this was a handy way to provide the computer with information that had to be readily accessible but didn't need to change. Early BIOSes used ROM, though Flash memory, which is also non-volatile but is faster and can be rewritten, is now preferred.

Router   A Layer 3 network device that analyzes incoming packets in order to make decisions as to where they should be sent. Routers are really special purpose computers; depending on the specific design, they can connect different physical networks and deal with multiple protocols.

Routing   The process of making decisions about where a packet or group of packets should go in a network is called routing.

Sampling   In order to make a digital representation of analog information, the original analog wave is sampled—checked at regular intervals. Each sample is given a numerical (binary) value. The result is that the digital system sends a stream of bits rather than an analog wave. The original wave can then be reproduced at the end. The more frequent the sampling, and the greater the range of values each can contain, the more accurately the wave can be reproduced.

SCSI The Small Computer Systems Interface, a parallel I/O bus that has been used for both internal and external devices, has been popular, but may be yielding to USB and/or FireWire.

Shell In operating systems such as Unix and its variants, the shell is a layer of the OS that sits between the user and the kernel. The user interacts only with the shell.

Sole sourcing When a vendor is the only one to provide a component, it is the sole source. Manufacturers try to avoid this, since multiple suppliers can be less risky to deal with.

Source code The written commands in a programming language, together with the comments that describe what they do, comprise a program's "source code."

Spaghetti code Second generation programmers derisively referred to much of the work of their predecessors as "spaghetti code." Their criticism was that the code was written in a meandering way, including the frequent use of "goto" statements. This approach made it very difficult to understand the program's flow and therefore very difficult to maintain.

Spatial compression Compression that operates within a given space, e.g. a video frame, is called "spatial."

Spectrum The electromagnetic spectrum includes all forms of radiation from radio to gamma waves. Spectrum is often described in terms of frequency "bands" or ranges. The information carrying capacity of all of this is vast. The Federal Communications Commission has recently had a series of "spectrum auctions" to sell some of this capacity for wireless telephone services.

Speculative execution A CPU that has circuits designed for speculative execution will execute the instructions after a branch just in case the program needs to go that way.

SRAM "Static Random Access Memory" chips are similar to DRAM. They are faster, but use more space per bit of storage, so are more expensive.

Statistical compression A form of compression that restructures the elements of a file or data stream such that those elements which are used most frequently get short symbols and those used least often get long ones. Often called Huffman coding after its inventor.

Structured programming As an antidote to what they considered the unreadable (and hence difficult to maintain) "spaghetti code" of first generation programmers, second generation programmers advocated more carefully organized and documented code writing, which they called "structured programming."

Structured Query Language Structured Query Language, abbreviated SQL, is a language that is employed for querying relational databases. Most implementations of SQL are specific to a particular database package.

Substrate The surface on which something is placed is called its "substrate." Most CPUs, memory chips, etc., use silicon as the substrate, though Gallium Arsenide (GaAs) and Silicon Germanium (SiGe) are gaining somewhat. Magnetic disks uses aluminum or glass as the substrate.

Superscalar A CPU that is "superscalar" has more than one pipeline.

Switch A Layer 2 device that connects networks of a specific kind—e.g. all Ethernet. Switches operate faster than routers, but unlike routers, they can't see beyond other switches of the same kind.

Switched circuit A dedicated path through a network that is not permanent, but can be established "on the fly" by a switching device.

TCP/IP The TCP/IP stack (Transmission Control Protocol/Internet Protocol) is usually considered to be synonymous with the Internet. In fact, while all Internet links use IP at Layer 3, many transmissions use TCP's sister protocol, UDP, in Layer 4.

TCP The Transmission Control Protocol, TCP, rides on top of IP and manages a connection for purposes of flow control, etc. Its sister Layer 4 protocol, UDP, is connectionless.

Temporal compression This is compression that works on a moving or "streaming" image by eliminating redundancy from one frame to the next in the stream.

Texture A texture is a predrawn pattern, stored and retrieved from memory as needed. A texture can convey complexity in an image that would otherwise require a great deal of computation. Heavily used in games.

Thrashing A poorly written program can find itself constantly moving pages back and forth between memory and disk. Called "thrashing," this makes systems very inefficient.

Thread A thread is a sub-process (program). It has no independent memory space, using instead resources assigned by its parent process.

Thunking "Thunking" is a term used by programmers to describe the process of converting 16-bit addresses to 32-bits. The technique is widely used in Microsoft's Windows family to provide compatibility with older software.

Time sharing The ability of a computer to run more than one program at a time was originally called "time sharing." The term "multitasking" is now used instead.

Trace The wires that connect devices within a chip are so tiny that they are called "traces."

Transactional database (OLTP) Transaction processing, also known as On Line Transaction Processing (OLTP), refers to a database that is accessed for the purpose of making changes to its records. For example, a library circulation system, which changes the status of a book from checked in to checked out (or vice versa) is responsible for transactions.

TrueType A vector font (font scaling) technology developed by Microsoft and Apple and used in their operating systems.

Bruce, Glen, and Dempsey, Rob. *Security in Distributed Computing.* Upper Saddle River, NJ: Prentice Hall PTR, 1997. Comprehensive and clear; the best introduction.

Derfler Jr., Frank J. *Using Networks.* Indianapolis, IN: Que, 1998. Highly readable.

De Wire, Dawna Travis. *Second Generation Client Server Computing.* New York: McGraw Hill, 1996. Both books by De Wire do an excellent job of explaining key concepts.

————. *Thin Clients: Web-Based Client/Server Architecture and Applications.* New York: McGraw Hill, 1998.

Dodd, Annabel Z. *The Essential Guide to Telecommunications.* Second edition. Upper Saddle River, NJ: Prentice Hall PTR, 2000. A clearly written best seller; focuses more on the telephone infrastructure than on computer networking.

Feibel, Werner. *The Encyclopedia of Networking.* Second Edition (first edition published as *Novell's Complete Encyclopedia of Networking*). Berkeley: Osborne McGraw-Hill, 1997. Indispensable; CD included with book contains full text and graphics.

Lu, Cary. *Understanding Bandwidth.* Redmond, WA: Microsoft Press, 1997. Lu, a fine writer, finished this excellent work just before his untimely death.

Luther, Arch C. *Principles of Digital Audio and Video.* Norwood, MA: Artech House, 1997. Everything you always wanted to know . . . And clearly explained, too.

Martin, James and Chapman, Kathleen Kavanagh. *Local Area Networks.* Englewood Cliffs, NJ: Prentice Hall, 1994. Old but still solid. Martin is The Man for computer and information system texts.

Noll, A. Michael. *Introduction to Telecommunication Electronics.* Second edition. Boston: Artech House Publishers, 1995. Thorough and clear.

Orfali, Robert; Harkey, Dan and Ewards, Jeri. *Client/Server Survival Guide.* Third edition. New York: John Wiley & Sons, 1999. Detailed explanations of this key area.

Pierce, John R. and Noll, A. Michael. *Signals: The Science of Telecommunications.* New York: Scientific American Library, 1990. The basics in accessible language.

Vaskevitch, David. *Client/Server Strategies.* Foster City, CA: IDG Books Worldwide, 1995. Subtitled "A Survival Guide for Corporate Reengineers," this work includes both clear explanations and thoughtful analyses. Vaskevitch is a senior executive at Microsoft.

Williams, Veronica A. *Wireless Computing Primer.* New York: M&T Books, 1996. Effective description of technology fundamentals.

The Computer Industry/Computer History

Campbell-Kelly, Martin, and Aspray, William. *Computer: A History of the Information Machine.* New York: Basic Books, 1996. Outstanding.

Caroll, Paul. *Big Blues: The Unmaking of IBM.* New York: Crown Publishers, 1993. Focuses on IBM's struggle with Microsoft. Contains good information, but the analysis is weak. For a more thoughtful interpretation, see Ferguson and Morris' *Computer Wars.*

Cringely, Robert X. *Accidental Empires.* Reading, MA: Addison-Wesley, 1992. An insightful history of the microcomputer industry from *Infoworld*'s gossip columnist. Unfortunately, does not include photos of Pammy.

Ferguson, Charles H. and Morris, Charles R. *Computer Wars.* New York: Random House, 1993. Simply brilliant, both on the IBM–Microsoft struggle and on the nature of the computer business. Still important despite its age.

Hafner, Katie and Lyon, Matthew. *Where Wizards Stay Up Late: The Origins of the Internet.* New York: Touchstone Press, 1996. Solid and readable.

Jackson, Tim. *Inside Intel.* New York: Dutton, 1997. Valuable insights on Intel's business strategy.

Malone, Michael S. *Infinite Loop: How the World's Most Insanely Great Computer Company Went Insane.* New York: Doubleday, 1999. Fascinating history of Apple Computer.

Negroponte, Nicholas. *Being Digital.* New York: Random House, 1995. Interesting stuff from the head of MIT's famed Media Lab.

Pugh, Emerson W. *Building IBM: Shaping an Industry and its Technology.* Cambridge, MA: MIT Press, 1995. A more scholarly analysis of IBM's troubles at the end of the '80s.

Shurkin, Joel. *Engines of the Mind: The Evolution of the Computer from Mainframes to Microprocessors.* New York: W.W. Norton & Co, 1996. Focuses on the early periods of calculation and computation. Well done.

Regular Reading and Reference

General access periodicals:

Business Week has excellent continuing coverage of technology issues, but there isn't space to explain how things work, rather the focus is on impact.

The New York Times' business page covers the computer and telecommunications industries very effectively. The weekly *Circuits* section is superb.

Scientific American has excellent articles on key technologies.

The Wall Street Journal has coverage similar to the *Times;* it's a matter of taste.

Specialized periodicals:

Infoworld (weekly) is breezy and quick, but essential if you want to stay up to date.

PC Magazine (every two weeks or so) is first rate; a must have for everyone.

e-Week (formerly *PC Week)* (weekly) has a little more depth than *Infoworld,* but lacks its competitor's crispness. It's reasonable to read both.

Interactive Week (weekly) provides a communications and media perspective lacking in the computer journals; a brilliant job of technical writing for the non-technical.

Wired (monthly) has some very good articles and a lot of "gee whiz isn't this new thing better than the old" articles. It also has layout and design that makes one think that the future will be a really hideous place.

Web sites:

http://www.cmpnet.com. Master site for *Electronic Engineering Times (eetimes.com), news.com, byte.com* and a host of others. *News.com* is the best site for daily updates.

http://www.zdnet.com. A vast resource from a major publisher.

http://www.tomshardware.com. An excellent site for hardware performance issues.

EDA (Electronic design automation), 129
ED/C (Error Detection/Correction), 304–305, 307, 373, 378
edge routers, 343
EDS (Electronic Data Systems), 252
EEPROM, 55
EGP (exterior gateway protocol), 343
electromagnetic spectrum, 268–272, 320
electromagnetic waves, 269–272
e-mail, 410
embedded processors, 117, 138
embedded systems, 199, 215, 259
emulation, 116, 188
encryption, 435–437, 459
ENIAC, xxiii
enterprise servers, 409
enterprise systems, 193–194, 250–251
EPIC (Explicitly Parallel Instruction Computing), 30
EPOC, 199–200
EPS (Encapsulated Postscript), 85
Ericsson, 200
ERP (Enterprise Resource Planning), 251–252, 258
errors
    in chips, 52
    in telecommunications, 289–291
    in packets, 297, 304–305
    see also ED/C
escrow, key, 442
Ethernet, 298, 310–311, 322–324, 330, 339–340, 352–356
    Fast, 355, 358, 447
    Gigabit, 446
    isochronous, 403
    Metropolitan Area, 426–427
    with ISDN, 375
European Laboratory for Particle Physics, 429
Excel, 187, 254
executable file (.exe), 205
execution
    CPU stage, 9, 11, 16
    speculative, 25–26
explicitly parallel instruction computing, 30
Extreme Ultraviolet Limited Liability Co., 108

fabless, 115
fabs, 22
Fast Ethernet, 355, 358, 447
FAT (File Allocation Table), 42, 44, 56–57
fat client, 400–401
fault tolerant, 165
fax machines, 275
FDDI (Fiber Distributed Data Interface), 357–358
FDM (frequency division multiplexing), 335
FEC (forward error correction), 290–291
FED (Field Effect Displays), 80
fetch, 7
    CPU stage, 10, 15
    fetch/execute, 17
    prefetch queue, 23, 43, 45
fiber optic cable, 35, 324–327, 361, 366, 373, 413, 446, 453, 460
    dark, 326
    non-zero dispersion shifted, 326
    unlit, 326
Fibre Channel, 446
field effect displays, 80
field programmable gate array, 33–34, 129
fields, in databases, 242
files, 9
    data, 41
    locked, 392
    program, 40–41
    saving, 44
    server, 392
    systems, 148
    transfer protocols, 296–301
    types, 84–85
    see also BMP, EPS, FAT, GIF, .jff, JPEG, PICT, .tif, TIFF
firewalls, network, 434–435, 447
FireWire, 61–62
flash memory, 54
flash RAM, 55
flat-file databases, 244
flat panel displays, 79–80
flicker, 78
floppy drives, 179
flow control
    in modems, 374
    in networks, 303–304, 308, 378
flow switching, 348
fonts, 82–83
form factors, 12

formatting disks, 42, 56
Fortran (Formula Translator), 216
forward error correction, 290–291
FPGA (Field Programmable Gate Array), 33–34, 129
frame buffers, 86–87
frame rates, 77–78
Frame Relay, 360, 374, 379–381, 386, 420
frames, 284–285, 288, 366
    Ethernet, 298
frequency
    bands, 268
    of waves, 270–271, 274–275
frequency division multiplexing, 335
FTP (File Transfer Protocol), 296
full duplex, 336, 361, 446–447
function call, 212

Gallium Arsenide (GaAs), 106, 327
garbage collection, 219
Gates, Bill, 176, 254, 258, 409
Gateway 2000, 66–67
GDI (graphics device interface), 146, 396
General Instrument, 123
General Motors, 252
geometry, 3D, 90
geosynchronous orbit (GEO), 385
GHz (Giga-Hertz), 78
GIF (Graphics Interchange Format), 85, 432
Gigabit Ethernet, 361–362
glue logic, 7–8, 65
GML (Generalized Markup Language), 220
Goldberg, Adele, 229
"goto" statements, 210
graphics
    accelerators, 87
    device interface, 146, 396
    interchange format, 84, 432
    systems, 80–93, 131
grayscale, 95
groupware, 410–411
GTE, 417, 435
guard bands, 273
GUI (Graphical User Interface), 147, 172
    Lisa, 181

H.323 standard, 455

HAL (Hardware Abstraction
  Layer), 153, 191, 196
halftoning, 95
handheld computers, 124
Handspring, 199
hard disks, 8, 42, 54
  evolution, 56
hard errors, 52
Harvard University, 253
HDSL (high data rate DSL), 370
HDTV, 127–128
head, on disk, 42
headers, packet, 308
Hertz (Hz), 19, 78, 270
Hertz, Gustav, 270
Hewlett-Packard
  see HP
hierarchical databases, 244–245
hierarchies, router, 341
high-level languages, 215–216
Hitachi, 120, 198
holography, 59
Honeywell, 166
hosts
  network, 307, 395
  Web, 448
hot swapping, 62
HP (Hewlett-Packard), 117, 119,
  167–168, 186
  8500, 26
  AnyLAN, 356
  printers, 97
  UX, 168
HTML (HyperText Markup Language), 220, 430
  Dynamic, 433–434
HTTP (Hypertext Transfer Protocol), 430
hubs, 329, 339
Huffman Code compression, 287
hunt group, network, 420
Hypercard program, 220
hyperlinks, 220

IA (Intel Architecture), 30
IBM, 55, 64–65, 68, 86, 110,
  115–116, 128, 163–164,
  185, 193, 196, 216, 231,
  252, 356, 361
  3270 terminals, 391, 393
  AS/400, 166
  DB2, 250
  e-commerce, 262
  Lotus 1-2-3, 253

information appliances, 398
  NC, 399
OS/2, 188, 193–196
OS/2 Warp, 196
OS/9, 199
OS/360, 163
OS/390, 162
OS/400, 166, 173
PC, 178
Power3, 157
software, 258
SQL, 243
System 3+, 166
System 360, 211
System 370, 162
System 390, 120, 162
VisiCalc, 253
WordPerfect, 256
Workplace OS, 196
Icons, 181
IDT, 115
IEEE (Institute of Electrical and
  Electronics Engineers), 169
  802.3+, 353, 361
  802.11b, 356
  1394, 61–62
IETF (Internet Engineering Task
  Force), 417
images
  display, 77–78
  bitmapped, 81–82
IMAP (Internet Message Access
  Protocol), 410
index, database, 238–239, 243
Inferno (OS), 199
information appliances, 201,
  398–399, 413
information hiding, 210–211
Informix, 246, 262, 395
infrared networks, 322
inheritance in OOT, 224–225
ink, solid, 99
inkjet printers, 98
instance of objects, 224
instructions
  branch, 25
  CPU, 15
  EPIC, 30
  iterative, 17
  pipelining, 24
  RISC, 27–28
  scaling, 30
  SIMD, 28–30
  VILW, 29–30

instruction sets, 16, 18, 116, 152
  compatibility, 113
integrated services digital network
  see ISDN
Intel, 67–68, 110–111, 124, 171
  286, 143
  386/486, 113–114
  4004, 109
  80286, 110, 178, 182, 185
  80386, 66, 110, 142
  80486, 100
  8086/8088, 16, 107, 109–110,
    177, 182
  and standards, 461
  AGP, 91
  Celeron, 112
  Chips & Technologies, 64–65
  clones, 113–114
  EPIC, 30
  Itanium, 30, 111, 113
  marketing, 119–120
  SIMD, 29
  see also Pentium
Intergalactic Digital Research,
  179
International Standards Organization, 308
International Telecommunication
  Union, 377, 455
Internet, 266, 330, 383
  and networks, 446–449
  appliance, 399
  architecture, 419–429
  backbone, 417, 426
  brownouts, 425
  graphics systems, 85
  growth, 444–445
  organization, 419–432
  origins, 415–416
  over cable, 372
  protocol, 296–298
  security, 434–437
  speed, 432–434
Internet Engineering Task Force,
  417
Internet Explorer, 258
Internet Message Access Protocol, 410
interpreted languages, 205–207,
  230
interrupts (CPU), 19
intranet, 434
I/O (Input/Output) bus, 8, 11, 38,
  40, 42, 61–62, 132

IP (Internet Protocol), 306, 308, 311, 316, 348
  addresses, 428
  and voice/video, 455–466
  IPv4, 428
  IPv6, 417, 428, 453
  see also TCP/IP
Iridium LLC, 385
IRIX, 168
IRMA boards, 391
ISA (Industry Standard Architecture) bus, 49
ISDN (Integrated Services Digital Network), 367–368, 374–377, 420, 422
ISO (International Standards Organization), 308
isochronous Ethernet, 403
ISP (Internet Service Provider), 370, 379, 385
  CompuServe, 418
  and LANs, 448
  university as, 416
Itanium, 30, 111, 113
ITU (International Telecommunications Union), 377, 455

Java, 117, 207, 227–228, 230–232, 246, 262
  beans, 434
  with NC, 397
Java Virtual Machine (JVM), 230, 232, 398
Jazz, 254
J. D. Edwards (Firm), 251
.jff files, 84
Jobs, Steven, 180
Joy, Bill, 167
JPEG (Joint Photographic Experts Group), 84, 283

Kaleida, 230
Kapor, Mitch, 253
Kemeny, John, 217
kernel, 151–152, 166–167
keys, encryption, 436–442
Kildall, Gary, 179
Kodak, 252
Kurz, Thomas, 217

label switching, 348–349, 433
LAN (Local Area Network), 196, 249, 266, 339–340, 352–357, 362–364, 453

coaxial, 324
e-commerce, 446–449
fiber optic, 325
peer-to-peer, 392
protocols, 298
routers, 342
segments, 353–354
software licenses, 392–393
voice transmission, 403
see also Ethernet
LAN Manager, 197
languages
  see Assembly language, high-level language, machine language
Lanier, 255
laptops, 79, 124
laser printers, 96–98
last mile, in networks, 368, 373, 399, 413, 454
  and pervasive computing, 459
latency, 52, 359, 380, 403
layers, in protocols, 306–311
LCD (Liquid Crystal Displays), 74, 79–80
  passive matrix, 80
  printers, 99
leased lines, 299, 313, 365–366, 379, 386–387, 420
LED (Light Emitting Diode)
  displays, 79–80
  printers, 99
legacy systems, 246–247
LEO (low earth orbit), 386
licensing, software, 392–393
light, in chipmaking, 108
line cards (ISDN), 375
link/state algorithms, 342
Linux, 147, 171–172, 200
liquid crystal displays
  see LCD
Lisa (user interface), 181
lithography, optical
  and pervasive computing, 458
  in chipmaking, 108–109
LMDS (Local Multipoint Distribution System), 383–385, 448
load/store, 17
local area network
  see LAN
locking
  of files, 392
  of records, 393

logic gates, 16, 107
loop, 234
  local, 368, 383–384
lossless compression, 285–286, 291
lossy compression, 283, 285–286, 291
Lotus Development Corp., 145, 187, 249, 253
  Lotus 1-2-3, 253, 391
  Lotus Domino, 411
  Lotus Notes, 411
low earth orbit (LEO), 386
lpi (lines per inch), 96
Lucent Technologies, 167
luggables, 124
luminance, 77
LZW (Lempel, Zvi, Welch) compression, 286–287

Mach OS, 170
machine language, 203, 214
Macintosh, 82, 249, 254
  operating system, 180–84
  see also Apple Computer
MAE (Metropolitan Area Ethernet), 426–427
MagCard, 255
magnetic domains, 54
mainframes, 120–121, 162, 245
MAJC, 232
MAN (Metropolitan Area Network), 381
markup languages, 220, 263
massively parallel architecture, 122, 156
Matsushita, 200
MCI/WorldCom, 299, 348, 417, 426, 435
media, in networks, 320
media processors, 33, 36, 124, 128
memory
  main, 46
  management by OS, 139, 151
  pages, 142
  physical, 140
  shared, 156–158
  storage, 39, 53
  substrates, 60
  virtual, 140–142
  see also cache, flash memory, DRAM, NUMA, RDRAM, SRAM

memory bus, 39–40, 49, 61
   see also synchronous bus, system bus
memory chips, 51–52
MEO (Middle Earth Orbit), 386
mesh, network, 350, 424, 427
meta-languages, 220, 430–431
method (in OOT), 222
metropolitan area network, 381
MFCs (Microsoft's Foundation Classes), 223
MHz (Mega-Hertz), 20, 78, 273
microcode, 162
microcomputers, 260, 391
   as terminals, 395–396
microkernel, 153, 170, 191, 396
micromirrors, 80
MicroPro International, 255
microprocessors (CPU), 14, 245
   architecture, 127–129
   codesign, 129
   vendors, 112
Microsoft, 42, 88, 100, 118, 123, 191, 245, 249, 258
   Access, 249
   Common Object Model, 409
   e-commerce, 262
   Excel, 254–255
   Foundation Classes, 223, 407
   source code, 171
   SQL Server, 250
   suites, 188
   Word, 256–257
   see also Internet Explorer, MS-DOS, Windows (Microsoft)
microwave networks, 321, 366
middle earth orbit (MEO), 386
middleware, 407
MIME (Multipurpose Internet Message Exchange), 410
minicomputer, xxiv, 122, 164, 166
MIPS, 117, 122, 124, 169, 191, 198
mission critical, 247–248
MIT (Massachusetts Institute of Technology), 129, 163, 253, 396, 416
MMDS (Multichannel Multipoint Distribution System), 383, 385
MMX (multimedia extensions), 28

modems, 301, 374
modes, in OS, 153
modular programming, 213
modulation, wave, 269–272
monitors, 78–80
   resolution standards, 73
Moore, Gordon, 22
Moore's Law, 22, 398, 451, 455, 461
motherboard, 12, 65–66, 118
Motif X/11, 166, 170
Motion Picture Experts Group, 282
Motorola
   68000, 109, 115, 142, 178, 181–183
   Dragonball, 199
   PowerPC, 114–116
MPEG (Motion Picture Experts Group), 282, 287
MRAM (Magnetoelectronic RAM), 55
MS-DOS (Microsoft Disk Operating System), 57, 88, 147, 149, 176–177, 184, 258
multicasting, 349, 385
multichannel multipoint distribution system, 383, 385
Multics, 166
multihoming, 425
multimedia, 45, 48, 68, 78
   extensions, 28
multiple processors, 51, 243
multiplexing
   in circuits, 302
   in networks, 333–334, 366
   wave division, 383
multiprocessing, 30–31, 153–158
   databases, 241
   e-commerce, 261
   preemptive, 155
multiprogramming, 143
multiprotocol routers, 344
Multipurpose Internet Message Exchange, 410
multitasking, 48, 142–143, 162, 261
multithreading, 144
multiuser databases, 393
multiuser operating systems, 149–150
MVS (Multiple Virtual Storage), 149, 162

nailed up lines, 313
Nantucket Software, 249
NAP (Network Access Point), 426–427
National Science Foundation, 417, 419
National Security Agency, 442
NC (network computer), 396–399, 413
NEC, 117
Net PC, 396–397, 399–402
Netscape, 171, 252
   as homepage, 433
   groupware, 411
NetWare, 163, 196–197
network loop, 33–344
networks
   access points, 426–427
   and databases, 244–245
   intelligence, 453
   interface cards, 358
   Internet, 446–449
   intranet, 434–435
   layers, 308
   peer-to-peer, 392
   pipes, 299–300
   of workstations, 54
   proprietary, 418
   virtual private, 434–435
   see also LAN, Regional Networks, WAN
Neutrino, 199
Newton, 125–126
NexGen, 113
NeXT OS, 170
NIC (network interface card), 358
NLM (Netware Loadable Modules), 197
nodes, 311–312, 314, 323, 339
   Ethernet, 352
Nokia, 199
Noorda, Ray, 197
normalizing, in databases, 243
notebook computers, 124
Notes, Lotus, 411
Novell, 163, 173, 197, 255, 257
NOW (Networks of Workstations), 154
NSA
   see U.S. National Security Agency
NSF (National Science Foundation), 417, 419, 426

NT
  see Windows (Microsoft)
NUMA (Non-Uniform Memory
  Architecture), 157

Oak
  see Java
object-based software, 397,
  407–409
object-oriented databases,
  245–246
object-oriented languages,
  229–232, 262
Object Request Broker, 408
object-to-object communication,
  226–227
OC (optical carrier), 367, 382,
  427
OEM (Original Equipment Manufacturers), 97
OLAP (Online Analytical Processing), 395
OLE (Object Linking and Embedding), 227–228
OLED (Organic Light Emitting
  Diode) displays, 80
Olsen, Kenneth, 118, 163–165
OLTP (Online Transaction Processing), 240–242
OMG (Object Management
  Group), 408–409
OOT (Object-Oriented Technology), 204, 221–232
  e-commerce, 262
opcode, 15, 26
Open GL, 93
open shortest path first, 343
Open Software Foundation, 170,
  408
open source, 171
operand, 15
operating systems, 10, 99–100,
  161–173
  command-driven, 177–178
  e-commerce, 261
  embedded, 199
  microcomputer, 175–201
  multiuser, 149–150
  open, 166
  proprietary, 166
  single-tasking, 177–178
  single user, 176
  very small, 198–200

  see also Apple Computers,
    CP/M, IBM, Inferno,
    MS-DOS, Netware,
    RTOS, Sun, Windows
optical computing, 35
optical interconnects, 35
optical storage, 58–59
optimizing compiler, 206
Oracle, 172, 246, 250–251, 258,
  262, 395
  in distributed computing, 409
  NC, 398–399
ORB (Object Request Broker), 408
OS
  see Operating systems
OSF (Open Software Foundation), 170, 408
OSI (Open Systems Interconnec-
  tion), 308–309, 461
OSPF (open shortest path first),
  343
outsourcing, 252
overhead, data, 290

PA RISC (Precision Architecture
  RISC), 119, 122, 169
packet storms, 343
packets, 284, 289–290, 297–305
  call setup, 314
  headers, 308
  routing, 312
  sequencing, 303
  switching, 302–303, 310, 316,
    416
  transmission, 336–337
page fault, in memory, 142
pages, holographic, 60
pair gain, 275
Palm Computing, 199
PalmPilot, 125–126, 410
palmtops, 125, 198
  see also webpads
Paradox (Corel), 249, 262
parallel systems, 154
PARC (Palo Alto Research Center), 352
ParcPlace, 229
parity checking, 289
partition, on disk, 57
partitions, memory, 139
Pascal language, 217
passwords, 150
path width, 22

PBX (Private Branch Exchange),
  147, 403–404
PC (Personal Computer)
  see microcomputers
PC-DOS, 176
PCI (Peripheral Component Inter-
  connect) bus, 49, 61, 63, 87,
  118
PCS (Personal Communications
  System), 320, 454
.pct files, 85
PDA (Personal Digital Assistant),
  125, 321, 458
PDP, 164–165
peering, in networks, 426
Pentium, 110, 257
  II, 110
  III, 26, 48, 50, 107, 109–110,
    112, 123
  Pro, 17, 110, 190
  Willametter, 111
  see also Intel
PeopleSoft, 251, 258
Perl, 433
Perot, Ross, 252
persistence, object, 408
Personal Communication System,
  454
personal computers
  see Microcomputers
personal digital assistant
  see PDA
pervasive computing, 129, 259,
  266, 386, 413
  and cell phones, 455
  and piconets, 457
  challenges to, 458–463
PGP (Pretty Good Privacy), 438
phase, wave, 270
photolithography, 106, 130
physical layer, 310
physical memory, 140
piconets, 321, 457
PICT file format, 85
picture elements
  see pixels
pipe, network, 299–300
pipelines, 23–25, 33, 110
pixels, 71–72, 75–76, 87
  Texels, 91
PKI (public key infrastructure),
  440, 459
plaintext, 436

plasma displays, 80
platforms, 168, 461
Playstation, 33
point-to-point topology, 329
polymer LEDs
   see LED (Light Emitting
      Diode) displays
polymorphism, 225
PON (passive optical network),
   327,
POP (point of presence), 422–423
POP (Post Office Protocol), 410
port cost, 362
portable computers, 124–126, 134
portable power sources, 125, 458
porting, 167, 216
ports, 149
Posix, 16
post office protocol (POP), 410
Postscript, 101
power, portable, 125, 458
Power PC, 115–116, 122, 183,
   196, 398
   604e, 22–23
   G4, 116
preemptive multiprocessing, 155
prefetching, 23, 43, 45
presentation (client), 395
Pretty Good Privacy, 438
PRI (Primary Rate Interface,
   ISDN), 376
printer drivers, 99
printers, 94–102
   dumb, 99
   smart, 100
private branch exchange, 147, 403
private key, in encryption, 437
privileged mode, 153
procedural programs, 209
processor bus
   see system bus
processor cycle, 31
processors
   see ASIC, CPU
   see also media processors
program, computer, 204
programming
   e-commerce, 262–263
   levels, 214
   modular, 213
   see also Assembly language,
      Machine language, High-
      level languages

Project Angel, 384
project modeling, 212
Project Oxygen, 129, 327
PROM, 55
protocols, 296
   layers, 306–311
   see also FTP, HTTP, IMAP,
      IP, TCP, UDP
proxy servers, 433
PSTN (public switched telephone
   network), 421
public key, in encryption, 437, 440
pulses, electromagnetic, 268
PVC (permanent virtual circuit),
   345, 359

QNX (OS), 199
QoS (Quality of Service), 317,
   347, 361–362, 381
   Internet, 428
   in video and voice, 455–456
Qualcomm, 454
quantization, 283
quantum computing, 36
Quattro Pro, 257
queries, database, 241–243
   see also SQL
Qwest Communications, 327, 382

RAD (Rapid Application Development), 234
radio, 320–321
   frequency interference, 50–51
RAID, 132
RAM
   see Flash RAM, MRAM
Rambus DRAM
   see RDRAM
RAMDAC (Random Access
   Memory DAC), 86
raster, 86
ray casting, 90
ray tracing, 90
RDBMS (relational databases),
   240–247, 395
RDRAM (Rambus DRAM),
   52–53
read only memory
   see ROM
read-only access, 150
read/write access, 150
Real Time Operating System
   (RTOS), 199

receivers, 273–274, 288
records, in databases, 242
Red Hat, 172
reduced instruction set computing
   see RISC
refresh, 52–53
refresh rate, 78
Regional Networks, 399, 420,
   423, 426
registers, 14, 16–18, 45
   stack, 19
relational databases, 240–244,
   247, 395
release candidates, 189
rendering, 92
replication, database, 406
resolution
   displays, 73
   printers, 94
reversible colors, 97
RFI (Radio Frequency Interference), 50–51
RGB (Red-Green-Blue)
   see Dot triads
ring topology, 331–332
   see also SONET, Token Ring
RISC (Reduced Instruction Set
   Computing), 26–28, 36, 110
   CPUs, 115–120
   PA RISC, 119
Rise, 115
Ritchie, Dennis, 166, 217
robot, software, 412
ROM (Read Only Memory), 5,
   182, 198
   see also PROM, EEPROM
ROM BIOS
   see BIOS
routers and routing, network,
   297–299, 302–303, 312,
   315, 341–342
   and Internet, 419, 421, 424, 427
   as firewalls, 434–435
   in LANs, 447
   in Regional Networks, 425
RS6000
   see PowerPC
RSA (Rivest, Shamir, Aldeman),
   437
RSVP (Resource Reservation
   Protocol), 348
RTOS (Real Time Operating System), 199

SAA (Systems Applications Architecture), 186
Sabre, 397, 405–406
sampling, wave, 278–281
SAP (Systeme, Anwendungen, Produkte), 241, 258
SAS (Firm), 259
Santa Cruz Operation, 168, 197
Sachs, Jonathan, 253
satellite, direct broadcast, 285
satellite links, 385–386
satellite television, 123
scalability, 397
    e-commerce, 261–262
    Internet, 417
    system, 158
    vector, 83
Scientific Atlanta, 123
SCO (Santa Cruz Operation), 168, 197
SCSI (Small Computer Systems Interface), 62
Sculley, John, 125
SDH (Synchronous Digital Hiercharchy), 381
    see also SONET
second sourcing, 110–111
secret key method, 436–437
security, network, 434–444, 459
    in agent software, 412
    in routing, 344
servers, 122–123, 261
    application, 395
    local network, 392
    terminal, 420
    Web, 132
set-top boxes, 123–124, 373
Sevin Rosen, 253
SGI (Silicon Graphics Inc.), 117, 168
SGML (Standardized Generalized Markup Language), 220, 430
shared memory, 156–158
shared nothing, 156–158
shell, 166–167
shrink-wrapped software, 234, 250
Siemens, 117
Signaling System 7, 382
silicon crystals, 106
Silicon Germanium (SiGe), 106
Silicon Graphics Inc. (SGI), 117, 168
silicon on insulator, 128

silicon substrates, 60
signal to noise ratio, 281
SIMD (Single Instruction Multiple Data), 28–29, 36, 111, 133
SIMM (Single In-line Memory Module), 48
simplex, 335
skew, 50
slipstream, 189
Smalltalk, 229, 246
SMMDS (Switched Multimegabit Data Service), 374, 381
SMTP (Simple Mail Transfer Protocol), 410
SNA, 344, 381
"sneakernet," 392
SoC (System on Chip), 129
soft errors, 52
software
    agent, 412
    engineering, 212
    gridlock, 248
    industry, 258–259
    radio, 455
    reliability, 459
    robot, 412
SOHO (Small Office/Home Office), 249
Solaris, 168
sole sourcing, 66
SONET (Synchronous Optical Network), 309–311, 357, 359, 377, 380–383
    and Internet backbone, 426
Sony, 117, 124
sound, as BLOB, 246
source code, 171, 204–205
spaghetti code, 210
SPARC (Scalable Processor Architecture), 117
spatial compressions, 282–284
spectrum, electromagnetic, 268–272
speculative execution, 25–26
splicing, fusion, 326
splitter, wire, 370
spreadsheets, 237, 253–255
Sprint, 299, 417, 424, 435
SQL (Structured Query Language), 243, 395
SQL Server, 395
SRAM (Static Random Access Memory), 39, 42, 46–47, 48, 55

SSE (Streaming Single-Instruction Multiple-Data Extensions), 29
stack
    in CPU, 19
    in protocols, 296, 306
standards, in computing, 460–463
Stanford University, 416
star networks, 328, 357
Star system, 181
statistical compression, 287
storage, 39–40, 44
    access, 44
    chip, 54
    CPU stage, 11, 17
    hierarchy, 9
    holography, 59
    memory, 39
streaming media devices, 194
    see also data streams
streaming single-instruction multiple-data extensions, 29
StrongARM, 198
Stroustrup, Bjarne, 229
structured programming, 209–212
structured query language, 243, 395
sub-dots
    see pixels
sub-notebooks, 198
subroutines, 205
substrates, 60
suites
    software, 257
    protocol, 296
Sun Microsystems, 117–118, 123–124, 167, 231–232
    NC, 399
    Solaris, 168
    SPARC, 117
supercooling, 34
supercomputers, 29, 121–122
superscalar (pipeline), 24–25, 110, 119
superusers, 150
surround sound, 288
SVC (switched virtual circuit), 317, 345
switch fabric, 347
Switched 56, 374, 378
switched circuit, 315, 407
    see also circuits, switching

switched multimegabit data ser-
    vice, 374, 381
switches, network, 329, 339–340,
    345–349, 453
    Ethernet, 354–355
    packet, 456
    see also routers and routing
switches, optical, 35
swouters, 348
Sybase, 172, 246, 250, 262, 395
Symbian, 199
symmetric multiprocessing, 155
synchronous bus, 51
synchronous transmission, 336
system bus, 39, 41, 49–50, 52
system on chip (SoC), 129
System V, 169
systems applications architecture,
    186

T-1 digital line, 299, 448
T-carrier, 366, 376, 382
tag switching, 348
Taligent, 229–230
Tandem Computers, 123
Tanenbaum, Andrew, 169
TAPI (Telephony API), 147, 404
tariffs, 366, 381
TCI, 371
TCO (Total Cost of Ownership),
    400
TCP (Transmission Control Pro-
    tocol), 306, 308, 311, 316
TCP/IP (Transmission Control
    Protocol/Internet Protocol),
    167, 296–298, 350, 453
    in Internet growth, 416
    as networking standard, 461
    packets, 361
    routing, 344
TDM (time division multiplex-
    ing), 334–335
technologies, emerging, 454–457
teleconferencing, 455
Teledisc, 385
telephone companies, 361,
    364–366, 379, 382–383
telephone network, public
    switched, 421
telephones, 275, 288, 383
    and databases, 404–405
    integration with computers,
        402–405

lines, 374
    see also cell phones
television, 75, 291, 333
    bandwidth, 273–274
    signals, 280–281
    see also cable television, digi-
        tal television, satellite
        television
temporal compression, 282,
    284–285
terminal-host network, 390–391
terminal-host systems, 149–150
terminal server, 420
terminals
    network, 389
    PC, 395
    VT-100, 461
Texas Instruments, 117
    DSP, 32
Texel, 91
texture,-ing, 91–92
Thermal wax, 99
thin client, 395
Thompson, Ken, 166, 217
thrashing, in memory, 142
thread migration, 155–154
threads, 144, 170, 232
thunking, 189
.tif files, 84
TIFF (Tagged Image File For-
    mat), 84
time sharing, 143, 162
time slots, in networks, 331, 347,
    381
Time Warner, 371
timing, CPU, 11
TLA (three-leter acronymic), 316
Token Ring, 298, 331, 340–341,
    354, 356–357
Toolbox, 182–183
toolkits, programming, 223
topology, 328
Torvalds, Linus, 171
Toshiba, 123
Total Cost of Ownership, 400
traces, chip, 22, 67, 107
transaction processing database,
    240
transform and lighting, 93
translation look aside buffers,
    141
transistors, 14, 20–21, 33, 46, 67,
    107, 129

logic gate, 16
    SRAM cells, 33
Transmeta, 125
transmitters, 273–274, 288
transport layer, 306–307
trapdoor, encryption key, 442
TrueType, 101–102
TSAPI, 404
tuning, in databases, 243
twisted pair, 322–323, 362
two-phase commit, 407

UDP (User Datagram Protocol),
    298, 306–307, 316
UI (User Interface), 147, 166,
    172, 181
UltraSPARC, 117
Unicode, 191–192
Univel, 197
universal serial bus, 62, 144
University of California, Berke-
    ley, 167, 416
Unix, 142, 147, 150, 157,
    165–169, 200, 396
    in Internet growth, 416
    TSAPI, 404
Unix System Laboratories, 197
UnixWare, 197
uplink, cable, 372
URL (Universal Resource Loca-
    tor), 430
USB (Universal Serial Bus), 62,
    144
U.S. Dept. of Defense, 164
    ARPA, 302
    DARPA (Defense Advanced
        Research Projects
        Agency), 416
U.S. National Science Founda-
    tion, 417, 419
U.S. National Security Agency,
    442
U.S. West, 371
user ID, 150
user mode, in OS, 151–153, 166
username, 150
UTP (unshielded twisted-pair),
    323, 355, 357, 359
UUnet, 417

vaporware, 195–196
variable, in programming, 223
Vaskevitch, David, 245

VAX (Virtual Address eXtension), 164
vCal standard, 410
VCR, 123, 369
VDSL (very high data rate DSL), 367, 370–371
vector computation (SIMD), 29, 122
vector images, 83, 432
vectors, interrupt, 19
vendors, 250, 262, 383, 392, 398, 400
VeriSign, 440
versions, 189
very long instruction word
    see VLIW
VESA (Video Electronics Standards Association), 61
Via Technologies, 66
video, 49, 305
    and IP, 455–456
    BLOB, 246
    high definition, 58
    in networks, 317
    on-demand, 369, 371
    standards, 61
videoconference, 455
videophone, 456
virtual circuits, 300, 311, 317–318, 348, 360, 365, 378–379
virtual memory, 140–142
virtual path, 345
virtual private network, 434–435
VisiCalc, 253
Visor (PC), 199
Visual Basic, 217, 249, 262
visual languages, 219
VL bus, 61
VLIW (Very Long Instruction Word), 29–30, 36, 111, 207, 231
VM (Virtual Machine), 149, 162
VMS (Virtual Memory System), 149, 164–165, 172, 1
voice
    and IP, 455–456
    encryption, 443
    in networks, 317, 370
    in packets, 305

PC integration, 402
    recognition, 257–258
VPN (virtual private network), 434–435
VT-100 terminals, 391, 461

wafers, 106
wait state, 45–46
WAN (Wide Area Network), 266, 330, 338, 381–386, 453
    routers, 342
Wang, 168, 255–256
Warp (OS/2), 196
wavelets, 432–433
waves
    division multiplexing, 383
    electromagnetic, 269–272
    light, 324
    radio, 320
    square, 268
Web, World Wide, 398
    caching, 432
    Consortium, 430
    development of, 429
    e-commerce, 261
    groupware, 411
    hosting, 448
    pages, 85, 220
    security, 43
    servers, 172
    speed, 432–434
webpads, 125
Whirlwind Project, 163–164
wide area networks, *see* WAN
width
    circuits, 13, 23
    CPU paths, 22
    traces, 22
Willamette, 111
Win32, 190–191, 198
Windows (Microsoft), 184–195
    1.0+, 142, 178, 184, 187
    3.0, 256
    95+, 67, 150, 178, 184–185, 188, 190
    2000, 150, 194
    CE, 126, 198, 399
    COM (common object model), 193

NT/2000, 163, 178–179, 185, 190–191, 396, 404, 407
NT, 118, 150, 164, 169–170, 178, 189, 197
NT servers & workstations, 192
OS/2, 185, 190, 256
WinFrame, 396
Win/Tel (Windows/Intel), 116
wireless networking, 125, 320–322, 356, 383
    see also LMDS, MMDS, satellite links
wire speed, 346
Wirth, Nicholas, 217
WLL (wireless local loop), 383
Wolfpack (Microsoft), 192
Word (Computer program), 256–257
word length, 23
WordPerfect, 187–188, 227, 255–257
WordPerfect Corporation, 255
wordprocessing, 255–257
WordStar, 255–256
workflow software, 411
workgroups, 249
Workplace OS, 196
workstations, 122–123
WorldCom
    see MCI/WorldCom
World Wide Web
    see Web, World Wide
World Wide Web Consortium (W3C), 430
Wozniak, Stephen, 180
wrappers in software, 228

X-25, 360, 374, 378–379
X.400 specification, 410
xDSL, 367–371, 448
Xeon computers, 48
Xerox, 181, 229
    PARC, 352
XML (eXtensible Markup Language), 220, 263, 430–431
X rays, in chipmaking, 108–109
X Window System, 396